ROCKY MOUNTAIN RADICAL

Myron W. Reed
(Photograph courtesy Western History Department, Denver Public Library.)

JAMES A. DENTON

Rocky Mountain Radical

MYRON W. REED,
CHRISTIAN SOCIALIST

University of New Mexico Press   Albuquerque

For my parents,

Amos and Essie Denton

© *1997 by the University of New Mexico Press*
All rights reserved.
FIRST EDITION

Library of Congress Cataloging-in-Publication
Denton, James A. (James Andrew), 1936–
Rocky Mountain radical: Myron W. Reed, Christian Socialist /
James A. Denton. — 1st ed.
p.   cm.
Includes bibliographical references and index.
ISBN 0-8263-1814-2
1. Reed, Myron W., 1836–1899.   2. Socialists — United States —
Biography.   3. Socialism, Christian — United States — History —
19th century.   I. Title.
HX84.R43D45   1997
335′.0092 — dc21   97-4846
CIP

Contents

Preface

Reverend Myron Winslow Reed, the foremost Christian Socialist in the American West from 1884 to 1899, is seldom found in the major works on Christian Socialism. Historians have usually identified late nineteenth-century Christian Socialism with W. D. P. Bliss, Walter Rauschenbusch, and George Herron, men from the Midwest or East. Yet, from his Denver pulpits, Reed preached a radical message of Christian Socialism — at least his contemporaries called it radical. He encouraged the government to manage the sources of production, advocated the "comfortable life" for all citizens, and touted America as the messianic nation to the world — the example of a cooperative republic in process. Reed declared, "There ought to be a new earth, and what ought to be will be."

Nurtured by nineteenth-century idealism, Reed believed in humanity's inevitable progress, especially that of American civilization, but he credited this progress to the God revealed in Jesus Christ. Jesus taught the principle of servanthood, the basic principle of cooperation, and represented the most profound revelation of God's plan though not its final one. By observing history one could see the improvement of civilization and God at work. Reed believed that the church must teach by example and guide humanity into the promised kingdom of God on earth, which was best represented by a cooperative republic. Teaching by example meant doing the things that would create justice, relieve suffering, elevate human culture to its fullest potential, and establish small communities that could serve as catalysts to prod the rest of society toward the kingdom of God. Reed and others wrestled with how to accomplish this task in an expanding society that seemed determined to replicate the social organizations of yesteryear. Reed envisioned the West, open to new ideas and with budding settlements, as an ideal place to create a community to serve as a model for the kingdom of God.

The post–Civil War era introduced a dimension of change to the American people they had never experienced. Darwin's *Origin of Species* (1859) challenged creation dogma and provoked a perennial debate. Urban churches catered to the wealthy, and ministers upheld the axiom that hard work led to prosperity. The economic system also produced some of the country's poorest citizens but gave them few options to alter their miserable existence. For many immigrants and young Americans, the promise of a well-paying job remained only a dream and many felt it would never come true.

This changing postwar social scene forced many Christians to rethink their traditional views. A Congregationalist minister who came to Denver in 1884, Reed preached "The Fatherhood of God and the Brotherhood of Man" and cried out for more justice and less exploitation. Reed intended to create a new community that would give people the opportunity for a comfortable life. He entered a city that had developed from entrepreneurs whose political descendants promoted a laissez-faire economy. A frontier with hidden wealth in the mountains drew thousands from the East who sought their fortunes in the gold and silver mines, but only a few hundred made it to the middle class. Multitudes returned home, and the wage-laborer, the African American, the Chinese all faced limited opportunity in this land of hidden wealth. How could anyone hear and practice Jesus' principle of servanthood if earning a living required all of one's available time?

One can view western expansion as flowing out of the actions of eastern capitalists, exploitative entrepreneurs, and ordinary settlers, with return on investment as the dominant theme. But within this process critics arose who challenged the capitalistic method, and who tried to create communities on a foundation neither wholly capitalistic nor hostile toward the American republican system. These radicals hoped to establish cooperative communities based on shared values, using the socialistic principle of governmental ownership of key economic resources to provide for the common good. Their struggle had significance because it kept alive a stream of critical defiance.

A study of this kind of radicalism in the West from 1880 to 1900 is critical for a broader understanding of the historical changes that occurred there. It was during these years that the settlers established many cultural and political institutions in the new western communities. Yet there have been few historical studies of socialism in the American West during these decades, thus leaving obscure the importance that such radical protest may have for historical inquiries into western society and institutions. Most of the published research about socialism deals with periods and issues after the founding of the Socialist Party in 1901.

In *The Forging of American Socialism* (1953), Howard H. Quint surveyed the antecedents of socialism in America and traced its progress from 1886 to 1901. Quint discussed both European influences and the distinctly American factors that affected the socialist movement. He claimed that Edward Bellamy's *Looking Backward* inspired American socialism much more than the European Marxists. It was this utopian vision of a better world that became a key concern of such Denver radicals as Reed, who translated the "better world vision" into the coming kingdom of God on earth. Quint provides essential historical background for this book, but his purpose was to survey the origins of twentieth-century American socialism and not to detail western radicalism.

Studies of western radicalism have usually been slanted toward labor history, but Reed's concept of the kingdom of God separated him from the more militant labor radicals. Reed envisioned a new community that would provide more than simply rights for labor; it would include the comfortable life for everyone, actualized through socialism. Among the histories of western American socialism, there have been few in-depth treatments of socialism in the Rocky Mountain region. For example, in 1978 James R. Green published *Grass Roots Socialism, Radical Movements in the Southwest, 1895–1943*, which was devoted to an analysis of western socialism. Green's story began in 1895 and explored the relationship between populism and socialism in the states of Oklahoma, Texas, Louisiana, and Arkansas. James E. Wright's *The Politics of Populism: Dissent in Colorado* (1974) emphasized the roots and growth of populism in Colorado from statehood through the 1896 election, but his treatment of socialism concentrated on activities after 1900. Two widely read histories of Denver, Lyle Dorsett and Michael McCarthy's *Queen City: A History of Denver* (1986 edition), and Stephen J. Leonard and Thomas J. Noel's *Denver: From Mining Camp to Metropolis* (1990), contain no elaboration of socialistic activities in Colorado. A study of sociopolitical radicalism is necessary to balance our historical understanding of the West as a place of conflict (see Patricia Nelson Limerick, *The Legacy of Conquest*, 19–32), which Reed defined as capitalistic competition versus cooperation.

This book documents Reed's thought and actions as a Christian Socialist who achieved national recognition for his epigrammatic preaching and his political activism. Chapters 1 and 2 discuss the theological, social, political, and cultural contexts in which Reed lived. Chapters 3, 4, 5, and 6 examine Reed's ideas and activities using the themes of politics, charity, labor, and socialism, and the discourse with his contemporaries and great thinkers from the past. The New Theology of the 1880s became Reed's major theological orientation, but he remained somewhat eclectic, employing whatever he understood would advance the coming kingdom. Reed desired to show the masses that they could find hope and help in the gospel that focused on this life, not the life to come.

It is a great pleasure to acknowledge those who helped make a first book possible. The idea was discussed initially with Professor Martin E. Marty on a summer visit to Chicago, and it grew into a Ph.D. dissertation at the University of Colorado at Boulder. Members of my dissertation committee made themselves available for counsel and confession, and Professors Ralph Mann, Lee Scamehorn, Patricia Nelson Limerick, and Ed Miller communicated more support than perhaps they knew. My adviser, Professor Mark Pittenger, walked with me through each page of the dissertation. His criticism and suggestions have made this book better than it would have been without him. And my colleague Tom Krainz gently criticized the chapter on charity. To all I am grateful.

The staffs at the Western History Department of the Denver Public Library, Colorado Historical Society, and Western Historical Collections at the University of Colorado Library cheerfully went the extra mile to find any requested information. The Indiana State Library in Indianapolis and Denver's First Plymouth Congregational Church were most gracious in allowing me to copy material not available elsewhere. No research can accomplish its objective without the knowledge and forbearance of library personnel. I was fortunate in meeting such people at each institution.

Last, but not least in importance, is the recognition I happily extend to my wife, Laquitta. She was my closest critic and did those tasks that make writing and research easier. And to my son Greg, who never let up with his encouragement even when I lost my direction. They share in my relief and exultation.

ROCKY MOUNTAIN RADICAL

Part One

Creating a New Community

*"There ought to be a new earth,
and what ought to be will be."*

Our Kind of Man

James Whitcomb Riley

(to Myron W. Reed)

The kind of a man for you and me!
He faces the world unflinchingly,
And smites as long as the wrong resists,
With a knuckled faith and force like fists;
He lives the life he is preaching of,
And loves where most is the need of love;
His voice is clear to the deaf man's ears,
And his face sublime through the blind man's tears;
The light shines out where the clouds were dim,
And the widow's prayer goes up for him;
The latch is clicked at the hovel door,
And the sick man sees the sun once more,
And out o'er the barren fields he sees
Springing blossoms and waving trees,
Feeling as only the dying may,
That God's own servant has come that way,
Smoothing the path as it still winds on
Through the golden gate where his loved have gone.

The kind of man for me and you!
However little of worth we do
He credits full, and abides in trust
That time will teach us how more is just.
He walks abroad and he meets all kinds
Of querulous and uneasy minds,
And, sympathizing, he shares the pain
Of the doubts that rack us, heart and brain
And, knowing this, as we grasp his hand,
We are surely coming to understand!
He looks on sin with pitying eyes —
E'en as the Lord, since Paradise —
Else, should we read, though our sins should glow
As scarlet, they shall be white as snow? —
And feeling still, with a grief half glad,
That the bad are as good as the good are bad,
He strikes straight out for the Right — and he
Is the kind of a man for you and me!

(Published in the Rocky Mountain News, 6 March 1888, p. 4; Indianapolis News, 30 January 1899, p. 1; Denver Republican, 2 February 1899, p. 1.)

ONE

A City Of Entrepreneurs

One December Sunday in 1892 the Reverend Myron Winslow Reed, sometimes known for his temerity, proclaimed to Denver's First Congregational Church: "There ought to be a new earth, and what ought to be will be. No one will assert that this is the ideal social system — this one we are living under." This brash minister had no doubt that a new social order was inevitable — it was God's will. "We are not satisfied with it [this social order]. It is a makeshift," complained Reed, the preeminent Christian Socialist in the western United States. Indeed the late nineteenth-century West, with its apparent fluid social and political structures, seemed the ideal place to build a cooperative society based on Christian Socialism. Socialism would provide equal opportunity for everyone, and with the right management the new western communities would prosper and human misery would decline.[1]

Reed proposed a Christian Socialist community as an alternative to a capitalism that devoured the poor and enriched the already wealthy. He claimed that there were some seven thousand men and women in Denver who believed in cooperation and who wanted to remake society. Reed remarked, "There must be a beginning. Why not here in Denver try Socialism?" But he encountered a strong tradition of profits gained from high-risk investments and a perennial labor pool that would work for low wages just to survive. Perhaps the cushioned pews creaked as the wealthy church members squirmed, but their hearts were intertwined with the spirit of those pioneer entrepreneurs who had persevered to build their thriving city.[2]

The first priority of the entrepreneurs who created Denver in 1858 was to obtain a profit from their investments, and only then would they turn their attention to building a more permanent settlement. "Denver never aspired to be a utopia, only a place to live and to make money," according to historians Stephen J. Leonard and Thomas J. Noel. The budding town overcame several competitors in its immediate proximity to prosper temporarily as a trading and mining-supply hub. The supply business was a lucrative one; in one twenty-four hour period, twelve hundred wagons traveled through Denver on their way to and from the mining camps. One can imagine the profit from the sales of supplies and those typical frontier requirements, whiskey and female company for the lonely men.[3]

The early entrepreneurs who came to Colorado had a variety of backgrounds but a common aim: to make money. These men believed that the prosperity they created would generate opportunities for others. Historian Gunther Barth described these town builders as men "who quickly grasped the economic potential of emerging towns and utilized this potential for personal advancement." Their objective was to build a city, accumulate personal fortunes, enjoy as much comfort in life as possible, and not worry about equality of opportunity.[4]

Should equality of opportunity assume a lesser priority than profit in a new community? Reed answered that the major objective for any new settlement in the American West must include equal opportunity for its citizens. He hoped to create a community in which the principles of the Sermon on the Mount would prevail and result in "a comfortable life for everyone." By "comfortable life" Reed meant that each person should have food, clothing, shelter, and time for recreation and thinking. Music, books, theater, and other cultural amenities made available to everyone completed the balance of the comfortable life.[5]

Reed did not begin life in comfort. He was born on 24 July 1836 in Barnard-Windsor County, Vermont, to a poor Congregationalist minister and his wife, both of whom were active abolitionists. Myron was the middle child in a family of two boys and a girl. The village church could not support a full-time pastor and his father farmed or hired out to provide for the family. Working to sustain a meager existence left little time for education, but Reed read whatever books he could find or borrow. Always strong-willed, and with an intense independent spirit, the teenage Reed left home after a family dispute and tried to find his own way in the world.[6]

Soon Reed signed on with a fishing vessel that worked along the Newfoundland coast. When he completed his contract, he found himself in New York without sufficient food, shelter, or a job. A chance meeting with Horace Greeley resulted in the lad becoming a recruiter for the emerging

Republican party. In this position he discovered that he had a talent for public speaking. Reed had the ability to establish instant rapport with an audience, even though his speeches were not spellbinding. It was a discovery that would eventually lead him into the ministry.

When Reed's family moved from upper New York state to Wisconsin in the mid–1850s, he reconciled with his parents and later joined them. Here, Reed farmed and continued to read when he had books and time. He became friends with the members of a nearby Chippewa tribe, and hunted and fished with them frequently. Through this association he learned about Native American culture and the injustices forced upon them by federal bureaucrats and unscrupulous Indian agents. He never forgot these friendships and in the West, Reed became a vocal defender of Native American rights.

In search of a vocation, Reed read for the law and passed the Wisconsin bar. His practice consisted mostly of civil suits and land litigation. Never a man of patience, Reed soon grew frustrated with the law's potential for societal change. Friends encouraged him to enter the ministry, pointing to his talent for persuasion through public speaking. Reed observed that his father's ministry often produced changes in people's lives; this possibility appealed to him. He ended his law career and entered Chicago Theological Seminary in 1861.

The Civil War interrupted Reed's education. His childhood in an abolitionist household probably influenced his decision to answer President Abraham Lincoln's call for volunteers. Reed joined the Eighteenth Michigan Volunteers and served from 1862 until the war's end. He earned the rank of captain, was wounded at Chickamauga, and marched with General William T. Sherman across the South. During the war, Reed contracted a disease of the colon that caused intermittent periods of illness and later periodic absences from the pulpit. Generally, he cherished the war experience because of the camaraderie and loyalty of the troops. In the Grand Army of the Republic (GAR), Reed served as national chaplain and commander of the Colorado–Wyoming division. He always considered the GAR an organization that nourished manliness, interdependence, and patriotism — values that he prized. During Memorial Day observances Reed delivered speeches that promoted patriotism and the nobility of soldiering. War made one depend upon one's comrades for survival; it brought out the character in men. Reed thought that society could learn something from such camaraderie.[7]

When the Union Army discharged him in 1865, Reed returned to Chicago Theological Seminary and graduated in 1868. Soon after graduation,

Reed became the pastor of the First Congregational Church in New Orleans from 1868 to 1873. Here Reed met Louise Lyon, a Connecticut lady and accomplished soprano who had come South to teach African Americans; they were married in Clifton, Illinois, in 1870. In a letter written to a Chicago friend on 28 November 1871, Reed mentioned the death of a baby that summer, who must have been their first child. He went into depression and had difficulty recovering from his grief. The infant's death and his own uneven childhood probably influenced his strong compassion for all children. He viewed childhood as the time to play, to learn, and to explore — not to work in some dingy factory or wake up hungry. Reed accepted a call to the Milwaukee Olivet Congregational Church in 1873 and here three children were born, two boys and a girl.[8]

Reed's children grew up in a caring family. Camping, fishing, or travel vacations usually included everyone. The older son, Paul, graduated from Rensselaer Polytechnic Institute, and he received a prize for the design of an electric light and power plant driven by water power. He worked as an engineer in Belgium before becoming a U.S. Naval officer. Ralph became an attorney and finally settled in Washington, D.C., where he worked for the pension bureau. Ruth married a local businessman, L. P. Carter, and lived in Denver until her death in 1933.[9]

Little information exists about Louise Lyon Reed's activities in Indianapolis and Denver. We know that she was active in several civic projects: the Social Science Association in Indianapolis, the Denver Glenarm Club, and the Colorado women's suffrage movement. In 1890 she published a book entitled *One Law: One Life*. The book outlined humankind's religious journey and emphasized that the divine resides within the individual spirit. A progression of learning experiences defined life, and one learned about God by doing his will. Three sources of knowledge were available: the prophets, the words of Jesus Christ, and the individual's conscience. Through one's obedience to the truth, according to one's level of understanding, one would advance to a comprehensive knowledge of God. The New Thought movement was prominent in Denver during this time, and its form of idealism that emphasized the practical results of thinking good thoughts probably influenced Louise Reed's argument.[10]

Mrs. Reed believed that by focusing the mind upon a life situation, one could expect a positive result. Mr. Reed was not so confident. One day a house painter passed their front door with a noticeable limp. Mrs. Reed had pity on the poor man and decided to take him on her mind — something good would come of it. Within ten days, the painter walked without a limp and seemed very cheerful. When Mrs. Reed announced the happy news, her husband burst through the door and overtook the man to inquire how he had recovered. The painter explained that he had an old artificial leg that made his stump quite sore. But finally he had obtained a new leg, the stump had healed, and he was as good as new once again. Apparently, Mrs. Reed did not convert Mr. Reed to her healing philosophy, but she did remain an active companion for him throughout his ministry.[11]

In 1877 Reed responded to a call from the Indianapolis First Presbyterian Church. He expressed no particular reason for his decision to leave Milwaukee, but after four years perhaps he felt that a change would be stimulating. In Indianapolis Reed gained statewide recognition as an outstanding preacher. He also astonished some Indianians when they beheld a minister who fished, hunted, smoked cigars, and had an affinity for flashy jewelry.

When Denver's affluent First Congregational Church engaged Reed as their minister in 1884, he came without any pretense concerning his priorities for his ministry. In Jesus' life Reed saw the best example of the principle of cooperation: "He that would be the greatest among you let him be the steward of all." Reed aimed to assist the coming Kingdom of God on earth in which cooperation would reign supreme, perhaps through socialism, but whatever the method, it would dominate. From its beginning the world's progress had its source in the Creator; inventions, medical advances, labor-saving devices, all the improvements in humankind's quality of life and intelligence about the world were the products of the deliberate, steady work of God. This progress was both an enlightenment and a preparation for the coming Kingdom of God on earth.[12]

For Reed humans had a duty to contribute what they could, according to their ability, to bring about the conditions in which the Kingdom of God could flourish. At a minimum, this meant equal opportunity for everyone, with the commitment to produce the comfortable life. That was the message of Christian Socialism. The western cities had not yet achieved the kind of settled social structure that inhibited innovation in thought and reform, and Reed saw this as an advantage for those who advocated a new social order. Yet, at the same time, an army of entrepreneurs populated this West, fed by eastern capital and protected by politicians who depended upon their successes to retain their own power.

By 1884 Denver was well on its way to replicating the structure, ostentation, and the seamy underpinnings of many eastern cities. Several of the city's earliest entrepreneurs were still alive and jealously guarded their economic and political power. They had achieved their goals through hard work and an uncommon persistence in spite of the disasters they encountered.

Reed's efforts to build a community founded on the principle of cooperation, one that eschewed the very capitalism these investors understood best, involved him in a previously unknown struggle for political and economic power. What had these entrepreneurs endured to create a city and a state? Was the West as fluid in social and political structure as Reed imagined?

From Mining Hub to State Capital

In one generation, from 1859 to 1880, Denver had become the financial and trading center of the Rocky Mountain West, a feat achieved only because of the gargantuan efforts of a few men who imagined a prosperous city at the foot of the Rocky Mountains. The city's location, the discovery of gold and silver nearby, the availability of leadership, and timing all combined to make Denver and Colorado possible. Denver's earliest leaders — William N. Byers, John Evans, David Moffat, and Jerome B. Chaffee — all demonstrated that the drive to make money could overcome any obstacle. How did these early leaders accomplish so much in such a short time?

One historian answers this question succinctly: boosterism. Arrogant, intelligent, persistent, and braggart individuals, these early pioneers made Denver the Queen City of the Mountains and the Plains. Perhaps the greatest booster of them all was William Byers. He left Nebraska for Colorado's gold fields in 1859 with a printing press and his dreams. When he arrived at the small Auraria settlement, he visualized a great city at the foot of the Rocky Mountains. Byers immediately began to make that dream a reality. Within a few days, he had published the first edition of Denver's first newspaper, the *Rocky Mountain News*. The settlement's "gold fever" fueled Byers's town-building energy. Location and fortuitous circumstances provided the opportunities that made Byers and others wealthy. It was the right location, the right time, and Byers met the right people.[13]

Stories of gold had spun out of the Pike's Peak region and were drawing people like magnets from the Midwest and East. But some people thought that the stories were preposterous, and they demanded something more credible than "miners' tales" before making such a move. Horace Greeley, always ready for new adventure, traveled by stagecoach to the new settlement of Denver in 1859 to learn firsthand if what he had heard about the gold discoveries were true. After a few on-site inspections convinced Greeley that indeed gold was there, he published the good news in the *New York Tribune*. Greeley's story "was one of the most potent influences which brought rapid settlement to Colorado."[14]

Many of the "'59ers" sought instant wealth, but others came with different objectives. Men like General William Larimer of Kansas came seeking gold, not only in mineral form, but in real estate. Larimer formed a town-building company and sometimes used hired guns to validate his claims. Yet his unilateral action brought a degree of order to Denver's real estate transactions. Byers willingly joined with Larimer to plan a city and organize the land into lots, but in time Larimer became impatient with Denver's infantile economy. He returned to Kansas in 1863.[15]

Larimer's departure produced only a temporary pause in Byers's promotional activities. He printed maps and published guidebooks for those who needed directions to the bonanza, and he continued to advertise Colorado's attractions through the *News*. Settlers poured in and flooded the area with wagons, tents, and a passionate rivalry for mining claims. The combination of success, failure, and a rapidly increasing population brought crime and disorder. In an effort to introduce order through the presence of the federal government, citizens petitioned for territorial status.[16]

In 1861 Congress designated Colorado a territory. William Gilpin, the great forecaster of western economic dominance, was appointed governor. But Gilpin lost favor with President Lincoln when, without authorization, he funded the First Regiment of Colorado Volunteer Infantry to protect Colorado against expected Confederate raids. President Lincoln removed him in 1862 and appointed John Evans of Chicago as the new territorial governor.[17]

A practicing physician in Chicago, Evans had accumulated a sizable fortune through railroad and real estate transactions. He had supported Lincoln's nomination in 1860 and came to Colorado with ambitions for a U.S. Senate seat. Evans's experiences taught him that business and politics must work together if one were to fulfill personal and political objectives, and these were lessons that he brought to Colorado. During his term as territorial governor, from 1862 to 1865, and later, he pushed for statehood and economic progress in the region. In one of these early statehood attempts, during President Andrew Johnson's administration, Evans and the Republican party schemed to elect William Gilpin as Governor and Evans as U.S. Senator of the new state. But President Johnson refused to proclaim statehood and declared the Enabling Bill invalid; Evans's senatorial ambitions died with that declaration. Unlike Larimer, this disappointment did not send him back to Illinois. Because he had seen the promise of a city bursting with potential for investments, Evans stayed to fulfill as much of that promise as he could.[18]

Soon after Evans arrived in Denver, he joined with Byers in the effort to build a viable city. Surveying the available natural resources in the Rocky Mountain region, the two believed in the inevitable growth of a major city. With this confidence, a small group of men started to meet regularly to discuss how Denver could become that major city. Although they could barely be called a power elite in the 1860s, several of these men weathered the town's worst crises and ensured its survival because of their initiative and leadership. Along with Byers and Evans, this early group also included David Moffat and Jerome B. Chaffee; all were members of the Republican party.[19]

Moffat, a New Yorker, was the least educated when he arrived in Colorado, with wagonloads of merchandise instead of mining tools. Fortunately, Moffat saw profit in supplying products rather than prospecting and when he met fellow New Yorker Chaffee, they joined in several profitable investments. One was the First National Bank founded in 1865 with Chaffee's earnings from a quartz mill. Elected cashier in 1867, Moffat molded the bank into the region's strongest financial center. Chaffee assumed an important role in Colorado's Republican party, mostly because of his wealth and territorial recognition.[20]

William Byers, John Evans, David Moffat, and Jerome Chaffee constituted an important part of the emerging core of leadership in the 1860s. They demonstrated their confidence in Denver and the territory with investments and vigorous promotion. They wanted to build a town that protected their investments and attracted settlers. Although their objective was heavily influenced by an expected return on their money, they also understood that a secure and safe environment would be necessary if their town was to appeal to new families and new businesses. Each man was inextricably tied to Denver's survival, and together they faced the challenges to its existence from 1863 to 1867.

Four major events threatened the future capital of Colorado: the fire of 1863, the flood of 1864, the Sand Creek massacre in November 1864, and the lack of a railroad link to the transcontinental line. Any one of these problems would have caused weaker men to retreat to more benign regions. But these investors refused to let their town and its financial promise fade away. The most tragic of the four, the Sand Creek massacre, occurred on 29 November 1864. In response to Indian raids and the murder of a white family, Col. John M. Chivington led his men on a raid of a sleeping Cheyenne village. When the morning light illuminated the village, more than 153 Indians lay dead. When Denver's citizens learned about the horrors committed by Chivington's troops, so many people spurned him that he finally left for California.[21]

In 1867 Denver was made the territorial capital, having won out over Golden, but the emerging power elite faced its most serious challenge yet to the town's growth. Evans, Byers, and others believed that the Union Pacific Railroad should route its tracks through Denver as it moved westward to complete the transcontinental line. The rail line through Denver would greatly strengthen the city's commercial position in the region. They were devastated when they learned that the railroad company had decided to route the line through Cheyenne, Wyoming. As this news spread among local businessmen, some left for Cheyenne, assuming that it would become the most influential city in the Rocky Mountain region. The year, 1867, was the most crucial in the city's brief history, for the decisions made and the actions taken would determine the location for the future metropolis of the Rocky Mountain states.[22]

These entrepreneurs never gave up. They held a series of meetings with other boosters to find a way to connect with the transcontinental line. Soon they announced that negotiations were under way to build a branch line to Cheyenne to assure Denver a connection. Evans had also reached agreement with the Kansas Pacific railroad company to build a line from Kansas City, Missouri, to Denver. Shortly after this announcement, a Kansas Pacific official informed them that the railroad was stalled in Kansas and would require a capital investment of $2,000,000 if they were to continue. Also, the boosters soon learned that competing promoters in Golden were going to build a rival branch line to Cheyenne. If this happened, then Denver would probably remain a small town on the plains.[23]

Other investors joined with Evans, Byers, and Moffat to convince residents that a railroad connection to Cheyenne was necessary to ensure Denver's future. On 13 November 1867 interested citizens organized the Board of Trade (precursor to the Chamber of Commerce). It was responsible for making crucial economic decisions for the community and then implementing those decisions. The Board held an open meeting the next night and pleaded with the citizens to support an emergency plan. The message was simple: if Denver was to survive, the railroad was absolutely necessary. In a few days the Denver Pacific Railroad and Telegraph Company was incorporated, with an initial capital stock of $2 million.[24]

Financing was a challenge, but finally Evans was able to secure a land grant of 900,000 acres, on the condition that the Denver Pacific connect with the Kansas Pacific and the Union Pacific. The National Land Company of New York was chosen to manage the sale of this land, and Byers became the company's land agent. In the meantime, the Kansas Pacific had raised enough money to start construction anew. On 22 June 1870 the first locomotive, named the "General D. H. Moffat, Jr.," rolled into Denver and guaranteed for many boosters the promise of a future. Crowds gathered to gaze at this symbol of achievement and prosperity. In August 1870 the Kansas Pacific opened, giving Denver two connections with the East. The railroad pushed Denver out of the village class and pulled it into the city class.[25] The financial involvement of Denver's leadership and their informal communication of confidence in the city's future played a crucial role in helping citizens overcome these crises.

This diverse group of men exerted nothing less than "a herculean effort" to put Denver on the commercial map. Their success stemmed from their common bonds of the vision of a city made for commerce and the love of a challenge to build something new. Work experience varied, age differences were wide, education, origins all diverse — but they had turned a small town into a possible metropolis. Denver's potential to become a great city was assured by 1870 because the emerging power elite had pooled their talents and their resources.[26]

The railroads had an immediate economic impact in the region. The railroads advertised Colorado, hiring renowned photographer William Henry Jackson to take pictures for promotional purposes. Incoming trains brought passengers and freight, making Denver the hotel and business hub of the Rockies. Outgoing trains carried products from Denver's factories and food-processing plants to the mountains and plains.[27] Denver was no longer a stagecoach stop, but a railroad terminus:

> Within a single generation, railroads transformed a pokey frontier crossroads into an industrialized regional metropolis. Without railroads, Denver would have withered, as did many other frontier towns. With their spider web of steel Denverites began bragging that they had built the Queen City of the Plains.[28]

Even with the railroads, the city's long-term prosperity still depended on the regional economy. The town rebounded in 1876 from the Panic of 1873 because of the Leadville silver bonanza. But the removal of the Utes from the mineral-rich San Juan mountain range, and from most of the rest of the state, in the early 1880s made the most important contribution. The *News* boldly proclaimed that Ute reservations in Colorado were "a violation of every principle which belongs to civilized government." Furthermore, progress would not be stopped nor thwarted by "any senseless sentiment or foolish legislation." This usurpation of the Utes's rights increased Denver's hinterland by twenty thousand square miles. With this large economic playground, Denver generated more confidence in its future.[29]

While achieving these economic successes, Denver's leaders pursued admission to the Union for Colorado. Statehood would give Colorado more voice in decisions affecting the state's resources and applications of federal policy. There had been several earlier attempts, but each had failed for various political reasons. Republicans knew that Colorado had the potential to put three electoral votes in the party's coffers for the 1876 presidential election. On 3 March 1875, after prolonged effort and some political maneuvering, Congress finally approved the Enabling Act for Colorado to enter the Union.[30]

Colorado's two territorial delegates, who worked tirelessly for statehood in this period, were Republican Jerome Chaffee and Democrat Thomas M. Patterson, one of the few prominent Colorado Democrats. Tom Patterson was born in County Carlow, Ireland, on 4 November 1839 and immigrated to America with his parents in 1849. The family finally settled in Crawfordsville, Indiana, where he learned the trades of printing and watch repair. After serving in the Union Army, Patterson returned to Indiana and built a successful law practice. The law was interesting and profitable, but politics proved far more fascinating.[31]

Tom Patterson's political ideas were more liberal than his family preferred. When he announced that he wanted to go West, they encouraged him to choose Colorado because of its Republican dominance. They thought a liberal Democrat would have little chance there to realize any political aspirations. Patterson arrived in Denver in 1872 and was elected city attorney within eighteen months. Three months later he was a successful Democratic candidate for territorial delegate to Congress — the first major post in Colorado filled by a Democrat.[32] Not everyone thought he was qualified. The *News* was skeptical:

> He is a comparatively young man; has been a resident of Colorado about two years; is possessed of considerable energy, cunning and ability; is a fair lawyer, and an interminable talker. He has not the caliber, character, brains, or experience to properly represent Colorado at the national capital.[33]

Yet this young upstart played a key role in the final approval of the Enabling Bill.[34]

When the state constitutional convention convened on 20 December

1875, the delegates faced several troublesome issues. One of the most problematic was what to do about regulating the railroads. The Granger movement was at its peak at this time and was demanding strict regulation of railroad rates. It was a critical decision for Colorado. Still a frontier state and in need of capital, Colorado relied on eastern and European money for major investment. On the other hand, there was a fear of large corporations and a desire to protect citizens against extortion and monopoly. But the need for capital to fuel economic growth dominated. The delegates agreed on a ten-year tax delay for the mining industry and favored corporations with loose controls on stock issue, annual meetings, and reports. In the last days of the convention, the delegates adopted a moderate decision that did not specifically authorize the state to fix railroad rates, but gave the General Assembly the power "to revoke or annul any charter when it was found to be injurious to the people of the State."[35]

The Convention finished its work on 14 March 1876, and the people approved the Constitution in July. President Grant issued the petition granting Colorado admission to the Union on 1 August 1876. As part of the deal to get the Enabling Act, Patterson had promised the Democratic party that he would deliver Colorado in the upcoming presidential election. Unfortunately for Democrat Samuel Tilden, Patterson failed and Colorado's three electoral votes went to Republican Rutherford Hayes.[36]

Tom Patterson became Colorado's first U.S. Congressman and Republicans Jerome Chaffee and Henry Teller were its first U.S. Senators. Patterson lost the 1878 election and returned to practice law in Denver. He earned enough money from mining litigation and criminal law to accumulate a sizable fortune. Some described Patterson as the best criminal lawyer in the West, but politics always remained his consummate passion. He became the leader of the state's Democratic party and a close friend and supporter of Myron Reed. Later, as editor and owner of the *Rocky Mountain News*, he was an annoying critic of monopolies and the Republican party until his death in 1916.[37]

Statehood created opportunities for investors, but it did not solve the problem of unemployment. A state friendly to outside investors and eager to welcome all newcomers would find that it could not have the best of both worlds. Capital investments were geared for one primary objective — to make money. Newcomers came with one obsessive idea — to reap the rewards of opportunities. Sometimes these two goals, while similar, did not fit together well. The drive to earn profits often pushed investors to quantify all costs and to ignore the human variables that conflicted with the profit margins necessary to satisfy investors. For the enterprising individuals who came seeking rewards for their labor and commitment, the large corporations recognized their value only in terms of dollars, but not as individuals with loyalty to the company. The issues were reduced to one burning question, "How much is a worker worth in *today's* market?" If the corporation could not return the required profits because of increased costs, then management usually cut the most visible, variable cost — wages.

Most men who came West to dig their fortunes from the gold mines failed. When they did not find instant fortune, few had the money to return home or to buy land. For those who had to stay, the only choice was to hire out for wages. Surplus manpower resulted in a large labor pool that favored the corporations and merchants. Those who had no jobs often had to depend on charity or beg on the streets. From its beginning as a territory, Colorado had its problems of poverty and the inequity of opportunity — especially in Denver. Serious poverty had existed since the 1860s and organized efforts proved insufficient to answer the growing needs. In 1860 Elizabeth Byers, William Byers's wife, assisted in the organization of the Ladies Union Aid Society, which eased for some the misery that resulted from no shelter and not enough food.[38]

As the new state entered the 1880s, labor problems grabbed the nation's attention. Concerns springing from striking workers and riots, wages, the eight-hour day, the work environment, and immigrant contract labor stirred the imagination of most Americans, and the West was no different from the rest of the nation. These were unsettling years for much of the country. In Colorado the boom and bust economy created tough times when mineral prices dropped. The western mining industry had grown from small operations to corporations with new technology and widespread use of immigrant workers. With more laborers than jobs, corporations could lower wages and manage costs during slack periods.

In those days of unemployment and turmoil, Reed supported the eight-hour day and labor's right to organize and negotiate with employers. When workers experienced forced idleness, Reed felt that the minimum any community could do was to provide relief until the person could find employment. The advent of organized charity in the 1880s suggested an efficient, sympathetic method of assistance during these periods of misfortune. Thus, Reed and other interested citizens organized the Charity Organization Society in 1887, the forerunner to Denver's United Fund, with the Ladies Union Aid Society as a charter member. The city's charities established an annual communitywide approach to fund raising.[39]

Optimism, Culture, and Upheaval

The positive assessments of Colorado's potential for growth fed the great expectations of most investors in the 1880s. Fortunately, the 1873 panic had left no lasting damage on Denver's economy. A booster remarked: "Who can guess the future of this great city? Before the ordinary course of events is likely to check our growth, Denver will at least double her present population and increase her wealth by at least one-half."[40]

On 1 January 1880 the *News* extolled the wealth of Colorado in articles that described the state's mining successes, its building boom that produced churches, public schools, and fine mansions, and its agricultural growth. The homes and real estate of the bonanza kings were particularly newsworthy on this New Year's Day. The *News* profiled the Tabor Block, the Windsor Hotel, St. John's Episcopal Cathedral, and U.S. Senator Nathaniel P. Hill's house, which stood on five lots, a "mansion of an imposing appearance and [it] makes a fine architectural ornament to the portion of the city in which it is situated." The wealthy had moved from Fourteenth Street to high land near the capitol, which became "Capitol Hill," a location more symbolic of their status. In truth, this move further insulated them from the poverty, noise, and unpleasantness of the flourishing city. The entrepreneurs agreed that these evidences of economic success confirmed a city worthy of investment and residence.[41]

Denver and Colorado experienced rapid development from 1880 to 1892. As the largest city between Kansas City and San Francisco, with a population of 35,629 in 1880, Denver functioned as the center for commerce, finance, and governmental bureaucracy in Colorado and the Rocky Mountain region. With no significant competition in its immediate area, Denver's market stretched from Cheyenne, Wyoming, to Pueblo, Colorado, as far east as the midwestern towns around Chicago and St. Louis, and even to the Pacific Coast. Railroads put the city on the regional trade map—literally and strategically—and in spite of the fear of monopoly, railroads enhanced the image of Denver as an urban center of eastern industrial status.[42]

By 1880 railroad track mileage in the state had expanded from 157 miles of track to 1,570 miles, and other enterprises experienced a similar boom. The number of farms had increased from 1,738 to 4,506, and laborers from 7,353 to 16,336; manufacturing establishments grew from 256 to 599 and their workers numbered 4,393, up from 937; and the numbers of mining employees had escalated from 2,478 to 34,675. In 1879 Colorado mines processed $25 million dollars worth of ore—a gain of 175 percent over the previous year. The railroad's success, which created jobs and business opportunities, spawned much of this expansion and injected more capital into the region.[43]

In less than one generation, Denver had progressed from a mining supply town to a state capital with railroads, churches, schools, theaters, and first-class hotels; it was now a metropolis at the foot of the Rocky Mountains with a promising future. Byers's dream had come true. Here was an authentic city built upon the courage and determination of the power elite — and the drive to make money! They continued to claim that success awaited those who would work and invest. Even though opportunities seemed weighted toward the financiers, the working class grew during these years.[44]

Economic conquests were not the only notable events in the Rocky Mountain West; Denver's culture aroused interest beyond the region. Educated and talented patrons of the arts found Denver an attractive place to live and visit because of its climate. One German musician described Denver: "In proportion to its size, its population, and its advantages . . . there is not a city in the old or new world that has a history equaled to that of Denver." One could find in Denver about the same attractions in music and art that one expected in the eastern cities. The Tabor Opera House opened on 5 September 1881 with Emma Abbot singing "Lucia." The Denver Musical Association performed Gilbert and Sullivan's comic opera, "The Mikado," at the Academy of Music; churches provided an ongoing variety of musical entertainment. The same German musician exclaimed, "Music in opera, in concerts, in churches, in conservatories and schools and only I am compelled to be a silent listener."[45]

The Glenarm Club, organized in September 1884 by Myron Reed, was responsible for some of the early success of music in Denver. As a component in the comfortable life envisioned by Reed, the Glenarm Club would make cultural benefits available to the larger public. The club proposed to study selected books and prominent authors; it scheduled lectures on contemporary topics such as the tariff, Matthew Arnold's criticism of American civilization, and Shakespeare. Occasionally, it invited someone well-known like Julia Ward Howe, composer of "The Battle Hymn of the Republic," or the Indiana poet, James Whitcomb Riley. Special events included classical musical selections that headlined the best musicians available to Denver, and it was reported with some glee that "cultured New Englanders" copied Glenarm Club programs. An early chronicler of Denver musical history concluded that the Glenarm Club would grow into a permanent and powerful organization for the presentation of music, oratory, art, and literature.

Membership grew to seven hundred in 1889, but the annual dues of two to four dollars favored the middle and upper classes more than the masses.[46]

Art was nourished by artists' clubs and exhibits in bookstores and selected private studios. The *News* often published notices about exhibits and artists' activities, and the Denver Art League offered public and private education in the arts. The University of Denver's Art Department held its first annual commencement on 9 June 1888 at the First Baptist Church, with William M. R. French, director of the Art Institute in Chicago, as the featured speaker.[47] The community did not lack a reasonable promotion of art and its advantages.

The *News* editor especially emphasized local support for art and literature when he importuned that gifts to enrich the city's culture should begin in the present. Why wait until death to endow cultural advancement? Today was the time to finance a library or an art school that would benefit the public for generations. Art had immediate, promising effects, declared the editor: "Art can engage in no better pursuit than to stimulate noble and healthful thought on all matters of human concern." There is no record that such appeals changed the decisions of the rich, but they did advance a definition of art's function in a growing city.[48]

Culture did not change politics in any significant way. The entrenchment of a new political elite was well under way by 1880. The leaders of the 1860s faded away and younger men assumed the responsibilities of economic and political direction. By the beginning of the 1890s, Colorado's railroads were largely under the control of eastern corporations or private investors. These "outsiders" made more deliberate investments that resulted in the steady growth of Denver. Its population had grown to 134,000 by 1900 — an outstanding feat. Denver's financial power now was in the hands of fewer than twenty men, and through their network of corporations and interlocking investments they dominated the community. The Denver Club, organized in 1880, sought to imitate British clubs, where men of power gathered to socialize, to discuss pertinent business issues, and to guarantee the safety of investments and growth.[49]

While the new power elite was digging in, the Republican party continued its dominance of Colorado politics. The eight territorial governors had been Republicans, and the party controlled the governorship for eleven years in the state's first fifteen years. The two Democratic governors had had to deal with a Republican-controlled legislature. Reed ran for Congress as a Democrat in 1886 and drew public and partisan criticism because, many felt, a minister had no business in politics. But the more serious charge was that he dared to oppose the establishment's economic policies in this one-party state.[50]

The entrepreneurs who founded Denver were no different from many eastern town builders. They tried to build a city that looked much like those in older sections of the country. Historian Gunther Barth maintained that Americans organized cities primarily for commercial and economic ventures — not for political, social, and economic reasons, as did the Europeans. To safeguard their investments and to make the city attractive for outside capital, the entrepreneurs used their political and economic power. By the mid–1880s, Denver resembled large eastern cities with its public transportation, telephone and telegraph systems, electric lights, and fire and police departments.[51]

The 1880s closed on a strong note of optimism. One could list high silver production, the Sherman Silver Purchase Act (1890), available and profitable railroads, and an escalating population. Merchants could look forward to a healthy business climate, and farmers could expect irrigation systems on the eastern plains to open more land for profitable crops. Had not Denver experienced its best decade of growth in new construction and the accumulation of wealth? As one booster said in 1880, "Who can guess the future of this great city?" But the 1890s brought the Panic of 1893 that sent Denver's power elite reeling with anxieties about continued progress and searching for answers to a clouded future. For Reed, the crises of the 1890s presented the potential for reform.[52]

As historian Henry Commager has noted, the 1890s were a "watershed" decade for the nation, and Colorado and Denver were no exception. On one side was an agrarian America dominated by domestic problems and the political, economic, and moral baggage from the seventeenth and eighteenth centuries. It was an America in process, sure of its destiny, and certain of its self-reliance. On the other side was modern America, urban and industrial, but with more international involvement. Problems once thought peculiar to the Old World were now its problems, and it was trying to fashion its traditional institutions and habits of thought to conditions that were new and partly alien.[53]

As a territory, Colorado had depended on the national government for many years; consequently, national issues received more attention than state issues. Memories of the 1880s' labor strikes and social upheaval across the nation remained vivid for many Denverites. Many Americans demanded that state and national governments control the actions of these radicals. Coloradans had similar attitudes toward labor agitation and the presence of

vagrants and "unwashed" immigrants in their communities. Mark Twain
expressed a popular sentiment in a letter to William Dean Howells, "We are
a pair of old derelicts drifting around, now, with some of our passengers
gone and the sunniness of the others in eclipse."[54] It was a time of transition.

The fall of silver and the Panic of 1893 were uncharted byways in the
path of development for Colorado's entrepreneurs. The depression toppled
the fortunes of many American entrepreneurs, including Horace Tabor,
Denver's silver millionaire and builder of the Tabor Block and the Tabor
Opera House. While political and financial leaders searched for answers to
these economic and social problems, there emerged several economic subcultures. Laborers, miners, farmers, and stockmen looked to the Republicans and the Democrats for solutions. Neither party proposed an acceptable answer to their dilemma. When voters looked for an alternative, the
Populist party appeared as a possibility.[55]

The silver issue brought enough Populists together in 1892 to elect
Davis H. Waite of Aspen as governor. They won no significant offices in the
1894 state election, and their future as a party ended in Colorado when they
united with the Democrats in 1896. Political reform in Colorado continued
to incorporate the Populist themes of more participation by the people in
governmental decision making and monetary reform, and these reformers
identified either with the established parties or independent movements.[56]

The entrepreneurs and their descendants again found the necessary
imagination and perseverance to put Denver and the state back on its way
to a profitable future. By 1898 they had emerged from the Panic of 1893
and planned to build a broader economic base. Colorado would take a
different path from the 1880s with more diversified businesses, but it also
would highlight the state's strengths — climate and tourism. The recovery
from the Panic of 1893 demonstrated that their marriage to investment and
Denver as the western commercial center could not be dissolved because of
economic misfortunes; the bond between them was made of impervious
financial mettle. The Queen City remained on the Rocky Mountain throne
with profit as her charm.

In 1884 Reed, armed with a vision of a new social order, became pastor of
Denver's First Congregational Church. He arrived in the midst of the
prosperous 1880s and called for change in the established social order, a
change that would provide a better life than that experienced under the
dominance of capitalistic industrialists. He asked not for equal possession
of goods, but for equal opportunity for all citizens. Reed stood in the
tradition of Edward Bellamy, Henry Demarest Lloyd, and Eugene V. Debs,
reformers who wanted ordinary working people to participate more in the

decision-making process of political and economic policies. They searched for a better way to realize the American Dream than by a capitalism that exploited people, glorified materialism, and dehumanized work with a technology that "mechanized" the worker so that she/he could be discarded as easily as a worn-out gear. Sometimes they proclaimed their message through Populism, sometimes through Socialism, and sometimes through proposals for cooperative industries and colonies. What would happen if the masses began to use their power to effect the changes demanded by reformers? These possibilities infuriated capitalists and frightened power-hungry politicians.[57]

In this budding Western region Reed saw the possibility of a new community that would use the principle of cooperation, not competition, as its foundation. Modeled after the New Testament teaching of Jesus Christ, it would embody the socialist idea of "From every man according to his powers to a man according to his needs." This community would make literature, art, music, and theater available to everyone without discrimination. Men and women of all races could participate in the political process and vote. For Reed, this "comfortable life" was possible in the West. The institutions of charity, politics, organized labor, and Christian Socialism could serve as vehicles to hasten the coming of the Kingdom of God on earth.

TWO

Cooperation:

Foundation for a New Community

The record of successes and the expectations for greater progress in the years ahead possessed Colorado's leadership throughout the 1880s; enthusiasm for regional promotion and confidence in the soundness of future investments abounded. New people filled Denver's streets, and businesses grew to meet their needs. But one new arrival stood out among the crowds. Myron W. Reed did not look like the ordinary minister of the nineteenth century. He presented a different appearance, carried a different message, and expounded a different theology from that of the average Christian minister. The *Omaha World* newspaper painted a picture of a man most unlike the conventional parson:

> Myron Reed . . . is dark and big, with a heavy black mustache and bold black eyes. He wears a broad-brim slouch hat, yellow plaid suit and loud jewelry, and chews tobacco as vigorously as Sam Jones did before the reformation. His style in the pulpit is what he calls "plain and practical." Having occasion to refer to the article popularly known as the spade, he calls it a spade without equivocation; and he has been known to indulge in the luxury of expletives of the milder form. He has had a varied life, having been successively a soldier, a workman in a printing office, a miner and a minister of the gospel.[1]

Fitz-Mac, a Colorado Springs columnist, elaborated on this description by pointing out, "He does not wear gloves, and I never knew a man of brains that did."[2]

Reed's unconventional appearance did not prevent Denver's First Congregational Church from installing him as its minister in 1884. From the beginning Reed insisted on a church that would make all people welcome, regardless of their economic class. One could expect to see on any Sunday evening a mosaic of the city's society scattered among the wealthy members. The new preacher's sermons and outspoken opinions provoked negative and positive reactions from church members and nonmember regulars. But he made it plain that neither his message nor his personality would change to satisfy his critics. He was simply Myron Reed—a man with a mission.[3]

When Reed arrived in Denver from Indianapolis, he undoubtedly was impressed with the city's progress from "mining camp to metropolis" and its potential for continued growth. Sometimes his vacations has lured him to the West and Reed had already grown to admire its beauty and pristine environment. When discussing with a friend the East or West as a possible home, Reed had expressed a preference for the West. The West had fertile ground in which one could plant new thoughts, thoughts of the comfortable life, but only a small window of time remained. Like older communities, western cities would soon acquire an ingrained identity and social structure that would be more difficult to change.[4]

Reed carried with him the intention to make a mark in the city's political and social life but on a different basis from the city's founders. Denver's wealth, its bright future, and its civic optimism were welcome attributes to reformers like Reed; he could use them to his advantage. The problems that needed solutions cried out for definition and Reed thought he was the man to define the problems and point to the solution—the cooperative community.

The Bible and Plain Language

Some described Reed as a man with an exasperating, independent attitude who possessed ideas that sounded too radical for most clear-headed citizens. Others said that in spite of his audacity, he attracted people because of his provocative sermons and this was his redeeming quality. Reed believed that society needed some modifications: a more equal distribution of wealth, more justice for the worker and the poor, and more cooperation among growing populations in the emerging urban communities. Sometimes his friends asked him to soften his words, but he answered each time: "While I serve you as a teacher my speech shall be free; when my services are distasteful you may dismiss me. I can speak no man's mind but my own."

As a preacher, Reed functioned as an interpreter who proclaimed the gospel
to all people so as to generate more understanding, but he always acted as a
member of the community, never placing himself above or separate from
the many. As a teacher, he had a responsibility he could not shirk—to
contribute to the growth of the kingdom of God on earth.[5]

When he had been separated from his family as a young man, Reed had
swallowed a dose of experience in the outside world that taught him about
life in a way he probably would never have known otherwise. He learned
that a tramp endured hunger, loneliness, and rejection, but in New York he
had been befriended by a warm and generous stranger. This act of unexpected kindness left a lasting impression that aroused Reed's compassion
for any luckless person he chanced to meet.[6]

In his poverty Reed learned that not all people who owned few material
goods and lived from day to day were guilty of immoral conduct or had
no will to work. His experience as a youthful wanderer convinced him
that many of these men would work, just as he would, if work were available. Reed never accepted that tramps or any unemployed person deserved
their fate; instead they deserved assistance to help them overcome their
misfortune.

A penurious childhood had placed limits on Reed's early education, but
when possible he had attended the local school. Subjected to a Puritan
discipline, he often challenged any strict enforcement. When he quarreled
with his father and left home, Reed's public schooling ended. With such
limited formal teaching, it required an enormous individual effort for Reed
to acquire his subsequent education. Always an omnivorous reader, he had
access to what he called a "library of old Puritan teachers" and Bulwer's
novels. He retained much of what he read and often used material from
Thomas Carlyle, Robert Burns, Ralph Waldo Emerson, Charles Dickens,
and Victor Hugo in his sermons. He also counted the abolitionists as a part
of his intellectual heritage.[7]

In his youth, Reed's family had entertained abolitionists and sometimes
attended their meetings. He saw the abolitionists assisting runaway slaves
on their way to freedom. These experiences impressed upon Reed the value
and necessity of individual liberty. To Reed, the abolitionists represented
justice for those who were powerless to win it for themselves. By their
deeds, they redefined the law and rewrote the social code for the black
slaves. They also exposed for Reed the law's fairness and unfairness. He
came to believe that the law as an instrument of justice required close moni-
toring. When it robbed any American of the republican ideal of liberty or

subverted the equal application of justice to all people, then every responsible citizen must demand changes in its statutes and its administration.[8]

When Reed decided to enter the ministry in 1861, he enrolled in Chicago Theological Seminary. The seminary featured a full-time faculty of three professors: the Reverends Joseph Haven, Samuel C. Bartlett, and Franklin W. Fisk. Haven and Bartlett, graduates of Andover Theological Seminary, had previous teaching experience and had been ministers in the Congregationalist church. Haven, an exponent of the Scottish "Common Sense" philosophy who taught doctrinal theology, proposed that theology had progressed a bit since the time of Jonathan Edwards in the eighteenth century. Thus it was now acceptable and obligatory to question contemporary theological positions to determine if their application to the modern world made sense. Haven also argued that one must do right because it is one's duty to do so: "We ought because it is right." This was a principle that Reed apparently adopted.[9]

Bartlett, professor of Biblical literature, emphasized Biblical exegesis in the Hebrew and Greek tongues. If students were to understand the Bible, then they must learn to read it in its original languages and appreciate its cultural setting. Bartlett later designed a system of daily study for ministers that included: arise at six; make time for tea and prayers and play with the children; have a reading time with the wife but no hard thinking between 9 p.m. and 10 p.m.; in bed at ten or sooner.[10]

Rev. Franklin W. Fisk, a Yale Divinity School graduate and professor of homiletics, served the seminary for forty-two years. Described by his students as "a hundred and ninety pound trip-hammer," he was an active physical man with superabundant energy. Fisk, an excellent raconteur and a remarkable conversationalist, could have passed as the model for the "manly Christian." Manly Christians in Victorian America were men who led robust lives, engaged in activities that demanded discipline and physical exertion, and demonstrated that to follow Christ did not mean a denial of manhood. The weakness of the pulpit, according to Fisk, had its source in the ministers' denial of the church's authority over society's political and economic organizations. This act of denial was not manly nor was it according to the gospel's imperative as Fisk understood it; ministers must courageously address the injustices in the social order and announce the gospel's demands for justice.[11]

Reed's preaching reflected the influence of all three professors. The themes of the progression of theology, Biblical interpretation that utilized exegesis as well as the latest scholarship relative to historical and cultural influences, and claims that economic and social justice were the rightful provinces of the pulpit appeared regularly in his sermons. The insensitivity of some churchmen to society's injustice and to a theological dogma that alienated the common people angered Reed. He regarded organized religion's methods to extend its spiritual authority as alien to Jesus' message. When churchmen exhibited concern about the declining church attendance of the lower middle class and poor, they typically emphasized the lack of personal morality and piety. In short, those who did not attend weekly worship lacked a sense of remorse for their sinful conduct. It seemed that some churchmen encouraged the poor to accept their lot in life and prepare for heaven. Reed held that if the church wanted to speak to the common people, then it must simplify its theology and use language they understood. Reed remained sensitive to historical changes and to the necessity for revisions in doctrine and ecclesiastical practice to match the evolution in the thought and needs of the people.

After graduation in 1868 Reed served churches in the South and Midwest until 1877, when he was called to the prestigious Indianapolis First Presbyterian Church. He had no difficulty passing the presbytery's examination for theological acceptance but he remained a Congregationalist. Reed made friends with the future president, Benjamin Harrison, who was an occasional hunting companion, and with James Whitcomb Riley, the poet and lecturer, who accompanied Reed on a European vacation. Church attendance increased under Reed's preaching, although some of these new attendees would not appear on that society's list of respectable citizens. A group of gamblers admired Reed and frequently attended the Sunday evening services. They never joined the church, but when he left Indianapolis, they rewarded him with a set of expensive jewelry. Reed attracted all kinds of people because of his ability to relate to them in a way that recognized their common frailties and their concerns.[12]

Participation in charity and other local affairs helped Reed attain a positive image statewide. Because of this recognition, some thought he ought to run for political office. A few newspaper friends offered to support him for governor of Indiana, but Reed did not encourage them. He became involved in the city's culture as a member of the Indianapolis Literary Club, an elite group which met for discussion and criticism of members' papers on contemporary topics and classic literature. Elected president for one year, Reed's presentations always assured a large audience and lively discussions. The Indianapolis Literary Club probably provided Reed with a model for the Denver Glenarm Club.[13]

Oscar C. McCulloch, a Christian Socialist and pastor of the Plymouth

Congregational Church, became more than Reed's ministerial colleague. To widen the church's outreach, McCulloch had transformed the Plymouth Church into an institutional church, one that opened its doors daily for general ministries to the total community. He had founded the Plymouth Institute, a people's college that offered a variety of courses and sponsored a series of popular lectures that included Matthew Arnold and John Dewey. Recognized for his charity work and elected president of the National Charity Organization in 1891, McCulloch felt that heredity was a major contributing factor to ongoing poverty. In *The Tribe of Ishmael: A Study in Social Degradation*, an examination of Indianapolis slum families, he looked for ways to break the perpetual cycle of pauperism. Supported by city leaders, McCulloch created a unified charity organization in 1883 to replace the existing haphazard ones. He built a Friendly Inn and Woodyard to provide work and lodging for tramps and the unemployed. McCulloch shared his ideas with Reed, who would later propose a similar Friendly Inn and an organized charity society in Denver.[14]

The friendship between Reed and McCulloch began in 1874 when Reed presented a paper on Matthew Arnold's *Literature and Dogma: An Essay Towards a Better Apprehension of the Bible* to the Wisconsin Congregational and Presbyterian State Convention at Madison. This dignified body considered Arnold's book dangerous and disagreed with Reed's conclusion that excessive concern with dogma had alienated the common people. McCulloch defended Reed; he had read Arnold's book and agreed with Reed's essay. Both men believed in a Christianity that stressed action, with less emphasis upon dogma. This chance meeting grew into a friendship that endured until McCulloch's death in 1891.[15]

Reed's treatment of Arnold's *Literature and Dogma* can serve as a prologue to his developing theology and his criticism of the church's effectiveness and its doctrine in the latter nineteenth century. He began by emphasizing that Arnold did not intend that one should harshly criticize the Bible or let go of its truths; instead, Arnold tried to show how one might seize the Scripture and never let it go. In the preface, Arnold assumed that "an inevitable revolution . . . is befalling the religion in which we have been brought up." To Reed this implied that religion attracted more common people than it had in the past, an argument with which he disagreed. For example, Reed argued, many common people in New England and its surrounding areas did not read the Bible nor did they attend church with any regularity. As Reed pointed out, in these states annual membership increases for the Congregational churches ran only four to six percent; even the spiritualist Fox sisters exceeded that percentage.[16]

What caused the common people to reject the church and the Bible? Reed agreed with Arnold that councils and bishops had robbed the Scripture of its original appeal by forcing its message into creeds and immutable dogma. Reed asked his audience to weigh carefully Arnold's call to remove the weights of anachronistic religious language and dogmatic baggage that unnecessarily complicated the gospel truths. The early church had labored and prospered for three hundred years without a catechism. In the next fifteen centuries, dogma, with its theologically precise creeds, had tried to convert the world, but the world had turned away. Ordinary persons could not reason from such terms as "substance, identity, causation" and arrive at any sensible interpretation of life.[17]

If one read the Bible with the understanding that it contained poetry, songs, history, and stories, not hard, scientific facts, Reed argued, then perhaps it could speak to the inner person. Jesus used ordinary language in his teachings and established a strong rapport with the people. The Biblical message came neither from the American Bible Society nor did it drop down from Heaven, but it grew within the person and God made it grow in a natural way. Reed favorably compared Biblical language with the language that might be contained in the conversation of two friends. When they shared a story or daily events, their words had no preconceived notions about them, but rather signified "heat and life," that is, passion and truth. Reed stressed that informal and direct communication with ordinary language struck the chords of meaning and facilitated understanding, whereas language cast in the rigid molds of a dogmatism that reeked of musty, ecclesiastical, storage vaults produced no feeling and little understanding among the common listeners.[18]

Reed believed that anyone with an open mind could find faith and the assurance that he or she belonged to God's community. Faith proved itself in good works, in activities that helped those in need inside and outside the circle of the church. When individuals accepted membership in the family of God through faith in Christ and altered their behavior to conform with Christ's example, that is, when they served God and humanity, then these actions authenticated their salvation. Reed asserted, "The sufficient proof of good health is to feel well." As Horace Bushnell had earlier stated, one's salvation awaited one's acceptance and then the living out of that faith confirmed one's salvation.[19]

But churchmen thought in terms of doing something with creeds instead of focusing on people, as had John Wesley, when he left the comfortable pulpit of the Anglican Church and preached to the coal miners on their way to work each morning. The exodus from the church had not been caused by good works. The masses had not been fooled; they knew the church emphasized the wrong word — wealth. Reed said, "It is the heresy of the head that is offensive."[20]

If the church could not reach people with its dogmatic message, then better to let it go. Newspapers, magazines, and popular novels all pointed up the doubts of the common people about the church's theology. Why could not the church accept what human experience verified in the gospel story; it was enough for salvation. Reed quoted Arnold to show that in Christ's teachings anyone could encounter genuine personal salvation: "They [Christ's teachings] have an ineffaceable, unforgettable stamp of reality." Reed agreed that the church required doctrinal statements, but he contended that correct or incorrect doctrine had no essential bearing on one's salvation. Man cried out for something simple on which to base his beliefs. The church stood a better chance of success with all classes of people if it became known more for its role as a servant to humanity than as an institutional embodiment of correct theology.[21]

Although Reed claimed that Arnold's essay taught him how to read the Bible with a more reasonable understanding, he had a stronger intellectual kinship with Horace Bushnell. Typical Bushnellian themes — an optimistic view of the world's progress toward the kingdom of God on earth, and a belief in America as the land of special promise — permeated Reed's sermons in the 1880s and 1890s. After the Civil War, Bushnell had written:

We are the grand experiment of Protestantism! Yes we — it is our most peculiar destiny — we are set to show, by a new and unheard of career of national greatness and felicity, the moral capabilities and all the beneficent fruits of Christianity and the Protestant faith.[22]

From Reed's point of view this grand experiment should not be limited to Protestantism. Judaism and Roman Catholicism should also be accepted as part of God's kingdom on earth. A Denver pulpit fortuitously appeared at the right time for Reed to prove his ideas in a receptive city.

"Just the Man for Denver"

In early 1884 McCulloch temporarily filled the vacant pulpit of the First Congregational Church in Denver, one of that city's wealthiest and most prominent churches, that counted among its members several distinguished civic and political leaders. The trustees inquired if McCulloch

could recommend someone for their open pulpit. Colorado's reputation for
a healthy climate inspired McCulloch to suggest Reed. Reed had experienced periodic illnesses resulting from his Civil War service and McCulloch thought the Rocky Mountains' benevolent atmosphere would be kind
to him. Familiar with Reed's love for the outdoors and Colorado's fishing
and camping attractions, McCulloch suspected this pulpit would appeal to
him, and this church presented a worthy new challenge for his old friend.[23]

For seven years Reed had filled the prestigious Indianapolis First Presbyterian Church pulpit and had earned a reputation as a social gospel advocate, an excellent preacher, and a potential politician. There were public
expressions of sorrow when he left, and the newspapers lamented the great
loss to the city. Reed explained his resignation by claiming that he had done
all he could in Indianapolis, and now he must move to a new field of
endeavor.[24]

His farewell sermon contained Reed's views of the essence of religious
faith, along with a pithy definition of personal salvation:

> Religion is made out of plain duties, plain even to children. Cease to do
> evil; learn to do well. Let him that nameth the name of Christ depart
> from iniquity. The sayings of Christ are dissertations, and the listener
> has that within which echoes them.[25]

According to Reed, righteous conduct would lead to religious faith. No
traumatic experience was necessary to introduce one to Christianity; rather,
one could decide on one's own to do right and then live in a way that
reflected that commitment. One's behavior must go hand in hand with
one's faith in Christ; the two cannot be separated. This faith had no elusive
qualities; it resided within each person and anyone could grasp it.[26]

In his evening address Reed outlined his views of the minister's function
and the futility of any accurate measurement of success. A minister worked
on the mind and heart in a way that one could not measure; a dynamic faith
in God and humankind, not concrete models, dominated the pastor's calling. Growth in faith and works was a process and did not lend itself to any
precise assessment. Reed saw this function as replicating the model of Jesus'
ministry, which meant changing people's thoughts, altering society, and
making the world more tolerant and pleasant. The important thing for the
minister was to persist with this message and to serve as an example. Reed
reminded the congregation that he preached a gospel that emphasized the
present, not the afterlife; he encouraged people to believe in the new world
to come. He expected the church to reflect equality: "Jesus Christ. . . .

intended as a result of his work to unite men, and women, and children in a commonwealth. We here believe that the Lord's supper stands for this democracy." Reed trusted that the kingdom of God would progress to fulfillment: "I have preached a vigorous discontent with things as they are, no satisfaction until things are as they ought to be, and the philosophy that things that should be, will be." With this hopeful message, he left Indianapolis bound for a new land.[27]

He arrived with his family at his new post in April 1884. While his health figured as one consideration for the relocation, Reed also felt that he could contribute to the political and social development of Colorado. In his initial interview with the *Rocky Mountain News*, Reed told the reporter that legislatures could not make men virtuous and intelligent by passing laws. The human race would figure out the values of right living and appropriate social conduct through the art of persuasion and the application of reason. Reed emphasized that the villains in society were not the poor, ragged creatures; instead, he identified them as:

> . . . the rich intelligent rascals, who sit in cushioned chairs. . . . [I]n my pulpit . . . I shall not appear as a special pleader for rich men. They have enough money to hire lawyers to talk for them; they may own some ministers, but they don't own me.[28]

As a parting, perhaps peace-making remark, he said:

> I do not want to shock or unnecessarily offend my people. I do not want to strike too high or too low a plane in my first sermons, but I do intend to preach what I honestly believe, and to tell my people what I think whether they like it or not.[29]

What Denverites yearned to hear was more about the city's progress and how it would continue. Economic expansion had captured their attention, and some probably considered their good fortune a result of God's blessings showered upon a deserving community. With its smelters, railroads, and small businesses, Denver had work for anyone who wanted it — so believed its civic leaders. The *Denver Republican* made a grandiose comparison when it described the city as "the Paris of Colorado" because of its regional influence on trade and culture. Eastern investors certainly regarded Denver as the financial oasis of the "Great American Desert," which confirmed for the city fathers their financial expectations.[30]

The *News* gave Reed the opportunity to declare his concerns about the ills of the human community and to let everyone know that he valued his independence of thought. The cares and needs of the poor bothered Reed more than the problems of the entrenched wealthy class. This opening interview set the tone for his ministry and the subsequent controversies that would plague his successes, but Reed would speak no man's mind but his own. His maiden sermon in Denver's First Congregational Church revealed his interests and his definition of the minister's task.

The sermon, entitled "Bezaliel [sic], The Inspired Mechanic," set out the three beliefs that undergirded Reed's theology and ministerial philosophy. First, Reed affirmed that God is in everyone. God had inspired Bezaleel, a common workman, to train and to work on the construction of the tabernacle. Reed used this scripture to illustrate that the best thoughts, which entered one's mind "in a flash," came from God. It signified the way God inspired people, especially in the task of moving the world forward according to the divine plan. Columbus provided another example of God's inspiration: even if he was not everyone's ideal of a pilgrim in 1884, Reed claimed that God chose Columbus to stumble across America. There was no divine discrimination among those whom God would select to further the growth of his kingdom. God used even the wicked and the weak in unfolding the better world: "Treasure may be carried in an earthen vessel."[31]

Second, the sacred and the profane could not be separated in this world. Reed reasoned that any artificial separation caused further divisions of the world, which allowed non-Christians to limit the sacred domain. Many skeptics professed that the profane realm included all contributions to the advancement of knowledge and the comfort of humankind. Reed listed the printing press, steam power, labor-saving machines — all inventions claimed by the profane community. But for Reed, humanity progressed according to God's wisdom and timetable. The Denver skeptics notwithstanding, Reed declared that all advancements in thought, machines, and institutional care resulted from God's inspiration.[32]

Finally, Reed attached great importance to this claim of God's inspiration. Simply, the world's development, in its totality, had its source in God's ultimate design for humanity. Reed proclaimed: "I want to stretch forth my hand and claim every good thing that is done under the sun as done by impulse of the Lord. . . . I do it to widen God's work." God's activity embraced all of society, not just the churches, the holy days, or protracted meetings; the kingdom of God slowly moved forward according to the New Testament plan. All things that promoted humanity's improvement contributed to the building of the kingdom on earth.[33]

This sermon framed Reed's basic message: the coming kingdom on earth proceeded from God's work through all people throughout the world. As people gained more understanding of the divine plan, and then applied that understanding to the problems of their communities, the commonwealth of Christ would slowly emerge and take shape. The progress of humanity in all things verified the work of God in one world — not in a world of two realms. The minister must teach these truths and maintain an open mind to changes within science, culture, or politics that affected the growth and health of human society. Inasmuch as these changes improved the human community, they confirmed the coming kingdom of God.

If the reaction to Reed's first sermon reflected to any degree the true local feeling about Reed, then one might assume a positive reception without any serious qualification in spite of his theology. The editor of the *News* commented:

> Rev. Myron W. Reed, who preached his first sermon as pastor of the First Congregational Church, yesterday, is a splendid type of the Christian gentleman in all the relations of life. He possesses brains and heart to an uncommon degree and charity is greater than creed in his lexicon. In the pulpit he is strong, clear and broad; out of it he is bright and genial as a day in June. He is just the man for Denver and Denver is just the place for him.[34]

The West was just the place for Myron Reed, and no mainline denomination in the West could claim a minister who had such strong convictions about charity, labor, and socialism; who weekly expressed these opinions in sermons; and who promoted reform through politics and local and state institutions. The rich socialized with Reed and supported his ministry, even as he criticized their stewardship and motives. The poor gravitated to Reed because he spoke for their concerns and tried through public and charitable agencies to relieve their misery. And the workers championed Reed as one churchman who understood the injustices they faced and who would put his livelihood on the line on their behalf. Almost everyone agreed that Reed's ability to cultivate loyal friends contributed enormously to his success as an outstanding preacher.

The New Theology and Princes of the Pulpit

The nineteenth century bequeathed to Reed the idea of human progress and the widespread optimism it brought to American culture. He typified at least two other prevailing attitudes: nativism surfaced in his endorsement of immigration restrictions for the Chinese and in his support of limitations on "assisted immigration" (immigration through labor contracts); he also possessed a strong sense of nationalism, with an intense dedication to the ideal of the American republic. For Reed, America figured in the plan for the coming kingdom of God; it symbolized the modern promised land. And, according to Reed, the church properly functioned as a primary agent in the transformation of humankind into a model community—one of cooperation. Reed's theology, inasmuch as he admitted to a theology, most closely resembled the New Theology that began in the late 1870s.

In an age when science, and particularly Charles Darwin's *Origin of Species*, bombarded the churches' teachings, many religious leaders sought a method of theological reasoning that could make the Gospel relevant to the modern age without sacrificing its basic truths. They had to deal with the impact of evolutionary theory on the origins of the world and humankind, as well as the scientific criticism of the Bible, which challenged Biblical authority and the theories of inspiration. These developments called into question traditional views of God, creation, and salvation. Now the church had to make sense of these developments in terms of its own theology. In the 1880s and 1890s "progressive" theologians developed the New Theology. Religious historian Winthrop S. Hudson summarized its advantages as follows:

> The great advantage of this New Theology was that it enabled its proponents both to maintain what to them was the heart of their inherited faith and at the same time to come to terms with the whole intellectual temper of the modern world. The stress upon self-authenticating religious experience permitted them to bridge the gap between the natural and the supernatural, and enabled them to give due recognition to the claims of science and of the scientific method. The acceptance of the idea of development made it possible to view the Bible in a way that was congenial to both their religious and their cultural orientation, allowed them to share to varying degrees the growing confidence in man and his future, and fostered an open-minded attitude toward differing opinions and new modes of thought.[35]

Industrialization and rapid social change after the Civil War added more problems to the church's agenda. Urban unemployment, aid for the destitute, a growing alienation between the churches and the masses and between wage labor and the capitalist—all these problems became exceedingly urgent as the century progressed. The New Theology allowed the church to reinterpret its message for broader appeal. The Social Gospel, with its imperative to seek solutions to social and political problems, complemented the New Theology's applied Christianity by pushing the church into a variety of programs to aid the poor and unemployed.

Historian William R. Hutchison has singled out Horace Bushnell (1802–1876) as the theologian who prepared the way for modernism in American Protestantism. Bushnell's writings expressed the New Theology's framework and made two important contributions to modernistic themes. First, he argued that one should interpret the language of the creeds poetically and not literally. Second, his environmental approach to religious nurture, with Christ as the moral force of God in society, fostered a growing confidence in the redemptive potentialities in the realm feared as "the world." He taught that we are born children of God and only need to live as such. As one became aware of God within and without, one grew in the knowledge of salvation and in the duty of right conduct. Bushnell placed great emphasis upon social institutions, particularly upon the nurturing powers of the family and the community of faith.[36]

While modernism was not yet a movement in the late 1870s, the idea of God's immanence and the adaptation of old dogma to contemporary language further encouraged a wider application of this new way of expressing traditional theology. In the 1880s Theodore Munger, a New Haven minister and disciple of Bushnell, attempted to define the budding New Theology and to explain how new truths work their way into human consciousness.[37] He defined the New Theology as the summons to a broader use of reason in religion. A reasonable interpretation of the Bible, according to Munger, accepted the divine inspiration of its writers but also held that the writers' culture conditioned their thoughts and language. Munger saw no antagonism between the kingdoms of faith and natural law. Instead of individual salvation alone, the New Theology also emphasized the solidarity of the human race. God was love and sought to save all people; God did not want to punish them. This theology declared in contemporary and plain language the spiritual truths suggested and validated by experience. The New Theology concerned itself with the "wider study of man." It dealt with real people and real problems — not the abstract beings defined by Calvinistic logic — and preached a hopeful message to human beings who struggled daily without the comfort of a loving God.[38]

Several Protestant ministers dominated America's pulpits in the late nineteenth century, and they addressed the task of mediating Christianity to America's changing society. Winthrop Hudson called them the "Princes of the Pulpit." Among these urban princes were Phillips Brooks, Washington Gladden, Henry Ward Beecher, and, one could add, David Swing and Myron Reed. All drew attention to the mission of the church because of their personalities and their pulpit skills. However one might criticize their theology, they labored to keep the church in the forefront of a society that often doubted its relevance in a growing industrial-commercial society. They did not agree on every issue, but they supported the new emphasis on God's love — not on his retribution — and on an individual's liberty to choose to do good. They believed that God worked through the whole of humanity, not just through the church, to effect his purposes and the coming kingdom of God.[39]

Phillips Brooks probably best exemplified the personality and eloquence of the preachers of the New Theology. As a minister of the same Boston congregation for twenty-five years, he often preached that "the spirit of man is the candle of the Lord." Humanity revealed God's goodness in its actions and humankind — not any organization of believers — provided God's instrument to accomplish his will. Confident of society's improvement, Brooks demanded no social reform program. He believed that poverty and injustice usually resulted from sin, but that they were temporary, "for there is a natural harmony which in the end will bring all diverse interests into perfect accord."[40]

Washington Gladden, Social Gospeler and Ohio Congregationalist minister, differed from Brooks in that he saw the need for reforms that would take place within society and within individuals concurrently. Gladden, focusing on the conflict between labor and capitalism, believed that the church would have to involve itself in this problem. For Gladden, the essence of Christianity was not in emotional experience, ritual, or specific dogma, but in specific ethical conduct. When a Christian followed Christ, it meant that he or she accepted that maxim "love your neighbor as yourself" as the ruling principle of life. God's Golden Age on earth would happen when the Christian law of love was applied to the problems of America's industrial society.[41]

While Bushnell buttressed Reed's views of the immanence of God and the path to salvation, two "princes of the pulpit," David Swing and Henry Ward Beecher, contributed to his conception of the ministry and the proclamation of the gospel in contemporary terms. David Swing, a popular Presbyterian minister in Chicago, preached a gospel that emphasized action more than simply profession of the faith. Some people erred by limiting their religion to faith, but Swing declared that one's faith must prove itself in one's deeds. Swing believed that one could not practice Christianity by simply believing and then refusing to become involved in the struggle against social injustice — a Christian committed to action. Furthermore, he stated that the culture of the Church Fathers who wrote the creeds influenced their doctrinal expressions. One could not understand any creed apart from its culture. After all, human culture changed rapidly, so that static creeds quickly became irrelevant.[42]

This position did not merely question the relevance of dogma, it urged the adaptation of contemporary meanings to old teachings. If dogmatic Christianity had no power to change people, then the gospel must be proclaimed as a way of living, not merely as recitation of correct beliefs. Religion that could not change human behavior had no practical effect in life. Swing's preachings were seen as very controversial. He was tried for heresy in 1874 for not preaching the Westminster Confession, a creed more than two hundred years old. After his acquittal, Swing resigned from the Presbyterian ministry and began an independent church in Chicago's Central Music Hall.[43]

As a seminary student in Chicago, Reed sometimes attended the Westminster Church where Swing preached to a congregation of approximately three hundred souls. Reed described Swing's sermons as old, probably written years before he came to Chicago. When the Chicago fire (1871) destroyed Swing's church and his sermonic notes, he had to write new ones that forced a restatement of his theology. Reed surmised:

If something like that could happen to all of us it would be well. We remember our old opinions too well. We suffer ourselves to be bound by them. . . . We must continually move on and out."

The organized church, Reed believed, had to do the same: it must always update theological beliefs so that anyone could comprehend their meanings and relate them to life — not to a lifeless, creedal dogma.[44]

Churches ordinarily did not modify creeds without debate among the clergy and laity and long periods of reflection. But by a happy circumstance, the Congregational churches had completed a revision of their statement of belief and introduced it in 1884, which coincided with Reed's arrival in Denver. In his initial interview with the *News*, Reed was asked what he thought of this new creedal expression. Reed commented that it seemed to improve on ideas that were three hundred years old and had done away with a good deal of dogma. The modernization of theological ideas concurred with his opinion that language commonly used best communicated the kernel of Christianity.[45]

In 1892 Denver's First Baptist Church sponsored a series of Sunday night services in which local ministers were encouraged to discuss why they had united with their respective denominations. Some ministers had previously exchanged pulpits to create understanding and cooperation, and this series kept that custom alive. For almost three months, the ministers of Denver's major denominations explained their basic beliefs and church polity.[46]

During this series, Reed took his turn to speak on "Why I Am a Congregationalist." He joined the Congregational church, he said, because of his childhood options: his father's church was the only one in the Vermont village where he grew up. He emphasized that the growing child assimilated the neighborhood's opinions as well as the church's teachings. Reed placed a high value on each congregation's freedom to develop and approve its creedal statement independent of the denomination.[47]

This sermon discussed three points that illustrate Reed's position with respect to creeds and the New Theology. First, Reed affirmed that statements of belief functioned best if they were brief and written in ordinary language. The First Congregational Church had only five articles of belief in its creed, which read as follows:

(1) We believe in God, the Father Almighty, the Being of absolute perfection, the Creator, Preserver and Governor of the universe, whose name is love;

(2) And Jesus Christ, His Son, our Lord and Savior, in whom through faith and repentance we have redemption and forgiveness of our sins and life everlasting;

(3) And in the Holy Spirit, through Whom we are renewed and sanctified, by whose inspiration the Scriptures are given to men; Who, with the Father and the Son, is supremely to be loved and adored;

(4) And in Divine retribution, through which shall be to every man as his work shall be;

(5) And in one church on earth and in heaven, and in one communion of the body and blood of Christ, and in the life immortal.

To this confession according to your understanding of the Word of God and according to your personal faith in Christ, do you now give your cordial assent?[48]

Matthew Arnold and David Swing would have approved of this creed's language and simplicity; it satisfied Reed because of its brevity. Bushnell, said Reed, represented the nineteenth-century theology of the Congregationalists more ably than Jonathan Edwards because he reinterpreted the

Christian faith according to changing conditions in contemporary life. Society had advanced in thought and civilized behavior since Edwards, and thus churches discarded "outworn doctrines" just as one discarded unnecessary items when moving.[49]

Second, the Congregationalists practiced the right of free speech and held this right in the highest esteem. Free speech guaranteed each person a voice in the congregation's decisions, and even though disagreements often arose, the final result produced a level of cooperation and harmony in the tasks agreed upon. To force dogma upon anyone against his or her will resulted in a continuing discord that threatened the institution. People must freely consent to the truth, and open dialogue facilitated the processes of understanding and agreement. Reed maintained, "Where people are allowed to speak and write freely there will be no revolution."[50]

Finally, the Congregational church understood that the road to God's kingdom on earth had many branches. No one denomination had the absolute truth, nor did any one religion. In Denver, Reed supported ecumenicalism, exchanging pulpits with Roman Catholics and Jews. On a return visit to Indianapolis, someone asked him what impressed him about Denver. Reed answered, "I saw a Jewish rabbi, a Catholic priest, an Episcopalian rector and a Congregational parson in one carriage going to the burial of a newspaper man who belonged to no church." For Reed, this symbolized God's universal love, which could not be contained in any one creed. Reed avowed, "We hold the truth, but we hold it with a limber elbow. . . . We sink the petty differences and lift up the great agreements." The God of love would bring agreeable people together into one community.[51]

Reed had followed Beecher's career since his appointment to Brooklyn's Plymouth Church. He admired Beecher for his preaching and perhaps for his unconventional conduct. Beecher's disheveled appearance, an unbridled independence, and little discrimination in his choice of friends bore some resemblance to Reed's own conduct. The charges against Beecher for an alleged affair with Mrs. Theodore Tilton in the 1870s did not cause Reed to rush to judgment. Acquittal by the court and the church restored Beecher's integrity; he regained the people's confidence—and for Reed that was enough.[52]

A week after Beecher's death, on 13 March 1887, Reed preached a memorial sermon in the First Congregational Church. He credited Beecher for elevating the minister's function from one of caretaker of a "sorghum Christianity" to one who proclaimed that God is love — that Christianity was a religion without terror, a religion that stressed the present life. Reed eulogized Beecher as one who "has done much for our conception of

God. . . . [God had] terrorized the children of men. Now he persuades. Now he rests his government not on the fears of men, but on their free consent." Beecher's eloquent message of God's love, drawn from a Bible reinterpreted for that age, left its mark upon Reed. Beecher's imperative that ministers preach upon every side of political life, that they relate the gospel to current issues, concurred with how Reed viewed the minister's task. The difficulties of knowing how and when to make clear the gospel's application to social concerns, and how to deal with people's apathy, troubled any minister. In an earlier sermon, Reed had somberly conceded that he could only try to make the gospel plain, but the listeners must receive any truth with an open mind and then decide how they must act.[53] Reed's message in Denver sounded the same notes found in the pulpit music of Swing and Beecher: he emphasized faith plus works, a God of love, and the sociopolitical responsibilities of the minister and the church.

On what basis can one include Myron Reed in the company of the Princes of the Pulpit? If one looks at personality and individual charm, then Reed compares favorably with a Brooks or a Beecher. But Reed did not possess the speaking skills of either man; no one accused him of being a great orator. He read his sermons with an uneven delivery, often without voice modulation or hand gestures, and his sentences were crisp and terse. His closest friends agreed that his sermons were more effective when read than when they first heard them. Yet the First Congregational Church was often filled to capacity, sometimes overflowing, and later, when he preached at the Broadway Temple, Reed's audience frequently exceeded fifteen hundred. These audiences included people from all walks of life: the rich, the poor, politicians, celebrities, and gamblers. The *News* regularly printed Reed's sermons; the *Denver Times* and the *Republican* published them now and then. Some fifty additional newspapers featured Reed's sermons, which permitted him to gain a degree of national and international recognition. In Indiana he was known as the "greatest preacher west of Brooklyn" (referring to Beecher), and even the English knew Denver as "the home of that great American preacher — Myron Reed." With Brooklyn's Plymouth Church vacant, reports circulated that Reed was the logical choice to succeed Beecher. But Reed told a *Republican* reporter that Plymouth Church had not contacted him, and if they did, he would not accept the position — he preferred to remain in Denver.[54]

In July 1887 the *News* profiled Denver's leading ministers and described Reed as "An Unique Genius." Already known as a man who quoted the classical authors, Reed now referenced contemporary novels and newspapers in his sermons, in an effort to reach ordinary folk. "Humanity is the great sea," said the celebrated infidel Robert Ingersoll, and Reed agreed: the church should sponsor a ministry that concentrated on the masses. Discussions of dogma could not compare with "getting the poorer classes out of the hells of this world." Because of his attention to the less fortunate and the positive publicity he received through the *News*, the majority of people were receptive to Reed's preaching. He accentuated doing rather than being, discussed everyday themes, and framed bits of wisdom and humor in epigrams that his listeners quickly grasped. One 1881 writer suggested about Reed's epigrams: "His thoughts come out like cannon balls, not merely one at a time, but each complete in itself and as compact as granite." A *News* reporter later commented that Reed's sermonic appeal rested not on his speaking ability, but on the "force and . . . evident expression of his own individuality." Perhaps it was this appealing individuality that earned him the reputation of an outstanding preacher.[55]

Despite these admirers, there were also critics, who did not agree that Reed's epigrammatic style communicated the thoughtful profundity that others adored. In 1887, when Reed was being touted as a replacement for Beecher, an (Aspen) *Rocky Mountain Sun* reporter described Reed's sermons as "made up of odds and ends" similar to a "crazy quilt" that finally resulted in a "showy absurdity that 'will not wash'.'" He declared that none of Reed's sermons would survive a thoughtful examination, but suggested that the average mind preferred these "catch-penny sentences that sound as if they might mean something" rather than a sustained argument. The reporter concluded that Reed spoke to the level of his audience, a talent that also reflected his limited knowledge.[56]

A *News* reporter criticized Reed's epigrammatic style after attending his church in 1889. On this occasion, Reed's sermon was "described as of the skirmishing order"; it lacked continuity of thought and attempted to condense too many thoughts into epigrams. The reporter complimented Reed for this skill and admitted that it made the sermon more interesting for many listeners. Yet, the reporter noted, most people required a process of reasoning, particularly when it involved religious matters, and without this logic, there would be mental dissatisfaction. After hearing these thought-capsules, the reporter inferred that Reed was a man of action and probably quick to make judgments.[57] But even with Reed's shortcomings, his critics agreed that the congregation listened intently until the very end.

Reed learned how to capture provocative ideas in simple language that was appealing and attractive to his audiences. These epigrams emphasized those ideas he considered most worthy of people's attention, and he carefully phrased them to convey thoughts that they could ponder and possibly

act upon. The following examples, gleaned from Reed's sermons, illustrate
how he used epigrammatic language to champion his major concerns:

CHILDREN, BOOKS, AND EDUCATION

The diet of a child's mind has much to do with the quality of his mind.
An injustice to a child will appear in the warped life of the man.
A preacher who reads books is so rare that he is much forgiven.
Read the best that has been thought and said. One face we inherit, the
other we make. The face we make and die with is made out of thoughts.
It costs more to arrest, try, and convict and hang a man than to endow a
kindergarten.

POLITICS

I am interested in politics because I believe that every political question
is a social question, and that every social question is a religious one.
It is a pleasant thing to me that the time has come when a priest and a
rabbi and a Protestant preacher can come together on a public platform not to dispute, but to agree as to some public question.
The charm of American life is its variety, its individuality, its invention.
The condition of these is liberty.
Where people are allowed to speak and write freely there will be no
violent revolution. That is the merit of a town meeting.

HUMANKIND

These perfect people make me tired. They are too good for human
nature's daily food.
It is beautiful to be a sinner and be conscious of it.
Great is the difference of race, color and previous condition; but one
humanity is common. All tears are salt; all blood is red.
Whatever the Indian of to-day is we made him, and he wears our
shoddy blanket and he eats our government steer.
If you wish to make men to be better you must make them happier.

THEOLOGY, CHURCH, AND THE KINGDOM OF GOD

It is high time to have less steeple and more bread. If the people knew
what the origin of steeples was, what they signified, they would not
build any more.
I was never more pleased in my life than when I discovered that God
was good and infinitely merciful. With my first money I bought all of
Theodore Parker's published works, and have been happier ever since.

I have never been able to feel any sense of blame because Adam was my father.

If a soldier does not keep his powder dry, trusting in God will not get his gun off.

The kingdom of God is strictly a republic . . . The golden rule familiar to us all obeyed would make a new Heaven and perhaps a new earth unnecessary.

America is the mixing pot of the nations — of the religions. We hope out of this mixing to secure the coming man — better than any who have come. So be patient, be merciful, be just. Hold fast to the American idea.

It is not a comfortable world while a single soul goes without.

SOCIALISM, TRAMPS, AND LABOR

I have lived to see socialism a respectable word and a socialist a respectable man.

You hear the phrase "Christian socialism." There is such a thing . . . the motto of this kind of socialists [sic] suits me very well. "From a man according to his power, to a man according to his needs." That is Christian.

Simply to see him [a tramp] makes a thoughtful man a socialist.

This society that permits such deadly parallels as we see, the gorged few and the hungry many, can not last.

I should find it exceedingly difficult to be compelled to be a tramp and not at the same time feel compelled to steal.

The question of woman's wages is a moral question.

The Socialist insists upon shorter hours for workingmen and on working hours for all men.[58]

Reed never achieved a national recognition for his sayings, as did Mark Twain, but the *Chicago Tribune*, in a review of Reed's book *Temple Talks*, placed him on a plateau with Ralph Waldo Emerson: "He is a master of style. In the art of sententious phrase-making he may be called a master of high degree. Not since Emerson has there been an American writer who excels him in this particular art."[59]

Regional recognition came more readily to this radical voice, as local newspapers advertised his abilities as a preacher and writer. The *News* published his series on the *Evolution of the Tramp* in 1886, and the *Denver Post* reprinted it in 1905. Articles for the *Republican* on personalities such as P. T. Barnum, the great showman, and Sarah Bernhardt, the actress, flowed from Reed's pen. A Reed sermon, "Night and Sleep and Rest," appeared in *Cosmopolitan*, a monthly magazine with a masthead slogan of "From every man according to his ability; to every man according to his needs."[60]

Scriptural lessons sometimes were eclipsed by stories about figures from literature, politics, or history. Men and women who could serve as examples to illustrate any theological theme would serve as Reed's examples: Jay Gould and George Pullman illustrated the avarice of capitalism; John Brown, the martyrdom of abolitionism; Robert Burns illustrated how a man could overcome stark Calvinism to find a merciful God; Charles Kingsley was characterized as a heroic socialist; and Minnie Freeman, a Nebraska schoolteacher who saved her pupils from a storm, demonstrated courage and love. Reed accentuated God's presence in these lives; although it was sometimes a gracious presence and sometimes a judgmental one, for Reed both evidenced God's plan to bring about the new community through all kinds of people.[61]

Like the Princes of the Pulpit, Reed sought to bridge the widening gulf between the church and the ordinary American by transforming theology and Biblical teachings into language understandable to the common person. His epigrammatic style appealed to all social groups, and even to politicians. Reed's sermons did not have the eloquence of a Brooks or a Gladden, but he communicated a gospel that called the church to confront, not accommodate, the social and industrial changes occurring in post-Civil War America.

A New Community

The doctrine of the Incarnation constituted a major theme in the New Theology, interpreted largely in terms of divine immanence. One could see God's spirit at work in the highest cultural ideals and in the noblest social institutions. Winthrop Hudson criticized the New Theology as too accommodating to culture and without any normative content.[62] But Reed maintained that Jesus Christ embodied the criteria for social behavior and that the New Testament outlined, in principle, the model for the kingdom of God on earth. Jesus' teachings would prove themselves by their results in life. Reed perceived two basic truths in Jesus' revelation of God: first, Christ revealed God as love and that defined his relationship with humanity; and second, Christ's life and teachings proclaimed God's standard for social behavior that, if diligently practiced, could generate a community based on the principle of servanthood.

If asked how to define God, Reed would answer, "Look to Jesus Christ." Attempts to encapsulate God in written statements of belief invited dispute before the ink had dried. The simplicity of Jesus' example magnified the gospel's appeal to the masses. According to Reed, Jesus expressed "the character of God, His mind and heart . . . [and] by his works we know God. This our God I trust."[63] Reed totally agreed with the New Theology's declaration that "God is Love." He believed that Jesus demonstrated this love through his life and death:

> Jesus Christ, who came from God to tell us about God, said: "The works that he does I do." So if you see what Jesus did when he was on earth, you see what God is doing all the time — healing the sick, making the blind see, giving people courage and hope, telling them when the sea is rough not to be afraid. Be afraid of nothing, not even of death. Be afraid of nothing but wrong thoughts.[64]

Reed agreed that governments conditioned the conception of God and that even scientific advancements, including evolution, could not alter God's character as defined in Jesus. He believed that people who lived under kings sometimes viewed God as more capricious than those who lived in a republic. Reed observed that strict Calvinism, with its notions of infant damnation and the election of a few for salvation, formed the basis of Robert Burns's early conception of God as a harsh taskmaster with little mercy. But, Reed noted, Burns found the God of love by caring for animals, children, and daisies. He sensed that God cared for him in the same way. Reed contended, "When one gets in sympathy with grass and leaf and flower, and little children and oppressed people and animals abused, he is getting to apprehend God."[65]

The truths that emerged from scientific investigations did not destroy God and current research would not affect God's nature. As knowledge of the world and of man progressed, so should one also expect progress in the science of God and religion. Reed asserted:

> I could never see why the theologians were so afraid of scientific facts. If a man desired to, he could not get rid of God. . . . The more facts he finds out, the greater his conception of the great Contriver of the facts.[66]

Jesus had reduced the Old Testament message to twelve words: "Thou shalt love the Lord thy God and thy neighbor as thyself." A second commandment intensified the first: "A new commandment I give unto you, that ye love one another as I have loved you." All principles of religious conduct flowed from these two statements and from the collection of Jesus' sayings in the Sermon on the Mount. The four gospels had recorded the most simple expression of this principle: "He that would be the greatest among you, let him be the servant of all." Servanthood included acts that strengthened fellow pilgrims and evangelized the principle of cooperation that would lead to the kingdom of God on earth — a new community.[67]

Thomas Bender in his book *Community and Social Change in America*, proposes that we think of community in terms of the bonds of mutuality and sentiment that historically defined community, not in terms of locales. Conflict within a community does not mean self-destruction; conflict forms a natural part of the relationships inherent in either the community or the larger society. The concept of a community within the larger society parallels Reed's idea of the kingdom of God on earth. People who accept the truth revealed in Christ and who work to build this community will experience conflict, but such disagreements will pale when mediated through free speech and the practice of Christ's two great commandments. Reed regarded such disruptions as evidence that not everyone understood or accepted the truth. Thus, the church Catholic had to find ways to make more effective the persuasive power of Christ's teachings. The new community would exist within the larger society as the example, the teacher, of what ought to be.[68] Reed claimed that Jesus showed the way to real community:

> We know very well that the church of to-day is not the thing that Jesus Christ had in mind. It is way one side of what He had in mind. . . .
> What is true of the church is true of society. . . . I believe in the coming end of the world — not in a burning or a drowning of the earth. . . . The fashion of this world passes away. . . . [It's] going to change.[69]

What could actualize this new community? The "Christ feeling," the love and the law within motivated men and women to lay aside violence, and to follow willingly the religion of Jesus Christ. How to acquire this "Christ feeling" was not always clear. Reed had a favorite axiom that he occasionally used to express that the kingdom of God on earth moved slowly toward fulfillment. "What ought to be will be" meant that God's purpose would come to fruition — in God's time. Humanity could not stop the growth of the kingdom, but it could hasten its coming by increased understanding and good works. The final judgment of good or bad works was left to God; people acted on the basis of their faith and understanding. But the new community's expansion relied on the cooperation that flowed from the principle of servanthood. The church must communicate, as effectively as possible, the definition of servanthood, and then trust the people to respond as best they could. The community would build on good works until it spread throughout the land, and its guarantee of success rested on the Biblical promise that God would establish the kingdom on earth.[70]

With this concept of community, Reed tried to transcend the separation in the city that resulted because of the alienation between rich and poor. He wanted to build institutions that lifted up the more noble thoughts of the American tradition and that brought people together with a common purpose. In Indianapolis Reed saw how McCulloch successfully operated an institutional church, a church that served the community by providing a variety of services. It offered domestic instruction, selected educational classes, lectures, meeting space for community clubs, and more. Denver could benefit from an institutional church that would teach the highest ideals of culture and that would move people in concert with the spirit of God toward the kingdom on earth. When church members voted to build a new edifice, Reed demanded not a pretentious building, but one that would remain open seven days a week with a variety of programs for the city's citizens. He expressed his wishes to the trustees by maintaining that God had fashioned him to work among the masses, not to build expensive churches. With his work clearly defined, he asked for a "plain substantial structure . . . where church work would go on every day in the week." The trustees agreed, and Reed initiated a seven-day program in the new First Congregational Church.[71]

Jesus Christ suffered in all things just as any person, and he knew the limitations of human existence. With this understanding, one could expect justice and mercy from God in his dealings with humankind. Reed often quoted the Old Testament patriarch Abraham, as he stood between God and the destruction of Sodom and Gomorrah: "Shall not the judge of all the earth do right?" Power creates a responsibility for justice; thus God had placed himself under obligation. Now humanity required a land that encouraged development and where the new community could germinate and grow as rapidly as possible. In his justice and mercy, God had designated America as that place on earth. Reed vigorously asserted that America offered the last refuge on earth for man to become what he should. "This is the last chance for the race. If this fails all fails. And that I will never believe." Reed saw America's obligation as that of a missionary carrying the idea of liberty into all nations. America was the world's messiah and even though she might slip backward temporarily, "she is predestined of God to wake up, and to wake the world up, until every yoke is broken and the oppressed free."[72] In America, God's new republic would mature and all the world would finally see the "City upon a Hill."

After three years in Denver, Reed's reputation as a minister was widely acknowledged. Citizens, not associated with the First Congregational Church, surprised Reed with an oil painting by the local artist J. D. Howland in appreciation of his work among the people of the city. The Honorable R. W. Woodbury, promoter, editor, and organizer of the Denver Chamber of Commerce, presented the painting and praised Reed's activity with the poor. Woodbury added that all who knew Reed could feel as if they belonged to his church, even if they did not attend.[73]

Reed responded with an appreciation for the good will of the people, especially those who had no binding association with his church. He had come to Denver "to be a mover in every industry; to be a helper in every effort to advance its literature, its art, and its commerce. . . . I strive to go out into the broad life of the city. That I think is the province of the modern minister." Reed closed by emphasizing that one could bring comfort to the distressed and the weak: let the able ones defend those who had no defender.[74]

But his achievements did not satisfy Reed. In the sea of humanity, there remained many who looked not to the church for help or perhaps never knew that the church would help. Reed's radical idea that every person had the right to justice and to a life that involved more than unbearable labor from dawn to dusk found expression in political and charitable activism. Politics and organized charity could contribute to the coming of the kingdom of God on earth, and Reed entered into both of these endeavors with abundant gusto after 1885.

REV. MYRON W. REED

This illustration of Reed appeared in the 31 January 1899 issue of the *Rocky Mountain News*. The legend reads "Familiar Figure in the Business District."

(Illustration courtesy Rocky Mountain News.)

FIRST CONGREGATIONAL CHURCH IN DENVER, COLORADO
(Photograph courtesy Western History Department, Denver Public Library.)

METROPOLE HOTEL AND BROADWAY THEATER

(Photograph courtesy Western History Department, Denver Public Library.)

Part Two

The Comfortable Life

"It is not a comfortable world,
while a single soul goes without."

THREE

Politics:

Power without Justice

By the mid–1880s the older entrepreneurs had begun to fade and younger men had assumed the reigns of financial leadership in Colorado. Political power remained in Republican hands and even the Populist victory in 1892 melted like spring snow in Colorado sunshine. European and eastern capital continued to play critical roles in the state's economic development. The "outsiders" who had established themselves within the informal hierarchy of Denver's inner power circle tied the city's economic health more closely to the East.[1] Some Colorado leaders opposed the financial leverage that resulted from close ties with eastern financiers. Tom Patterson associated the Republican party with eastern investors and sought ways to neutralize their powerful influence in Colorado. Myron Reed entered the state as an outsider, but he brought no capital to invest. Instead, he hoped to participate in building a community that would provide a greater degree of justice and equal opportunity in the West. To accomplish this objective, he believed that the West would need the right kind of political representation.

Any political change in Colorado that threatened state and federal economic policies or patronage would be difficult, however. The Republican party could draw on its organizational and financial strength, nourished since the territorial days, to maintain the status quo, and Democratic candidates rarely won congressional seats or gubernatorial races. The elections of 1886 and 1888 illustrated the strength of the Republican party. In both elections, the Democrats selected what many observers thought were formidable candidates. But in 1886 Reed lost the First District congressional seat, in a disputed election, to Republican Judge George G. Symes; and in 1888 Republican Job A. Cooper won over Tom Patterson, the most recognized and strongest Democrat in the state. Political reformers like Patterson and Reed chafed under this one-party domination and searched for a candidate who could crack the Republican wall that circumscribed their power in Colorado.[2]

The Manufacturers' Exposition in 1886 afforded Tom Patterson the occasion to deliver an important political speech. Denver businessmen had originally organized the exposition in 1885 to exhibit Colorado's products, and the event received good publicity and drew people from across the Rocky Mountain region. The fall timing of the exposition and large attendance figures combined to make it a fortuitous affair for speakers to promote their particular political agendas, including which policies might be necessary for continued economic development in the state. Democrats and Republicans took advantage of this occasion when they could.

The second Manufacturers' Exposition opened in Denver on 7 October 1886. This annual event had important consequences for mining, commercial, and agricultural industries. It attracted potential capital and provided a showcase for the state's products. Tom Patterson opened the exposition with a speech that extolled the accomplishments of Colorado's businesses and the state's remarkable history. He also criticized the railroads (usually identified with eastern capital) for rate discrimination and for consolidation through pools that served to restrict competition.[3] Patterson called for more state regulation:

> The claim they make that they are purely private enterprises is without foundation. They exist and do business only under rights conferred by statute law. Because they are public in their nature and exist solely for public use, the people conferred upon them part of the sovereignty which would otherwise belong to the State.[4]

He acknowledged the essential relationship that existed between the railroads and the state's future, but he also alluded to the East's interests in railroads. According to Patterson, Colorado required such regulation so as to insure the continued development of its businesses and to create opportunities for its working people.[5] Patterson and Reed felt that Colorado must win its political and economic independence from eastern capital.

The Republican party had long been a political home for Reed before he moved to Denver. He had recruited young people for the New York State Republican party in the 1850s. Attracted by the party's reform spirit, he had faithfully supported it until the 1884 presidential election. The "Mulligan letters," indicating that Republican Senator James G. Blaine (Maine) had accepted money from the railroads, and later revelations that further embarrassed Blaine, repulsed Reed. He felt that he could no longer remain a Republican if Blaine represented Republican morality. In 1884 Reed switched parties and voted for the Democratic candidate, Grover Cleveland. Considering the accusations leveled against both candidates in the 1884 campaign, it is rather surprising that Reed was able to vote for Cleveland.[6]

Reed brought to Denver his idea that the world moved toward God's kingdom on earth as revealed in the teachings of Jesus Christ. The old theology had been formulated under kings, and thus it reflected outdated theological ideas. But, Reed declared: "The theology of a republic is taking shape now. It will be quite different from that of King James's time; it will measure obligation by power. The greater the power, the greater the obligation." Reed grounded this theme of obligation in the oft-quoted Old Testament text: "Shall not the Judge of all the earth do right?"[7]

Jesus summed up the gist of Christianity for Reed when he said, "Whoever would be greatest among you let him be the servant of all." To possess power meant that one had an obligation to serve humanity. The greater the power, the greater the obligation. But power also permitted one to serve in a broader, more forceful way the progress of the coming kingdom of God on earth. Less abuse of animals, a growing sense of justice between the employer and the employee, and a move toward women's suffrage, all demonstrated this benevolent power at work. Ideal conditions did not always exist, but changes from the old ways to the new ways nevertheless occurred from time to time — enough to nourish the hope that the new community would happen. Public institutions in the American republic contained the possibility for reform and progress toward the kingdom of God. A republic emphasized the good of the whole society over the individual and engaged the masses; it could serve as an example of a cooperative community.[8] Reed immediately involved himself in politics — one of Colorado's promising institutions.

The 1886 Campaign

On 17 November 1885 the *Rocky Mountain News* printed an editorial, "The Church in Politics," which argued that ministers had an obligation to speak out against rampant political corruption in any community. Although some people judged any minister who dared to sermonize on politics as "bold indeed," the minister properly represented a moral voice that should not remain silent when political corruption exercised a dominating influence in elections. In quoting an eminent New York divine, the *News* emphasized that any prophetic denunciation should target the vices and sins in politics generally, not those of any particular political party.[9] The editor summarized:

> If the political tricksters who manipulate partisan politics, even to the extent of claiming to run this church or that religious institution in the interests of their respective candidates, were held up to public scorn and condemnation, as they ought to be, there would be less of bossism and more individuality in our political elections.[10]

Reed preached against corruption and boss rule in politics shortly after he arrived in Denver. The state had the reputation of "boodle politics," which applied to the party in power's decisions concerning patronage and campaign financing. In his sermon, "The People's Peril," Reed held America up as the best example of liberty and republican government that any nation could emulate when moving toward the same objective. The founders of the republic did not intend that there should exist two classes: a business and professional class and a political class. Every man, regardless of his vocation, should not forget the public interest. Each citizen should exercise his liberty and participate in the decision-making process of republican government by voting in the election. When politicians came to believe they owned an elective office, then any subsequent loss of their privileged position filled them with outrage. Reed believed that this feeling of ownership resulted from the close association of politicians with other politicians, which in effect removed them from the concerns of the people. "He cannot possibly represent the people, he has not been with them, does not know what they think or how they feel," Reed complained. Politicians, like ministers, should mix with the people and learn their problems.[11]

America began as an experiment to determine whether or not people were wise enough and moral enough to govern themselves. This country's government rested on the consent of the governed, on the free choice of the mind and heart. If Americans allowed political bosses and corruption to continue, then the republic would die from internal rot and decay. "Now meddle with this free choice, persist in meddling with a free vote and a fair count, and the republic ends. It does not wait to die and linger along — it is dead," Reed wrote. The voters held the city's future in their hands. If vote buying were allowed, then how would that appear to newcomers who wanted to invest and to live in Denver? "We have enough Huns here now, and [enough] Dagos here now. Men with money are apt to think of all these things before they invest their money."[12]

According to Reed, European immigrants who had grown up in countries that practiced corruption and revolution had not learned what government by consent required. Earlier immigrants, he believed, had come to America with education, a means of support, and a passion for liberty. But "assisted immigrants" (those who made their way to America by virtue of labor contracts and travel loans) would work for pennies to escape starvation. Europe dumped its paupers in America. These recent immigrants were not the building blocks needed for the strengthening of the Republic.

This danger, that political corruption would undo the republican ideal, extended far beyond Denver, Reed believed. It reached across the Atlantic Ocean to England. Any damage to the theory of government by the people "is the grief of all the brave lovers of liberty," he preached. America had an obligation to Almighty God, even to the whole earth, that government by the people should not cease. Therefore, this experiment of citizen participation in governmental decisions must not fail or civilization would regress to the time before 1776. The American republic symbolized hope to all nations who had glimpsed the blessings of a government based·on the people's consent. Reed contended that England was moving toward this form of democracy, and America, as her example, must maintain the freedom of the ballot and the idea of liberty.[13]

While this concern for free choice seemed appropriate to most concerned citizens, a larger issue troubled others. Reed, along with Patterson and other reformers, pondered how they could upset the long-held Republican dominance. As Colorado's leading Democrat, Patterson could assist Reed if he decided to enter politics. As owner of the *News*, Patterson regarded Reed as a public figure who deserved the paper's attention. The *News* not only published Reed's sermons but reported his activities in Denver and the Rocky Mountain region. Occasionally, Reed wrote an article (with no byline) on a topic of interest. When Reed wanted to take his son Ralph on a camping trip, he asked Patterson for funds and in return promised an article for the paper. Reed benefited from such positive press, and the *News* made a major contribution to the size of his regional audience. Reed's entree into Colorado politics would not have been possible without Patterson's political savvy and friendship.[14]

Patterson had amassed a sizable fortune from his law practice and shrewd real estate investments. But politics remained his preferred vocation, for here, he thought, he could affect the state's political and economic policies. Although a wealthy man, Patterson identified more with the downtrodden

and ordinary people of Colorado than with the elite. Associated with the
News since 1890, Patterson never mitigated his opinion when it concerned
political corruption, the repression of individual rights, or the monied powers' manipulation of public policy. In 1892 Patterson acquired the controlling interest in the *News* and made it the vehicle for the expression of an
alternative to the Republican party's dominance. His use of the *News* as a
voice of reform, whether for the Democratic party or for the Populists, and
as an ongoing critic of political bossism (or "the Gang") constituted perhaps his most significant contribution to state politics. For forty years, from
1876 to 1916, Patterson was the acknowledged leader of the Colorado
Democrats, and Reed often joined him in campaigning for the Democrats
or the Populists.[15]

On 5 October 1886 Patterson chaired the meeting of the Colorado
Democratic Convention in Denver, assembled to nominate candidates for
the fall election. In his opening address, Patterson emphasized that the
1873 demonetization of silver had occurred on the Republicans' watch, and
while he did not question the sincerity of the Republicans' support for
silver's free coinage — who could trust them? Patterson admitted that President Cleveland's views on silver did not agree with the Colorado Democrats' position, but the party towered above any one man. He declared that
only the Democratic party could restore silver to its rightful place in the domestic and international money markets.[16] Furthermore, Patterson asked
the voters to take notice of how the Republicans had used their taxes:
"Commencing with 1879, those who have assumed to represent the people
of this state, have been engaged in the most extravagant, if not the most
profligate and dishonest use of the people's money that can be traced to the
reckless conduct of any political party in any state in the country."[17] He
then detailed the appropriations for the previous several years, illustrating
the excessive spending of the opposing party. The Democratic party went
on record as opposed to any boodle or bonanza bossism during or after the
campaign, and its candidates would uphold that conviction. The Republicans denied these accusations and implied that Patterson and his cronies
controlled the Democratic slate; only the Republican ticket could truly
represent the people.[18]

As their first major business the next convention day, the Democratic
delegates passed several resolutions. One resolution left no doubt how the
party felt about the importance of silver: it favored silver's free coinage and
asked the federal government to press the international community to consider its adoption. Several resolutions denounced the Republicans' controlling influence in state and local politics and federal appointments. The

Democrats blamed the Republicans for the conflict between capital and labor because of the Republicans' charitable attitude toward the formation of corporate monopolies. The convention also demanded that the state's new General Assembly limit the railroads' rates and regulate charges for irrigation and drinking water. The convention then turned to the nomination of its candidates.[19]

Charles S. Thomas, Patterson's law partner, nominated Reed to oppose incumbent Republican, Judge George G. Symes, for the U.S. House of Representatives. Thomas described Reed as "a man whose reputation for ability, for integrity, for purity of heart and nobility of soul, stands without a peer within the broad limits of the state of Colorado." The party viewed Reed's popularity with the workingman throughout the state as his chief strength in the coming battle with Symes. Patterson seconded the nomination. In Indiana, Reed had been considered for a number of elective offices, including governor, U.S. congressman, and mayor of Indianapolis, but the Colorado candidacy marked his first campaign for political office.[20]

In his acceptance speech, Reed made two remarks that his opponents pounced on to demonstrate that he could not effectively represent Colorado's interests in the 1887–88 Congress. First, he characterized the tariff as a local issue. Referring to a remark made by the 1880 Democratic presidential candidate, General Winfield S. Hancock, Reed noted that the tariff issue had emerged from a process of give-and-take among different sections of the country with respect to the protection of industries and as a result, "the common country goes on all protected and all helped." In a decade when the tariff never left the national agenda, not all Colorado businessmen could accept the "local issue" definition, particularly as applied to industries in their young state. Colorado needed protection to interest capital in its budding enterprises. Reed's oversimplification allowed Republicans to brand him as a "free trader," and the *Denver Republican* hammered home the theme that Colorado could not afford a man in Congress who did not support a protective tariff.[21]

In the latter part of his acceptance speech, Reed focused on ideas that meant more to him than the tariff. He portrayed the country as a united people who cared for one another. As evidence of this harmony, he mentioned the relief provided by the nation and Coloradans for Charleston, South Carolina, which had suffered severe damage from a "rotary earthquake." To Reed, this act of sharing signified the evolving spirit of Jesus' servanthood and provided certain evidence of progress toward a new community. With a hope for continued improvement, Reed assured the delegates that he would bitterly oppose "the system of industry which puts

Vanderbilt at one end and a tramp at the other, and I will attempt by work to abolish both." Politics, according to Reed, could be an agent of social reform in the creation of a new community. But in a closing anecdote, he used a mild expletive that became his second blunder. Reed told the story of an American general in the Mexican–American War who found his troops surrounded by the enemy. With no escape route in sight, the general had turned to his troops and shouted: "Boys, damn it, charge them." The *Republican* used this story to illustrate Reed's attitude toward Mexican Americans, and then compared his remarks with "the cheap demagogy of a ward politician."[22]

A preacher's entry into politics caused concern among some Denver citizens who believed that the pulpit was the only appropriate place for a man of the cloth to serve the community. The *News* editorial had not advocated that ministers enter the grimy, earthly world of politics, but only that they make the necessary moral judgments concerning politicians' unscrupulous behavior. Ministers had a duty to uphold standards of morality in their preaching and in their personal conduct — to serve as examples for their communities. How could a preacher perform as a politician and set a moral example at the same time? Most politicians and voters thought that a minister did not have the necessary qualifications for the business of politics and that he had a sacred calling to devote all his energy to the church. One could not serve effectively in both capacities. Reed's ministerial colleague, Dean Henry Martyn Hart of St. John's Episcopal Cathedral, said, "I am sorry that Myron Reed has gone into politics. I fear that he will fall between two interests." It seemed that Colorado politicians and church members felt that politics and religion belonged to two different spheres. Society needed government to maintain order, to protect the legal rights of citizens, and to safeguard property, whereas the church and its ministers cared for a community's spiritual needs. But Reed saw no separation between the sacred and the secular spheres, and he believed that a minister could faithfully serve God both in politics and in the pulpit.[23]

When the Republican convention nominated William H. Meyer for governor instead of the incumbent Benjamin H. Eaton, the Reverend Bayard Craig of the Central Christian Church used his pulpit to criticize his fellow Republicans for selecting a nominee "of less principle, a man in harmony with the prevailing political methods." Craig declared that he would "not knowingly vote for any man whose life is a violation of honor, chastity or sobriety." He closed by asking his listeners to work for the "supremacy of right methods in the politics of the city and the state." The *News*, partial to the Democrats, editorialized that this independent thinker understood that his party's convention was controlled by a few unprincipled manipulators. Earlier, a number of Republicans, charging corruption in their state organization, had formed the Independent Republicans. Craig seemed to lend credibility to the corruption charge with his public criticism of the party's gubernatorial nominee. The *Republican*, on the other hand, depicted Craig as misguided and without sufficient facts about the candidacy of William H. Meyer.[24] Craig's remarks showed that even as many religious leaders disagreed with Reed's candidacy, some ministers continued their criticism of political corruption and encourage those men who challenged its sources.

The *Republican* had immediately attacked Reed after the Democratic convention, but the *Denver Times* waited a few days before publishing its views on the contradiction of a minister in politics. The *Times* was more conciliatory toward those who would leave the pulpit for the smoke-filled back rooms of politics. Its editors noted that history had confirmed that preachers and politicians did not happily mix, and that that feeling certainly existed in 1886. But time and the examples of Henry Ward Beecher, David Swing, and Oscar McCulloch, all of whom had encouraged ministerial involvement in political issues, had softened some hearts. Now, it seemed best, editorialized the *Times*, to let the individual make the decision whether to run or not. The editors suggested that the euphoria over Reed's candidacy would probably only last three weeks, and they concluded with this advice: "Judge Reed leniently. Vote for Symes."[25]

The *Republican*, in contrast, took a rigid, far less conciliatory line as it continued its criticism of Reed's entry into politics. In an ongoing editorial campaign throughout October, the newspaper reiterated three points: (1) a minister, by virtue of his calling, had no business in politics; (2) Reed's campaign illustrated his demagoguery; and (3) Colorado's interests prohibited any free trader from representing the state in Congress. Wool growers and lead-mine owners required protection if their industries were to survive. The newspaper first stressed that the nature of a minister's vocation implied a lifetime commitment to the Christian church, and to leave that responsibility revealed more about a man's character than words could describe. A minister who used expletives usually lost the trust of his congregation. While professing high regard for the religion of Christ and for the minister's vocation, the *Republican* concluded:

> But it does not regard the office of a preacher as one that can be taken
> up and thrown down at pleasure, or preaching as a business in which a
> man may engage until he finds more profitable employment. It fails to

comprehend how Mr. Reed could give up his sacred calling to go into politics. Whatever his motive, his action has lowered the standard of religion without elevating the standard of politics.[26]

The *Republican* further noted that members of Reed's church were unhappy that Reed had made this decision. Some said that his effectiveness in the community was over. A gambler remarked that Reed was "a great fellow to make religion attractive" and he always played the limits on wickedness, which meant that Reed would go as far as conscience and propriety would permit. J. R. Hanna, a cashier of the City National Bank and a prominent member of the First Congregational Church, commented to a *Republican* reporter, "We don't want a preacher in politics. I consider it a great mistake on Mr. Reed's part, to say nothing of its influence on the church."[27]

The *Republican* depicted Reed as a demagogue who could not be trusted. The newspaper cited articles from the *Indianapolis News* to show that when Reed had lived in Indianapolis, he had supported the gold-bugs and free trade. According to the paper, these articles proved that Reed's conversion from Republican to Democrat reflected more the opportunist than one who had a genuine interest in Colorado: "Therefore it does not surprise any one, the members of his congregation least of all, that he has accepted the first chance to get office that offered itself."[28]

When Reed addressed his congregation on the Sunday after the convention, he spoke to these concerns. The *News*, *Republican*, and *Times* all printed abridged versions of his sermon the following Monday, but the *Republican* later published a full stenographic report, claiming its readers had demanded it. The *Republican* accused the *News* of deliberately suppressing the sermon, knowing that it would injure Reed's candidacy among thoughtful, conservative people. But the abridged versions excluded no remarks that could have placed Reed in a better or worse light.[29]

When Reed defended his candidacy on that Sunday morning, the church had to turn away more than five hundred people. Most noteworthy, many seated in the sanctuary had dust on their shoes from walking on dirt paths across the back country "to hear the great preacher and people's champion." Reed emphasized the sacred calling of every one in the congregation: "We have our duties to do in this world. These duties involve risks. We take the risks and do the duties according to our portion of what Victor Hugo calls 'the universal conscience.'" One could not separate the secular from the spiritual. The total world we inhabit belonged to God. In order to introduce any spiritual truth to the masses, one had to make their conditions better. Why talk of eternal things when hunger and cold blocked the message? First feed and clothe the needy and then offer the gospel. Reed wanted to create a more comfortable life for everyone, especially the masses, so that they could then hear the spiritual truths.[30]

A person could not look inside another man and assess his motives perfectly; only God had that power of judgment. But one could measure a man by what he did in a community — the test of works. Reed declared, "There is not a man who has his foot on a laborer's neck, or his hand on his throat, but dislikes me. All that sort of men would be glad to see me made to be silent." Reed urged his listeners to look at his accomplishments in the community and examine his preaching, including the series on the "Evolution of the Tramp." He had tried to make his opinions visible in his works and intelligible in his sermons, he asserted. This nomination did not mean the abandonment of his profession; instead, it meant a chance to promote those ideas which he had discussed since 1884. He believed in the ballot and urged the people to place in office candidates "more from the class who ride in an omnibus and less from those who ride in cabs." Let the common people judge the competency of the candidate, Reed argued. Reed tried to persuade the congregation that his campaign would turn on the concerns of those who had been forgotten in the mainstream of economic development and political decision making. Would the people elect a minister who promised them justice and a political voice, he asked. The *News* apparently thought they would and downplayed the argument of the opposition press "that there is no proper place in politics for a preacher, but we do not think that this view will be accepted by thinking men in any community in Colorado." But the *Republican* wondered, "What would become of the religion of Christ if all its preachers should imitate Mr. Reed?"[31]

In the 1880s political campaigns provided entertainment as well as information to help the voter decide how to cast his ballot. Voter turnout generally was high in presidential elections; voter participation registered a high of 81.8 percent in 1876 and 77.5 percent in 1884, when James Blaine lost to Grover Cleveland. Based on these returns, we may assume an intense interest in Colorado's 1886 congressional campaign somewhat comparable to these national responses.[32]

The press jumped into the political morass with entertaining stories and their own political agendas. The Denver newspapers stimulated and embellished the campaign with their daily reports, especially those related to Reed. For example, it was reported that the Democrats had promoted Reed's identity with the workers and the poor in Denver; he would voice their concerns and battle the rich megalomaniacs. But Reed did not measure up to this image on every occasion. The *Times* cheerfully reported that his sympathies for the masses appeared only when he had a large audience. The Swedish Methodist Episcopal Chapel, a small, struggling congregation of working people, arranged to raise money for their church by sponsoring a series of lectures. When Reed arrived to deliver the first lecture, many ticket holders had not come and a small audience greeted him. Reed remarked, "I cannot speak to so small an audience; and I shall advise the other gentlemen you have mentioned as lecturers in this series, to decline." He then turned abruptly and left![33]

For the *Times*, this demonstrated that Reed's concern for the poor went no further than his political ambitions — a charge that both the *Republican* and the *Times* raised again and again. The Colorado Republicans depicted Reed as a "born-again" Democrat, a cunning renegade who would align himself with any political party to realize his personal ambitions. The above-described reaction to a low turnout for his speech was not atypical. Reed could be short-tempered when he felt that he had been misinformed or unfairly imposed upon. Of course, these interpretations were his own and fit a personality that reacted spontaneously with a fierce independence to any situation that provoked him, no matter how small. Whatever Reed might have later thought about his behavior remains unknown; there was no rebuttal published concerning this incident.[34]

Nathaniel Hill, Colorado's Republican senator from 1879 to 1885 and a trustee of the First Congregational Church, owned the *Republican*, but the paper nevertheless continued to castigate Reed. After his senate term, Hill had remained politically active and undoubtedly involved himself in this campaign. In Denver's competitive newspaper market, Hill controlled the *Republican*'s editorial page. Although his paper consistently criticized Reed for running and for his tariff position, Hill approved $1,000 raises to Reed's salary each year until Reed resigned in 1894. That year, Reed's annual salary was reported to be $7,000 — a great deal of money in the 1890s.[35]

Hill and Patterson disliked each other and their newspapers served as the cannons for their feud — volleys were fired regularly. Once, when Patterson's daughter objected to an undignified attack on Hill, Patterson rejoined, "Even if so, it had been effective." In 1886 the *Republican* identified Patterson with John Arkins, then owner of the *News* and a Reed booster, and placed Reed, Patterson, Arkins, and the *News* in the same category — cheap demagogues. When Reed received endorsements from labor, the *Republican* countered with rebuttals. If Reed received any positive support from the Indianapolis press, the *Republican* offered another opinion. The Republicans belittled Reed's Civil War service and always reminded Colorado voters that they had been the reform party during the Civil War. They appealed to African American voters, reminding them that freedom from slavery had come through the Republican party and "it is little less than base ingratitude for a colored citizen to vote the Democratic ticket." No less a hero than President Ulysses S. Grant had led the Union Army to victory over the Confederates, and now, according to the *Republican*, Myron Reed, a newly converted Democrat and a lowly Union captain, had maligned this great American.[36]

The defamation occurred in an 1884 Memorial Day sermon when Reed disparaged the Wall Street brokerage firm that Grant had founded after his second term. Unauthorized borrowing by Grant's partner had brought about the firm's bankruptcy, and Grant had been forced to write his memoirs to earn money for his family. Reed equated Wall Street with a highly regulated confidence game, and had little sympathy for anyone who lost money in the game — including Grant. The *Republican* recalled Reed's remarks for its readers, suggesting that any true patriot would not impugn the Civil War hero as did Reed. Reed had earlier preached a sermon honoring Grant, after his death on 9 August 1885, and the *News* reprinted it on 26 October 1886 in response to the *Republican* exposé.[37]

To further illustrate Reed's alleged chameleon character, the *Republican* gave front-page coverage to campaign speeches by Willard Teller and Frank Goudy, two prominent Republicans. Teller attacked Reed for his tariff position, his hollow platitudes without solutions, and his born-again Democratic faith. According to Teller, Reed was an opportunist who had never committed to the Republican party and showed no ability to represent Colorado in Congress. In rebuttal, the *News* characterized Teller, an attorney for the Union Pacific Railroad, as a man with a corporate ring in his nose. Reed had supported laborers' rights against the Union Pacific Railroad, the *News* argued, and this explained Teller's opposition. The *News* predicted that the honest laborer would decide for Reed, who was the genuine champion of human rights.[38]

Frank Goudy, a promising young Republican from Gunnison, Colorado, also assailed Reed's character. Goudy portrayed Reed as a minister who had thrown aside the Bible and his ethics when he accepted the nomination. Goudy saw Reed "not as a minister, but as a politician who has stepped down and out of the pulpit on the level of ordinary sinners." Goudy did not clarify his relation to such sinners, but he claimed to have seen Reed step inside a saloon and drink several glasses of beer (probably true). "Does this not show the parson to be a hypocrite, if he is not true to his own teaching," asked Goudy. He further contended that the *News*, by its support of Reed's candidacy, had assaulted the very religious principles that Reed claimed to represent. Goudy appealed to the audience to vote for the Republican ticket and let the corrupt *News* and its parson go their way.[39]

The election results were too close to call on election night. As the days passed, it became clear that the Democratic gubernatorial candidate, Alva Adams, had defeated Republican William H. Meyer. The *News* celebrated with drawings of a crowing rooster for Adams and an exhausted rooster for Meyer. Within a few more days, however, the official count declared Judge Symes the winner in the congressional race by fewer than a thousand votes. Reed had run a strong race; Symes's earlier opponent, in 1884, had lost by 6,726 votes. Even political pundits in Washington, D.C., took note of the tight race, but such news did not console Reed; he preached a shorter sermon than usual that Sunday.[40]

What did Reed accomplish in this campaign? If he intended to infiltrate Colorado politics with his vision of a new community, he failed. If he hoped to shake up the established power group in Colorado, he did, for a short period. This would explain the strong opposition of the *Republican* and the *Times*—they thought that he could win. Indeed, one prominent citizen, Major W. S. Peabody, admitted that Reed had scared the ruling party. Reed had gained the support of the masses because he had followed his own advice and gone out among them. He had camped with the miners and mixed with the ordinary folk, and he had tried to understand their concerns. They thought of him as their spokesman, not as just another minister. His demeanor and his politics made Reed different from other preachers in the West.[41]

A reformer's path has many rough places, and perhaps Reed drew some encouragement from the near-success of Henry George's 1886 New York City mayoral campaign. Reed agreed with George that the land belonged to the people; he had been a single-taxer since he had read George's *Progress and Poverty* in Indianapolis. George had urged his readers to follow the road of liberty. The problems created by American progress demanded a solution that would generate opportunities so that all people could secure their "inalienable right to the bounty of the Creator," George wrote. He, too, had sought to actualize his ideas through politics. The New York City Central Labor Union had asked George to represent them in the 1886 mayoral election. At first George had hesitated, but then he had agreed to run if the party could produce a petition bearing thirty thousand signatures of voters pledging to vote for him. While the petition circulated, George had received a visitor from the incumbent Democrat's office who assured George that he could not win, and that his candidacy would "raise hell" and further split the Democratic party. If George would withdraw, this emissary promised him a seat in the House of Representatives in the next election. George roared in response: "I do not want the responsibility and the work of the office of Mayor of New York, but I do want to raise hell! I am decided and will run."[42]

The failed New York mayoral race had nevertheless increased George's national visibility. Perhaps Reed thought that if victory also escaped him, still his views on labor's rights, civic responsibility, and the tariff would position him well for a future race. Reed did indeed raise some hell. He returned to his pulpit after losing, but he never abandoned politics and its potential role in the creation of his new community.

Reform and Populism

In the state elections of 1888 and 1890, Reed joined with Patterson and stumped the state for the Democratic ticket. The 1888 election had greater significance for Patterson than for Reed. The Democrats had nominated Patterson for governor, and his campaign emphasized the accomplishments of the Cleveland administration — civil service reform, a U.S. Treasury surplus that made a lower tariff sensible, and a reduction in railroad land grants. Patterson's message centered around the workingman's predicament and the power of the Republican industrial barons. He claimed that tariff reductions proposed by President Cleveland in 1887 would protect American jobs and industries, whereas the Republicans were plotting to maintain protection so as to increase the capitalist's power over the worker.[43]

The Democrats played to the labor vote. Reed drew headlines for his speeches against "brass tag" labor: mine owners — Reed called them "Republican protectionists" — hired immigrants at wages lower than union scale and issued each one a brass tag that identified the worker for purposes of wages and purchases from local merchants. A union miner received from seventy-five cents to a dollar for each ton of coal mined, whereas brass tag laborers earned only fifty cents. Reed argued that brass tag labor disgraced the United States, and he named the Colorado Coal and Iron Company as a brass tag employer. Such laborers came from China and the "pauper-ridden districts of Europe," and they probably would return to their homes and not become productive U.S. citizens, Reed argued. He opposed this practice because he felt that these laborers had no interest in America, and by working for such little pay, they created an unnecessary and dangerous disruption in the state. Immigration solely to create a source of cheap labor for the corporations resulted in a loss of opportunity for Americans and contributed nothing valuable to the cause of labor. A *News* report described them: "These men work for nominal wages, live worse than cattle . . . do not care to learn our language, do not care to become acquainted with our political institutions, and taken altogether are not a desirable class of labor."[44]

A well planned and executed campaign did not produce a Democratic victory. Historian James E. Wright has shown that in the 1880s Colorado's voters generally followed tradition rather than class or cultural ties. The Republican party represented tradition because of its role in establishing Colorado's statehood, in promoting federal involvement in the state's economy (i.e., irrigation projects), and in tying national policy to state issues when it helped them. A protectionist tariff aided Colorado's economy, the Republicans claimed. The 1888 Republican victory demonstrated the strength of that close link with tradition, despite the Democrat's attempts to identify with the workers' cause. Patterson lost to his Republican opponent, Job A. Cooper, by ten thousand votes.[45]

The Democrats offered the governor's nomination to Reed in 1890. At different times in his career, Reed had expressed some interest in this office. While in Indiana, he had been approached about running for governor on the Republican ticket, but Reed seemed too aloof and the Republicans had not pressed him for a decision. The *Republican* reported that in 1886 Reed would have preferred the governor's nomination, but had agreed to run for Congress instead. Whatever the reason, Reed decided not to run for governor in 1890, but he did travel the state in support of the Democratic ticket, making speeches and socializing in his usual indefatigable manner.[46]

The 1890 election began a realignment of the state's political parties. Prior to 1890, third parties of one description or another had provided citizens with a way to express their dissatisfaction with the two major parties. The Prohibition party, organized in 1884, had had little success on its own but it supported candidates from the main parties who favored its platform. Governor Benjamin Eaton, elected in 1884, had endorsed the Prohibition position, but it was the Republican Party that secured his election. In 1888 the Union Labor party had backed the Denver Methodist minister Rev. Gilbert De La Matyr, a former Greenbacker and Prohibition proponent, for governor. The party's platform took the basic pro-labor stance of equality of opportunity and equal protection under the law. The Independents, a group of local reform leaders, put together a state ticket in 1890 that included both Republicans and Democrats. Their agenda included the Australian ballot, free silver and the abolition of national banks, government ownership of railroads and telegraphs, state ownership and management of all ditches and reservoirs, and the eight-hour day. They hoped to benefit from a weakened Republican party, which had been divided by an internal squabble over bossism and corruption. None of these parties was able to present a serious challenge to the two major parties, however, and the Grand Old Party again won the governorship in 1890.[47]

By 1890, however, there existed several economic subcultures — laborers, miners, farmers, stockmen — all of whom had suffered economic dislocation without fully understanding its causes. The traditional party structure was characterized by what Wright calls "brokerage politics": the propensity to satisfy critical demands only as they arose so as to avoid any full-fledged political revolt. But brokerage politics presented no lasting, acceptable solutions to the demands of these groups. Democratic and Republican responses to the changing socioeconomic order failed to deal with substantive matters of state policy. Dissenters reasoned from their political experience that any third party movement had to coalesce around an issue of broad appeal. For many concerned Coloradans the People's party had identified such an issue — the remonetization of silver.[48]

The Colorado Populist party grew out of the Farmers' Alliance and the Independent party movement. Initially, silver and agrarian interests dominated the party, but by 1892 labor concerns had become the top Populist priority. *The Road*, a weekly journal for the commercial traveler, soon became a voice for Populism because of editor Herbert George's political interests. He saw that silver had the greatest attraction for Colorado voters, and *The Road* promoted silver as the most critical issue in the 1892 election.[49]

Patterson, with his controlling interest in the *News*, also made a major contribution to the success of the Colorado Populist party by stressing the issues of the demonetization of silver, the strangle-hold of the Republican "money power," and the need for government to be more responsive to the people. Traditional political affiliations persisted, and the Populists understood they had to break these old partisan bonds. The free coinage of silver aroused feelings of pride among Coloradans and fueled a determination to discard any eastern policy that would restrict their progress. A Populist appeal to the reform spirit of the early Republican party caused many dissatisfied voters to think of the Populist movement as a war against the injustices wrought by the wealthy monopolists.[50]

These ideas appealed to Reed. He reasoned that a party that stressed the republican ideal of government by the people and intended to build a community on that basis demanded every right-thinking person's support. Reed extended that support to the issue of women's suffrage by promoting suffrage from the pulpit and by offering his church as a meeting place for suffrage leaders. The Populist's origins seemed to Reed analogous to those of the antislavery Republicans: "The People's party reminds me very much of the movement of 1856. The men in many respects are alike." Framing the issue in these terms made it seem like a crusade against gold-bug enslavement.[51]

After a bitter struggle and mainly due to Patterson's efforts, the Democrats fused with the Populists. Reed's name surfaced as a possible nominee for the First District congressional seat in the 1892 election. Publicly and privately, Reed made it known that he had no interest in any political office, but some friends thought he would run if given the chance. Herbert George assured the party that Reed would accept the party's offer to run upon his return from a vacation. Acting on this information, the Democrats and the Populists approved Reed's nomination and awaited his confirmation.[52]

When Reed returned to Denver, he sent a letter to the *News* expressing his regrets, but explaining that due to his current obligations, he must refuse the nomination. The letter confirmed Reed's sympathy with the Populist movement, for he saw it as an attempt to return control of the government to the people. Reed affirmed that he agreed with that emphasis, but he also believed he could serve the community best through his profession. Also, he noted, his congregation would soon begin construction of a new church building. And Reed planned to launch his institutional church that would keep its doors open to the community seven days a week. Obviously, the building project and its funding would demand most of his attention. When speaking to the Glenarm Club that fall Reed said: "Now, Denver is permanent. We speak of Denver now as our home. . . . I want you to believe me when I say that, except for something I might do for the people of this state that would be more useful than I could do here, I would never leave it." Although he declined political office, Reed would not withdraw his support from those candidates he favored, nor would he refuse a "useful" political appointment.[53]

The silver issue united enough silver Democrats and Populists in 1892 to elect Davis Hanson Waite of Aspen, a radical reformer and labor supporter, as governor. At a special state silver convention, Governor Waite went on to achieve national notoriety for his "Bloody Bridles" speech. He stated that if the monied powers blocked attempts to reform by the ballot, then a fight would follow, "for it is better, infinitely better that blood should flow to the horses' bridles than our national liberties should be destroyed." This striking emphasis on liberty seemed to call for violence in the minds of many Coloradans, and the national publicity became a source of embarrassment to the state. Reed defended Waite's language, describing the offensive phrases as "figurative" and used to create effect. He compared the language with that contained in newspapers, or even in the Bible, and wondered why people objected so strongly.[54] The new Populist administration took further advantage of Reed's reform interests. In addition to serving as chair of the State Board on Pardons and the president of the State Board of Charities and Corrections, he now became the only male member of the three-member board of control for the State Home and Industrial School for Girls in Denver. Expressing his dissatisfaction with the release of too many "penitentiary birds" and the limited time he had for such important work, Reed resigned as chair of the State Board of Pardons in August 1893. Known for leniency, Governor Waite had pardoned one man who had never served any part of his sentence. Reed may have found that his time became more limited as Waite's penchant for clemency increased. He had little tolerance for decisions that mocked the justice he believed appropriate for the crime.[55]

In 1894 labor dissatisfaction resulted in a strike at Cripple Creek over changes in hours and wages. Governor Waite took this opportunity to endear himself to many working men by his use of the state militia to prevent the owners' posse from overrunning the strikers' position on Bull Hill. Waite had intended to implement reform, but the Panic of 1893, Republican control of the state legislature, and an armed conflict with Denver City Hall over his appointive authority revealed his weakness as an administrator and made him a political liability.[56]

Silver continued to be an emotional and partisan issue during 1893 and 1894. When India ceased coining silver on 26 June 1893, Colorado's silver mines shut down and miners lost their jobs in large numbers. Reed joined the Colorado Silver League to promote silver interests in the East. Westerners did not think that easterners understood the benefits of monetizing silver. Boston's *Arena*, a magazine of social reform, did publish articles about silver's importance, but Reed contended that the voice of a western newspaper was needed: "To the bulk of people east of the river the argument for silver is unknown. It will never be published in a hostile newspaper."[57]

In July 1893 the Silver League sponsored a meeting in Denver to inform people about the local and national importance of the free coinage of silver. On 11 July 1893, Reed spoke on "The Situation" at the Broadway Theater. His speech combined the themes of silver, the debilitating impact of monopolists and trusts upon the people, and current politics as a crusade of good versus evil. Reed called for free and unlimited coinage of silver at a ratio of 16 to 1. He appealed to both the West and the South: "Silver down, wheat down, cotton at 4 cents a pound; that makes a triparte alliance a holy alliance of South and West. What more do we need?" Reed suggested that any western or southern congressman who reneged on the silver issue should be wary upon returning to his home state. "Let his people not shoot him," Reed suggested. "That would be hasty, inconsiderate and a discredit to the people's sense of law and order. No, just soak him in standard oil and burn him." To Reed, Henry George's 1886 New York City mayoral race had demonstrated the possibility of victory. George had run on one issue only, the land and its use, and he had "made a phenomenal run." Reed believed education was the most effective method to convince people of Populism's correct analysis of their problem and the rightness of silver's cause. "We must go on with Western pluck and Christian faith."[58] For Reed, Populism represented another means to bring about more justice and to move closer to God's kingdom on earth.

During the 1894 Populist convention, Reed's name emerged again as a possible candidate. The Populists discussed Reed's possible candidacy for governor or lieutenant governor, but, vacationing in Montana, Reed did not receive the convention's message in time to wire his answer. His chances, in any case, bordered on slim to none because Waite had put together a powerful organization for his own candidacy. Waite took the nomination in spite of Patterson's opposition. Reed campaigned for Waite's reelection, but the Populists won no important offices in the 1894 state election. And the fusion of the Populists with the Democrats in 1896 effectively ended the party's future nationally and in Colorado.[59]

Reed made two speeches in 1894 expressing his belief that the wealthy industrialists cared more for profit than for the working man's condition, and that those who worked to bring about a new community must prepare to protest unjust laws. In speaking to a Populist audience at the Denver Coliseum, Reed targeted Andrew Carnegie as an example of power without justice. Carnegie had gone to Jerusalem to find the exact spot where Satan had tempted Jesus with incredible wealth, Reed noted sarcastically: "He wants to know if the offer is going to be repeated: he wants to be there." Carnegie revealed the selfishness and the chicanery of the money-power: He donated money to charities, received praise from the religious newspapers, and then robbed workers of a fair day's pay. To protect silver and to reform the nation, Reed urged, everyone had to do missionary work: "Inundate the East with literature . . . until Colorado's opinion is the opinion of the country, and the opinion of the country is that of the world."[60]

During the Cripple Creek strike in June 1894, Reed expressed his sympathy for the miners on Bull Hill. When some church members took exception to his position, Reed resigned and established the Broadway Temple Association. In a speech to a union group that evening, Reed described Jesus as an anarchist — one who needed no law because the law resided within him — which resulted in negative publicity nationwide. In September 1894 Reed spoke at the Coliseum on "Politics of Today" and referred to those remarks that had earned him a national reputation. This reputation put him in the same company with Professor Richard Ely of the University of Wisconsin, Professor George Herron of Grinnell College, and Governor John Altgeld of Illinois, he declared — all of whom professed a brand of socialism. Yet all of these men believed that laws should dispense justice for all people, not just a few: "If you want me to respect the law you must make the law respectable. . . . My God, My friends, man is more than property! He makes property. He is not for the state: the state is for him." Reed referred to the abolitionists John Brown, William Lloyd Garrison, and Wendell Phillips; all three had challenged the laws of slavery and were vindicated because their cause was right, he maintained.[61]

Reed supported the Populist movement because it emphasized government by the people. Justice in the Omaha Platform meant returning to the voters a measure of control over their economic and social lives. Silver had functioned as a broad issue that united voters with differing interests for a political victory, but the monopolists' abilities to control economics and politics showed no sympathy for the masses and that was the real issue.

Reed believed that the potential for justice resided in the ideal of the republic. The people would not tolerate injustice for too long now because they were more intelligent and aware of their power to change things. Reed looked to the middle classes to bring about needed reforms in politics, not because they possessed any natural ability or social rank, but because of their ambition and education. They had the drive to create a better life; they had known economic scarcity but had risen above it. For Reed, this translated into positive change, and evidences of God at work; he wanted to support that work if he could. *Waiting for the Signal: A Novel* (1897) fictionalized the Populist movement as a revolutionary force and made Reed an example of a churchman's rare support.[62]

The Populists were a weak political alternative in March 1897, but in a raucous convention they agreed to join with the Democrats and field a ticket for the Denver city elections. They nominated Reed as their candidate for president of the Board of Public Works. That Sunday, Reed explained to his Broadway Temple congregation that this office directed city projects and would permit him to provide jobs so people could buy food and shoes for their children, thus reducing the drain on charity funds. He assured them that the Temple would continue as usual. Unfortunately, Reed lost.[63]

After 1896, Colorado political reform incorporated some Populist remnants but it became more closely identified with the established parties or other independent movements. Third parties in Colorado, except for the Populists in 1892, had little success over the long term. Reed's greater effectiveness, however, was not as a politician but as an advocate for the poor.[64]

Modern Charity:

Creating Opportunity

The misery that affected people's lives often caused Myron Reed to forget the science of modern charity and respond with whatever he had to bandage the hurt. A man went to Reed for some financial assistance and when asked if he had seen Reed, he answered that he had found him "crying in the parlor." No one had died, but an old woman stood before Reed telling him about her troubles; he listened and he helped.[1]

Myron Reed's notion of charity differed from the prevailing nineteenth-century view that helping the poor without careful screening would create dependent paupers. This view, advocated by Josephine Shaw Lowell of the New York Charity Organization, held that only the most distressed people should receive relief, that one should strenuously avoid duplication of assistance, and that one must not assist those who drank, gambled, and refused to help themselves.[2] Relief functioned only as a temporary measure because the American economy provided opportunities for people to help themselves. Reed believed, however, that organized charity should accomplish three things: people in distress should receive aid to help them through their misfortunes regardless of their morality; organized charity should create opportunities that would allow the recipients to work and function as useful citizens; and finally, charity's administration had to show a measure of kindness. The tramps and the unemployed were victims of an uncaring monopolistic system and had little control over their economic fortunes; some kindness would encourage them and help restore their sense of worthiness.

Since its beginnings in 1859, Denver had lived with the problems of poverty. In the 1860s fortune-hunters came and went, and those who stayed often had no money to return home and few chances to earn it. Conse-quently, poverty became a serious problem. The small settlement relied on the sale of mining supplies and what few support businesses there were required even fewer wage laborers. Organized efforts to meet the needs of those without any source of income proved insufficient. Jerome Smiley, an early historian of Denver, surmised that a great many of the destitute per-sons appeared unworthy of aid and attention.[3]

Many people shared this attitude in the nineteenth century, including a fair number in the emerging town of Denver. But compassion also surfaces in every era, and a few notable women in Colorado provided the early leadership that established a relief fund for the needy. Elizabeth Byers was instrumental in organizing the Ladies Union Aid Society, which was Den-ver's first nonsectarian charitable organization. All funds raised through the Society went to the poor. The Society not only helped those who wanted to go back home, but it fed and clothed homeless women and children whose husbands and fathers had deserted them. Women like Byers maintained charity's presence in Denver through the 1860s. In 1874 Frances Wisebart Jacobs, president of the Hebrew Benevolent Society and wife of Denver merchant Abraham Jacobs, extended her work beyond the Jewish commu-nity when she helped organize the Ladies Relief Society. In 1887 Jacobs merged the Ladies Relief Society into the Charity Organization Society, a coalition of Denver charities that combined to make fund raising more efficient.[4]

Churches struggled to meet expenses but still found money to furnish food, shelter, and medical care. Protestants, Jews, and Catholics worked together to assist the needy, regardless of their creed. Devoted workers like Rachel Wild Peterson and the Reverend Thomas Uzzell, Congregational-ist pastor of the People's Tabernacle, helped the destitute without preach-ing at them or judging their worthiness. Uzzell, who ministered to Denver's very poor, had the ability to raise money in tough times, and provided food and clothing to those down on their luck. At Christmas time, Uzzell would raise money for a children's dinner; it was well publicized and funded by regular donors. During the 1880s and 1890s one could not mention Colo-rado charity without referring to Jacobs and Uzzell.[5]

Associated Charities

Myron Reed came to Denver in 1884 with some experience of charity organizations. His friend, the Reverend Oscar C. McCulloch, pastor of the

Plymouth Church and founder of the Indianapolis Charity Organization Society (COS), had recruited Reed to perform various duties in the COS. McCulloch, a Christian Socialist and advocate of Henry George's single-tax plan, had invited S. H. Gurteen, who had started "organized" or "scientific" charity efforts in Buffalo, New York, to speak at the annual Indianapolis Benevolent Society meeting in 1879. The initial structure of the Indianapolis COS resulted from Gurteen's visit.[6] McCulloch stated the main objectives of the organization: to relieve all deserving cases of destitution; to prevent indiscriminate and duplicate giving; to make employment the basis of assistance; to protect the city from imposture; and to reduce vagrancy and pauperism and ascertain their true causes.[7]

Visitation, investigation, cooperation among all agencies, and the maintenance of a central registry of cases to prevent duplication formed the principal means for accomplishing these objectives. In March 1883 McCulloch had organized a businessmen's syndicate — the precursor of the community chest — to solicit funds once a year. The advantages, according to McCulloch, included one annual fund drive, more time for agencies to do legitimate work, and an increase in confidence in the COS as leading businessmen circulated among the people. Reed had worked closely with McCulloch as he canvassed for donations each year. One anecdote from this period illustrates Reed's kindness when predicaments required immediate aid. McCulloch had asked Reed to manage the COS while he was away. When he returned, McCulloch found that Reed had given away most of the fund's money, without bothering to investigate the worthiness of the needy's claims. McCulloch never repeated that mistake.[8]

When Reed moved to Denver, the idea of and effective organized charity came with him. In "Denver's Demands," a sermon preached on 24 November 1884, Reed pointed out the advantages of attacking poverty at the earliest stages of Denver's growth: "The day of opportunity for good things is when a city is young. An old city can only doctor its evil and nurse its infirmity. A young city can prevent both." Reed advised the people to establish the institutions that would shape the life and progress of the city before the window of experiment gave way to a closed door of established routine. One had to address pauperism before it became an institution. Such a task would require the participation of citizens who knew how to get things done. Oftentimes, these people had jobs other than that of professional alms gatherers, but Reed noted examples of men who had done more than just work every day. One such man, Horace Bushnell, took time outside his ministerial duties to establish a park in his city that would serve posterity. Reed admonished his listeners to act quickly: "It would be a pity in a young, new city to make a blunder, to suffer a neglect that by and by the coming citizen could only regret and could not remedy."[9]

Reed served on the advisory committee of the Ladies Relief Society, and soon met with Jacobs to plan for the organized fund-raising he hoped would supplant the practice of individual charities doing their own fund-raising. The *News* gave the program advance publicity by interviewing Jacobs and Reed. Jacobs explained that the Ladies Relief Society enabled people to help themselves. People wanted to work and would work if given the proper direction; any work that matched one's abilities and experience had two values — income and individual pride. A system also allowed one to deal with more cases. At any contact point in the system, the indigent would receive a card and directions to a station where she/he could get help.[10]

Reed told the reporter about his experience with McCulloch in Indianapolis, where the system had become a central clearinghouse for all charities in the city. A meeting, scheduled for 30 November, at the Tabor Opera House would outline the organization of such a system for Denver and would feature speakers such as Tom Patterson and Colorado Senator E. O. Wolcott. All churches in the downtown area had been asked to cancel their Sunday evening services so as to allow their members to attend.[11]

On the Tabor Opera House stage that evening sat a number of state and city dignitaries, along with an ecumenical representation of clergy. Mayor John Routt presided and introduced Colonel J. A. Bentley, who read a report on behalf of the Ladies Relief Society's advisory committee. The report described conditions of want existing in Denver and the excellent work the Ladies Relief Society had done in meeting those needs. Bentley carefully noted that not only did individuals have a duty to help the hungry and sick, but "it is also a social obligation, which no community can disregard." Poverty unanswered led to pauperism, crime, and finally to social disorder. The best interests of the community — preservation of property and law and order — demanded an approach to charity that could handle the increasing number of requests resulting from the city's growth. The uniting of all charity agencies in a common cause would establish a central location where applicants could receive aid and be directed to the appropriate agency for assistance. The advisory committee then recommended that other charity agencies combine with the Ladies Relief Society to coordinate fund-raising and record-keeping. After this proposal, the speakers for the meeting added their support: Patterson spoke on "Modern Charity vs. Ancient Charity," and Wolcott addressed "The Defect in Official Charity." Following this meeting, the Ladies Relief Society continued their annual meetings to publicize their budget objectives and the beginning of their soliciting campaign. Some agencies cooperated in a common fund solicitation, but any significant coalition of Denver charities would have to wait until Jacobs and Reed could work their persuasive powers.[12]

Denver's economy suffered from boom-and-bust cycles, and in the mid–1880s a recession reduced the number of wage-labor jobs. Enough people roamed the city looking for work that merchants and property owners became uneasy. The charitable agencies needed financial support if they were to supply the essentials for these people.[13] In the midst of these conditions, Reed preached on the themes: (1) wealth equals power and obligation; (2) charity's obligation begins at home; (3) and one should judge charity's economy by its consequences, not by dollars spent. These sermons explained Reed's concept of charity and the obligations of those who believed that life progressed toward something better.

In the first sermon, entitled "A Public-spirited Man," Reed declared that "the exclusive feeling is passing out." All around, one could see evidence of mutual concern and governmental decisions to preserve the natural beauty of the country. For example, the state acted in the public interest when it protected the beauty of the country, such as at Yellowstone Park and Niagara Falls, and made these areas accessible to all people. Likewise, a public-spirited man acted in the interest of the community when he performed benevolent acts. The significance of these acts was that they were not part of any official duty, but that they were acts of kindness performed simply because someone was in distress. Reed contended that wealth revealed a man's character; it endowed him with power, and how he used this power showed his true character. The Bible furnished an example of how wealth enabled man to create something new from old institutions. Joseph, son of Jacob, whose brothers sold him into Egyptian slavery, gained power and access to wealth as he matured. When famine came, he had used his power to help the hungry, including his brothers who had sold him to slave traders; Joseph's wealth had created an obligation for him to provide for those in need. Reed preached that wealth equaled power in Colorado, and those with power had an obligation to their neighbors. The community's benefits were available to everyone, and the most fortunate must extend a helping hand to the less fortunate. The crisis, not the letter of the law, dictated the kind of charity required. The charity of the rich could help the poor to bridge their misery.[14]

In his second sermon Reed acknowledged the great need for charity throughout the United States, but he argued that Coloradans should first focus on their own needs. "I advocate more attention to the motto: 'Charity begins at home,'" Reed preached. The man who lived closest to Reed was his neighbor, and "It is so arranged in this life that my obligation is never greater than my ability." Reed believed that Colorado's charitable endeavors should begin locally and then radiate out as far as they could go. Reed declared that so-called "assisted immigrants, Huns, Poles, and Chinese" — those immigrants brought into the country by corporations as a source of cheap labor — were the cause of much of the social disorder ascribed to the poor. Those immigrants who had come to America of their own volition, with the intention to become citizens, should be welcomed, Reed believed, but now America had enough people. Building a new community that practiced justice for all demanded an intelligent and servant-minded populace, and Reed believed that only those who were committed to that way of life could function as viable participants in developing the kingdom of God on earth. "To bind these together, to make these all intelligent, to set the feet of the children on the path to the school house, to give them plenty of the spelling book and the Bible is a large work." One could not blame the new immigrants totally; rather the corporations were at fault for enticing them to leave their homes to work for a pittance. Immigrant wages were usually insufficient to support a wife and children, but they came, nevertheless, expecting to return home with money to make life better for their families. Reed complained that these immigrants had no commitment to America, and by taking jobs at low wages, they robbed committed Americans of their rightful economic opportunities.[15]

The last sermon examined the theme of the economy of charity. Charity distributed properly and in the right amounts would prove more economical than prisons or poor farms. If one desired to protect property from the pauper who turned thief, then one must develop institutions that would produce better men — no matter what the cost. Reed criticized the public attitude that asked for more economical management of institutions without considering their product: "Crime small and great can only be stayed by education of the mind and of the heart. . . . The test of an institution is not is it cheap, but is it bettering men? If it is it is cheap no matter what it costs." In the matter of the tramps, Reed insisted that over time it would cost the city less to provide work than to let them remain idle and hungry. One had to take away the bent toward crime, which usually resulted from the lack of work, food, shelter — and a friend. Economical charity must contain the element of sentiment, a caring feeling because a fellow human being suffered. This sympathetic outlook flowed from the spirit of Christ: "The world will not be made a happy place by money nor miracle but by the spirit and mind of Jesus Christ. Let that spirit and mind be in us."[16]

These three sermons presented broad themes to establish principles for

examination, debate, and action. Reed had developed his views from attending the National Conferences on Charity and from his experiences in
Indianapolis. He accepted the practical effects of organized charity because
the system allowed people to gain support to work for economic independence. Not everyone had the ability or the drive to succeed, but those who
did documented for Reed that the journey toward the new community
moved forward. His obligation, and it was the same for anyone who worked
for the new community, lay in continuing to spread the truth and to agitate
for institutions that dispensed justice and protected liberty. Providing assistance that put people on the road to economic opportunity was the primary
goal of charity.[17]

The 1885 plea for combined effort finally resulted in the Charity Organization Society of Denver in 1887. This organization featured a fund-raising
team who solicited donations in all the city's districts. They maintained a
central point where applicants could secure directions to a place of assistance. Disadvantages included inadequate fund-raising to handle all who
needed relief, and lack of citizen involvement that resulted in too few workers. Reed kept the idea of "associated charities" alive by using his pulpit. He
criticized the many who did not spend time or money in the cause of
charity; always the bulk of the labor fell upon a dedicated few. "A large class
of people do not touch it [charity] with so much as the tips of their fingers,"
complained Reed and this inequality grew tiresome. Without money or
volunteers, it was conceivable that the city would have to dispense with
charity altogether: "The man who will not give anything . . . will not be so
altogether comfortable as he is now. . . . As long as poverty is soothed,
palliated, it is quiet. When it is desperate it is noisy and dangerous."[18]

In Colorado and America, events would soon conspire to make men and
women hungry and little children homeless: "There are gigantic schemes
now at work whose chief result will be the making of the many poor. The
lords of industry are increasing." What the country needed was a plan to
abolish "the wholesale manufacture of poverty," or at least discourage it.
Reed suggested that the government could expand what aid it now provided to include all categories of the poor with a new tax. The burden
would then be somewhat equalized. But realizing that such a plan probably
would not receive adequate support, he proposed instead an organization
modeled after the one in Indianapolis. It presented an attractive alternative
to the present system and would improve efficiency and beneficence in
Denver.[19]

The program of "scientific charity," as it was practiced by an estimated
forty charity organizations nationwide, now became the objective of Den-

ver's benevolent societies. Modern charity stressed the coordination and regulation of existing charities to avoid duplicity and to weed out "the unworthy." The volunteer "friendly visitors" were sometimes too intrusive, but they did help the poor by encouraging and advising them about possible jobs. Modern charity not only attended to the obvious needs of the indigent, it also tried to address the causes of poverty. Reed defined the work of modern charity as multitasked: (1) to limit the spread of pauperism by establishing kindergartens and more public schools; (2) to involve the poor in work programs that preserved their self-respect while they looked for permanent jobs; (3) to provide facilities to help those who could not help themselves, facilities such as hospitals, orphanages and newsboy homes, and havens for troubled girls; and (4) to assist anyone in true despair regardless of their creed, home city, or morality.[20]

This last task sometimes created tension between Reed and those who wanted to weed out "the unworthy." Reed employed a loose interpretation of "the unworthy." His public policy statements harmonized with the definition of modern charity, but in one-on-one situations, Reed would give aid to anyone who asked for it. One of his admirers recounted the story of the tramp who had wandered into his office and asked for a handout but was politely refused. In a little while, Reed entered the man's office and asked if there were any coin in the treasury. The man replied that the Broadway Temple Association was operating on deficit funding, to which Reed responded, "Well, let's press it for another ten." After he received the ten dollars, Reed had found the tramp and with a handshake transferred the money. Reed thought that any charitable program must first meet a person's basic needs and then endeavor to create opportunity for those who wanted to work. He believed that most people would work and society had to create the means of employment or face the consequences of the rebellious, hungry masses.[21]

The Charity Organization Society finally became a reality in 1889. The push for an organized effort by Denver charities increased markedly in 1888, largely because of Reed's persistence. Other contributors to this effort were Father William O'Ryan, Rabbi William Friedman, and Dean Henry Martyn Hart. On a Sunday night in April 1888, Reed's sermon highlighted Denver's organized charities. He told the story of London's "Jinx's Baby." Jinx, a London workingman, had too many children to feed and he tried to find a relief society, among the many in London, that would take the youngest child and place it a good home. Unfortunately, the baby did not fit any of the categories that defined need in London. In desperation, the father had thrown the baby into the river. According to Reed, an impoverished person could fall outside the acceptable definitions of a worthy recipient in the present system and receive no help of any kind. That possibility should not exist in Denver.[22] To avoid duplicity and to assure help for those in despair, Reed stated the objective of the organized charities:

> What we ask for in Denver is so complete a system of charities, so closely organized, that no living being in perishing need of anything shall lack that thing. So that once a year we can pay our money and feel reasonably sure that the poor of all sorts and conditions will be cared for promptly and wisely.[23]

Reed then outlined generally how such an organization would function:

(1) Schedule an annual meeting in which each component would report to the public on moneys spent and the number of cases handled;
(2) Establish a yearly visitation of volunteers from different agencies to obtain pledges from businesses and individuals and to distribute this money among the members of the organization;
(3) Representatives from the various societies and the state, city, county, and churches would form a committee to meet at a predetermined frequency to review cases and determine, when practical, which agency could best fulfill each request;
(4) Create a record system that would allow periodic reviews of the cases treated and that would contribute information for budget and activity planning in the next year.

Reed closed with the charity's principal objective: "The aim of all charity is not simply to feed and clothe, but to keep, build up and reinforce self respect, to prevent poverty as far as possible and pauperism in any way." In any charitable system, nothing took the place of "a warm hand, a good heart under the instruction and guidance of practical executive brains." Reed acknowledged that the poor had complex problems and required time and love, but he insisted that the city would benefit from the success and efficiency of organized charities. Assisting people until they could find work would cost less than prisons and poor houses.[24]

The *News* editorialized that "insurmountable prejudices" existed within the various relief societies. These groups had narrow interests and/or ties with religious groups that might work against any unified effort. Yet, the editorial also proudly noted that in Denver "the people are not frightened with a new idea," and it concluded optimistically that individuals still retained "the right to relieve distress wherever it is encountered, in the old-fashioned way." But Reed continued to participate in a number of charitable efforts: a women's hospital, kindergartens, a safe home for girls, and a Union soldiers' home. He labored to unite these benevolent causes for efficiency, and to establish more reliable systems of financial support. He did not believe that the city's poor fit the description of "genteel poverty": those brave souls who did without but put forth a good appearance. He judged that Denver had the resources to prevent poverty, aid its poor, and in so doing, create better citizens.[25]

In 1888 the annual meeting of the local charities provided an occasion to rally public support for organized charity. Speakers included the Reverend Frederick W. Slocum, Jr., of Baltimore, an experienced participant in organized charity who hailed from the city in which the system had originated. Slocum agreed with the nineteenth-century adage that indiscriminate alms-giving caused pauperism, and he believed that reforming the instincts that led to poverty defined charity's true purpose. This statement apparently agreed with the *News*'s view that modern charity would abolish pauperism in Denver and allow the city's charities to concentrate on only those valid claimants who truly deserved help — the insane, dependent children, and the destitute sick — in the *News*'s words, "the only valid claimants that ought to exist in a city that is enjoying unexampled prosperity."[26]

Reed hesitated to form such hasty conclusions about the expected results of scientific charity. The complexity of poverty's causes and people's different reactions to disasters introduced variables that often reflected individuality and background; these factors cautioned him to wait for results before deciding about scientific charity's effectiveness. In this changing world people had difficulty finding their places, and Reed had no doubt that society needed more support systems to ease them through the trauma. For example, the city could provide work programs, job training, and make education more available through additional public schools, all working in concert with charity. He also agreed that the division of labor principle widely advocated in industry applied equally to charity. It stretched the money and more people received help. With the drive for efficiency and a few available volunteers, Reed feared that the critical ingredient of personal interaction would suffer. If a central office administered the programs too rigidly, or if there were no friendly visitors to meet with people, then dispensing charity would become too impersonal to accomplish the objectives of providing encouragement and work. For this reason, he campaigned for programs like the "Flower Mission," an organization that would send volunteers with flowers and food to the sick and hungry. More importantly, the

Flower Mission brought a cheerful face to the sufferers and maintained a touch of care and human friendship in charity.[27]

Unworthiness, for Reed, was a relative condition, and his universal approach to the needy sometimes caused tension. Reed and another avid charity worker disagreed, for example, over whether the worker's charity should be accepted into the Charity Organization Society. Dean Henry Martyn Hart of St. John's Episcopal Cathedral had been active in charity work since his arrival in Denver. Although he claimed that Denver's new charity organization copied the society that he had organized in Blackheath, London, in 1869, he did cooperate with Reed in the development of the associated charities. Hart's Investigation Office proposed to rid Denver of tramps begging in the streets and to protect innocent people from unethical employment agencies. He thought that his office qualified for admission into the organized charities. Reed and most of the committee members thought otherwise. Hart had not submitted an application by the required date, and his organization did not appear in the collection books. Hart wrote a letter to the *News* and the *Republican* complaining that the fall solicitation had been completed without including the Investigation Office. The *Times* published Reed's reply, which described Hart's infrequent attendance at meetings, noted that Hart's office duplicated the work of the Ladies Relief Society (which, in any case, did the work more thoroughly), and besides the Dean canvassed poorly. Reed did not publicly express his opinion, but he would not have agreed with Dean Hart's practice of purging the city of tramps; these were men who, in Reed's view, had genuine needs, and who might not deserve the epithet of tramp. If a Christian had the duty to show charity to all people, then why discriminate against a particular group? To help someone through his misfortune seemed more kind than pulling him off the street and sending him on his way. Finally, Hart acknowledged that he had made a mistake and had nothing critical to say about Myron Reed. He then submitted a proper application to the newly organized charity society.[28]

The organizing meeting of the Charity Organization Society of Denver took place on 28 January 1889 at the Albany Hotel. The constitution followed the general articles of the Buffalo, New York, society.[29] The Society adopted the following objectives:

The Society was organized for the general purpose of promoting the welfare of the poor, and the suffering and the friendless in the City of Denver.

The chief objects and methods shall include:

(1) The promotion of cordial co-operation between benevolent societies, churches and individuals;

(2) The maintenance of a body of friendly visitors to the poor;

(3) The provision of temporary employment and industrial instruction;

(4) The prevention of imposition and the diminution of vagrancy and
pauperism.[30]

Twenty-two societies representing the Protestant, Jewish, Roman Catholic, and nonsectarian interests composed the first federated society. The
delegates elected Reed as president, five vice-presidents (including two
women), a secretary, and as treasurer J. S. Appel, a merchant and civic
leader.[31]

The birth of the Charity Organization Society seemed to reinforce the
opinions of other urban leaders that Denver had just become a better place
for them to send their helpless poor. Other cities could send their needy to
Denver and then use their benevolent funds for other purposes. At the
Society's February meeting, there was a discussion of the increasing numbers of outside paupers who had arrived in Denver and of what the appropriate action might be. When investigators determined that these poor
arrived from cities with a one-way ticket and no reliable means of support,
they immediately bought them a return ticket home. Reed warned of the
potential impact of these incoming migrants:

> The East is shipping its paupers to California, and California is busy
> shipping its paupers to the East. Denver is the half-way house of the
> victim. The question just raised is one of the most important our
> organization will have to contend with, and it should receive immedi-
> ate careful attention.[32]

Denver had limited resources, and Reed designated that this money be used
for its own citizens, not for transients or castoffs from other towns. He
contended that each town should assume responsibility for its own paupers;
that was what caring for one's neighbor meant. The Society did not object
to helping people in transit to their homes or to a new job; their objection
centered on the professional pauper—the individual who shunned work
and preferred handouts. Although the *News* published no decision by the
Society at this meeting, the transient problem continued and became extremely critical during the Panic of 1893.[33]

While Reed wanted to avoid supporting the professional pauper and the drain on Denver's funds, he could not discard his belief that charity applied to people in genuine need, wherever they might live. This conviction also included farmers in eastern Colorado. When these farmers experienced drought and crop loss in 1890, they asked for help. Reed believed the farmers represented an infant industry that deserved as much protection as any industry in the country. Denver's charities raised money for misfortune in the city, but why not help these farmers by using Arapahoe County taxes to relieve their distress. Reed urged: "If the county commissioners will take prompt hold of this matter — give these people what they need, no taxpayer, whatever he feels, will ever say a word. The justice of the action will make the meanest taxpayer dumb." This proposal further underscored Reed's position that charity should begin at home and then spread when funds would permit it. The county commissioners did not accept his suggestion, but Denver's private citizens collected money to assist the farmers.[34]

Later that month, Reed resigned as president of the Charity Organization Society. Even organized charity could not cure the problems of apathy and lack of shared responsibilities: it seemed that the same few volunteers did most of the work and others stood on the sidelines. The continuation of these problems prompted Reed's resignation; probably his lack of patience and frustration over trying to coordinate so many societies caught up with him. The *News* portrayed Reed as the life of the Society during the two years of its existence, but no amount of pleading could convince him to stay. But Reed praised the Society. It had graduated from an experiment to a living, efficient institution that worked to make life better in the city and the state, he said. No one was indispensable to the Society; some competent person would arise to fill his shoes. As he departed, Reed said to the annual meeting that even though his official duties ceased, his support of the Society would continue. And he did return to the presidency in 1892. Reed did not explain the reason for this return, but his interest in charity and his friends' lobbying efforts probably contributed to this decision.[35]

The Panic of 1893

Most Denverites entered the 1890s confident that prosperity would continue. This confidence was shattered when silver's decline precipitated the Panic of 1893 and created a bend in the road of ongoing success and prosperity that Denver's political and economic leaders never expected. Many American entrepreneurs, including some of Denver's notables, lost much of their wealth. Horace Tabor, who had migrated to Colorado from Kansas in 1859, saw his "rags-to-riches" fortune in mining and real estate turn again to rags. One observer sadly reported, "His clothes became shabby and he drove about town with an old gray horse and a dilapidated buggy." Tabor had been worth $5,000,000 in the early 1880s, but as Denver's postmaster he earned $3,700 in 1898.[36]

Yet Tabor had better luck than most Denverites. The Panic of 1893 spelled catastrophe for many laborers and marginal members of the "middle economic" community. People who lived in the "Bottoms," a slum of tents and shacks planted alongside the South Platte River in the midst of industrial pollution, had endured miserable conditions for years and likely never felt the depression's effects. They were the recipients of the welfare ministry of the Reverend Thomas Uzzell of the People's Tabernacle. A *News* reporter wrote: "This condition exists in a 'city which really has no very poor people,' in 'rich, progressive, prosperous Denver.'" Homeless children roamed the of Denver. Some hired on as indentured servants for local employers; others joined gangs and added to the problems of an already overtaxed police department. Unemployment approached 50,000 in the state, and 14,000 in Denver, or 33 percent of the adult male population. All types of vagrants and luckless people crowded the city asking for work, food, and a place to sleep. The unemployed so overwhelmed Uzzell's resources that he announced he could no longer feed single men because of the pressing needs of women and children.[37]

The State Board of Charities and Corrections met on 5 July 1893, and President Reed asked the board to address the emergency conditions in Colorado: "The indications are that assistance will be called for upon a scale not before known in Denver. The outlook is gloomy indeed for the miners and they will probably flock toward Denver." The Board recognized that the laborers' fate was no fault of their own and resolved to meet the catastrophe by combining public and private organizations to provide work programs along with relief.[38]

The unemployed wanted work, not relief, and conveyed their requests through public demonstrations. These luckless individuals who clamored for jobs reinforced Reed's conviction that generally men preferred to earn their bread rather than live off public charity. To alleviate immediate distress, civic leaders offered a temporary solution — a campsite beside the South Platte River. The state supplied three hundred tents plus food, and the militia imposed military rules regarding admission, visitation, and food rations. Even though the rules were confining, the camp provided a welcome refuge for many workers and their families. They could obtain food for their children and enjoy shelter while looking for work. The Board of Public Works used some men in municipal projects such as street repair, laying sewer pipe, and painting. But for many wage laborers these temporary projects ended too soon for them to earn enough money to leave the camp. Lack of funds reduced the number of work projects and the number of unemployed workers living at the camp increased.[39]

Camp Relief quickly translated into a liability. Each day people flowed into Denver, increasing the camp's population. Too many people, combined with fear that these vagrants would become dependent upon aid, or might form a mob to take what they needed, caused many citizens to call for the closing of the camp. The mob lynching of one Daniel Arata, an Italian bartender who had killed a man because he had not paid for his beer, heightened the people's anxiety. Italians had never been wholly welcomed in Denver because they were Roman Catholics in a predominantly non-Catholic city and because they spoke little or no English. This intolerance manifested itself in job discrimination; Italians were only hired for menial tasks and were usually denied better-paying jobs. This prejudice had driven many Italians to the "Bottoms" and kept them in poverty. Thus, it was the mob action that disturbed the good citizens Denver, more than the lynching of one Italian.[40]

On 30 July, in a decision not without political repercussions, the Executive Relief Committee announced that the camp would close. With the fall election approaching, the Populists accused their opponents of pushing hard for the closing because of their anxiety over so many unemployed in Colorado. Evidently, the Executive Relief Committee viewed the camp as a threat to public safety and as an attraction that would draw more transients to Denver. Money supplied by the Executive Relief Committee for reduced railroad tickets to hometowns and eastern cities probably accounted for a substantial exodus of the unemployed.[41]

During the Panic's early days, a spirit of benevolence hovered over Denver. In July 1893, the *News*'s articles reflected the noble ideal of providing care for all in need; the wealthy owed that much to the poor. Denver's magnanimous spirit even prompted a gesture to relieve distress in New York City. But as 1894 approached and the indigents kept coming, that noble ideal deteriorated. Denverites adopted the attitude: let's assist Denver's citizens who have been deemed worthy, and let the outsiders and Jacob Coxey's army fend for themselves. The arrival in Denver of the western Coxeyites on their way to Washington had complicated relief efforts. The Denver Home Guards had provided meals and tents to the Coxeyites, who had camped on the banks of the South Platte River in a camp that became

known as the River Front Park. But for some Coxeyites, Denver's generosity reduced the urgency of their mission to get to Washington and frightened local citizens. Herbert George, the Populist reformer, helped fund
supplies for the Coxeyites to build boats to float down the Platte River to
near Omaha and join another contingent to continue traveling East. This
plan turned into a disaster when the inexperienced travelers tried to navi-
gate the river with the small boats; at least two men drowned and some
swam ashore, but many kept on going.[42]

The *News* advocated the "old fashioned" method of one-on-one assistance to alleviate overburdened relief agencies. The Panic functioned, according to Reed, as an equalizer among men. He saw millionaires transformed into tramps and tramps more at ease in their misfortune because of
the unexpected, but deserving company. Reed observed: "It is a day of
judgment on fictitious value. . . . I think there is already a kindlier feeling
between man and man. The fence between the rich and the poor is not
nearly so high. A common danger brings men together." During these
terrible times, declared Reed, we must feed the hungry, but continue the
fight against child labor and for the rights of oppressed women; he implored the people not to give up on the state and its objectives for a better
life. This disaster should not become an excuse to forget what had made
Colorado a desirable place to live; instead, let the citizens come together in
mutual assistance.[43]

The tests of worthiness for Reed continued to be a person's physical and
financial condition, and he did not inquire if the person had reached any
particular moral standard. The blame usually fell upon the monopolists and
the people who let corrupt politicians govern the country. Reed used Andrew Carnegie, "the bullet-headed hero of Homestead," as an example of
a capitalist who imported cheap labor and disregarded the native-born
American who needed work. Coxey's Army showed that some people would
seize the moment to challenge the government's lack of action in the midst
of the Panic. What would result from this march on Washington? Reed
ventured no prophecy, but he did discern the presence of God among the
marchers, working to bring about the new community: "I do not believe in
any man who does not believe in God, and God in current events."[44]

Criticism soon developed about the Charity Organization Society's formal policies and possible duplications of charitable efforts. But the struggle
to find enough work and resources to handle the destitute continued, and
Reed claimed that, under the circumstances, charitable agencies and the
city had done well. The city had proved that it could cope with a severe
depression like the 1893 Panic. Denver demonstrated its resourcefulness,

for example, in the Maverick Restaurant that served five-cent meals, and in the Reverend Tom Uzzell's rabbit hunts in 1893 and 1894 that supplied meat for the poor in Pueblo, Colorado Springs, and Denver.[45] Reed remarked to his congregation:

> There is no city in the world that has mastered the emergency better than we have. I have no excuses to make for our Maverick restaurant, for our Helping Hand, for our charity organizations. . . . I am as proud as ever of my city and state.[46]

Reed worked as hard as anyone. A spring illness prevented him from being as active as he wished. It could have been the illness or the frustration of too many people and little money, but Reed once again resigned as president of the Charity Organization Society effective 20 August 1894. He said that he could not give the required time to the job. Within two weeks Reed left for Hot Springs, Arkansas, to rest and recover from his sickness. The Society regretfully accepted the resignation, called him the "father" of the society, and thanked him for his untiring efforts in making it a success.[47]

As Denver's citizens struggled with the depression, light finally broke through the black economic clouds. Civic leaders moved toward more economic diversification and encouraged new, non-mining related businesses to locate in the state. They described Colorado as the "Switzerland" of the West and promoted tourism. Bankers devised plans to work with depositors to keep money in the state despite the many bank failures. Denver's Chamber of Commerce encouraged increases in sugar beet production and the cultivation of more varieties of fruits. In 1895 civic leaders organized annual Festivals of Mountain and Plain — three-day carnivals complete with parades, entertainment, and displays of Colorado's agriculture, mining, industrial, and mercantile products — that favorably compared with New Orleans's Mardi Gras. Advertised nationwide, the Festivals attracted tourists and promoted agriculture and commerce. On 1 October 1898 Denver's business leaders issued a "Business Proclamation" in a booster issue of the *News* that included a pledge "to co-operate in all feasible and practical ways to promote the future growth, prosperity and solid upbuilding of our state." These actions enabled Denver to cultivate a more diversified economic base to safeguard its future.[48]

Reed believed that public institutions such as the Charity Organization Society had the potential to mold humans into suitable inhabitants for the Kingdom of God. He saw God's power in the lives of the men and women who dedicated themselves to helping people get through their times of misfortune—most of the time. As he grew older his penchant to speak his mind caused a dispute with Mary Lathrop, Denver's first woman attorney and a Quaker, about how one public institution, the State Industrial Home for Girls, was being managed. Reed criticized the Protestant "widows and old maids" who counseled the girls for not having the "tact to do their job" and suggested that "a washtub" might be more suitable for their talents. Ms. Lathrop reproached Reed for his thoughtless remarks about the Protestant women engaged in this work—and for paltry salaries. She reminded him that old maids and widows, both Protestants and Catholics, had recorded significant accomplishments in improving life for young ladies. Reed did not publicly respond to this deserved criticism, but on his good days his demeanor was more positive toward everyone.[49] Reed believed that institutions would grow from the American republic's fertile ground of justice and liberty, and he believed these institutions should reflect those ideals. Reed defined the republic's religion:

> The religion of a nation ought to be the embodiment of its highest intelligence and in harmony with the outcome of the deepest thoughts, the deepest experience, the richest culture, the finest institutions of the best and wisest minds that nation counts among her children.[50]

Life did not move along without some rough and tumble times and neither would the kingdom of God on earth evolve in a smooth and certain manner—only God knew the method and timing of the coming kingdom—but humanity could not prevent it. Reed envisioned the task of those who understood God's purpose for humanity as being one of removing the obstacles to the development of justice and liberty: "The great force is a live man in love with his errand." If one gave people the opportunity to earn enough money to feed their families, gave them time for thought, for music and books, and let the good within them take over, then, Reed maintained, they would contribute to a community that contained more justice and liberty. But we must accept that this type of community required cooperation: "If all the world could still take care of itself there would still be gravy for her bread; also jam, if she preferred jam. But to do that, we must get together."[51] Reed knew of no easy way to bring about charity or to show the love of God:

> There is no cheap way of helping folks. . . . [A] "charity organization" does good, but it becomes mechanical. It is a good thing but it needs a supplement. . . . You must help directly. You must see the man you

help. Official charities are bloodless and cold. Official religion is show and noise. The theory of liberty never loosed a fetter. It is liberty incarnate in Frenchmen, and Irishmen, and Americans and Cubans, that make men free. . . . A man also who believes in man and in God has the old power of Jesus Christ.[52]

Christians proved their faith by their actions and illustrated their commitment to the use of power to effect justice. The injustices perpetuated by the wealthy industrialists upon their laborers cried out for this dedication to fairness in wages and working conditions. These industrialists made any future for the worker uncertain by their collusion:

No man by observation of a harvest can tell what wheat will be worth, or coal, or any necessary of life. No miner can tell how many days he will be allowed to work, nor at what wages. Competition had some mercy in it, but there is no competition in a "trust." Unless this ill-named abomination can be killed, the crop of crime and poverty will be well tasseled, well filled and very large.[53]

Laborers deserved a quality of life that would enable them to cultivate their minds and their bodies without fear of losing their jobs at the hands of greedy monopolists. Reed intended to introduce as much justice into labor and capitalism as his position and activities would permit.

FIVE

Labor:

A Frontier with Opportunity and Conflict

The relationship between labor and capitalism captured the public's imagination during the 1880s and 1890s. The propaganda of labor organizations inspired the public to look with horror on the terrible working conditions and wage manipulation by greedy employers. On the other hand, strikes and the accompanying unruly disorder conditioned the public to view the strikers as troublemakers, or even worse, anarchists. Henry Ward Beecher of Brooklyn's Plymouth Church, perhaps expressed the general opinion of many American church leaders when he reacted to the 1877 railroad strike, the forerunner of more labor problems in the 1880s:

> It is said that a dollar a day is not enough for a wife and five or six children. No, not if the man smokes or drinks beer. It is not enough if they are to live as he would be glad to have them live. It is not enough to enable them to live as perhaps they would have a right to live in prosperous times. But is not a dollar a day enough to buy bread with? Water costs nothing, and a man who cannot live on bread is not fit to live. What is the use of a civilization that simply makes men incompetent to live under the conditions which exist?[1]

Beecher's income allowed him to live on considerably more than a dollar a day and he could afford to urge workers to bear poverty in more civilized ways. The traditional view of wages taught that they were beyond human influence, subject to economic laws that operated much like nature's laws. With this attitude, religious leaders condemned the violence, blamed the workers, and supported methods to reestablish order. But some ministers

96

thought that if labor's complaints were submitted to men of reason on both sides, solutions could be found. Church members and ordinary citizens became anxious when clerics like Myron Reed supported labor in its efforts to rectify these perceived wrongs; they believed such encouragement might provoke a general uprising against society. But to Reed, a dollar a day was not enough, and he believed the established social order presented a sizable obstacle to a sensible settlement of the labor problem.[2]

For Reed, the greed of the monied power prohibited a civilized discussion about alternatives. Too many corporate magnates and politicians were more interested in return-on-investment than they were in the humanitarian needs of the workers. Reed believed that employment should be available for all who would work, dependent upon their ability, and that wages should be paid according to the worth of one's labor, not according to some previously determined value that only considered the investors' profit margin. Given America's resources and its willing labor force, no man should have to go without food. Any workingman deserved enough money to buy food for his family.[3]

How labor and capitalism solved their disagreements would affect all citizens — including women and children. The problems of women's wages and child labor were also clearly fraught with moral issues. There was no justification for the sweatshops that women endured to make a few cents for their families. Women certainly deserved jobs with better pay than sewing overalls for fifty-five cents per dozen. A young state like Colorado should not be allowed to replicate the child labor system as it was practiced in England and Massachusetts. The conditions of childhood molded the child. If children only experienced long hours of labor, inadequate food, and no education or loving care, then they would mature with an attitude toward the world that might take years to change, if ever. The proper nurture of children demanded time for play, time to develop their minds and bodies — not time in a dark, dirty factory. If the country desired to form good citizens, then these injustices must be corrected.[4]

When Reed examined the causes of these injustices, he determined that they rested upon the wage system. He recognized that limited family incomes forced some women and children to work. But neither society nor the family could afford to neglect a child's education. The home suffered, too, when an absent mother worked to put food on the table. The nation's glory resided in its homes, not in its factories. Reed declared, "If woman and child labor are the necessary fruit of the wage system, then that tree will have to be cut down."[5]

Over time, this assessment of the problem between labor and capitalism led Reed to believe that if ballots failed, if strikes produced no mutually satisfactory arbitration, then labor must organize just as capitalists had organized. He disagreed with ministers like Beecher, for Reed saw that workingmen needed an organization with some leverage to represent their interests. The Knights of Labor, perhaps the most successful national labor organization in the 1880s, had an active group in Denver, led by the avowed socialist, Joseph Buchanan. The Knights had elected Terrence Powderly their Grand Master Workman in 1879, and the union had prospered under his leadership. It had championed the eight-hour movement, called for the abolishment of the wage system, admitted women into its membership, demanded equal pay for both sexes, and emphasized cooperation as a means to combat the competition inherent in industry and commerce. Reed agreed with these ideas, and soon after his arrival in Denver he joined the local Knights of Labor assembly.[6]

Labor, properly organized, could force a summit with the capitalists on a somewhat equal footing. Undoubtedly, reasonable men would discover that their problems affected the whole community and therefore demanded a solution in which all parties would benefit. In Reed's opinion, the principle of cooperation formed the basis for any solution. Labor necessarily had to appeal to the public in a straightforward way, just as capitalists had done, to gain their support. The truth would persuade Americans of the fairness of the workers' grievances. Reed confidently expected that, using its voting power, the public could push corporations and the government to search for common ground. The church, as the country's moral conscience, could act as a mediator, bringing these factions together to make them understand the tragic consequences if they reached no agreement. With this objective, Reed addressed the conflict between labor and capitalism, emphasizing its crucial importance in Denver's prosperous, developing community.[7]

In her essay on "The Adventures of the Frontier in the Twentieth Century," historian Patricia Limerick suggested that we examine the concept of *la frontera* as a way to understand the interactions among the various peoples in the West. The concept of *la frontera* describes the borderland between cultures or groups that includes the possibility for cooperation as well as conflict. This frontier possesses no inevitable tranquillity, nor does it symbolize a place of equal opportunity. *La frontera* introduces the possibilities of peaceful coexistence along with the realities of power and greed. The conquest of the West appropriated land from its ancient owners, and entrepreneurs migrated from the East to develop that land without acknowledging the rights of those who were already living there. Struggle was necessary if justice was to prevail. The concept of *la frontera* provides a useful way in which to think about the relationship between laborers and capitalists in the 1880s. Denver can be viewed as a borderland, with the potential for cooperation or conflict, between labor and capitalism.[8]

Labor Must Organize

In the first year of his ministry, Reed reminded his congregation and Denver's civic leaders that growth from "mining camp to metropolis" had been a recent accomplishment. As citizens with a measure of responsibility in a young community, they had the opportunity to prevent pauperism and ignorance before these traits became well established. A glance at older cities demonstrated that within a very few years the prejudices and practices of Denver's citizens would determine that city's response to the unfortunate souls in its midst. The administration of intelligent charity with kindness and financial aid would assist these luckless souls to cross the bridge of bad times and stop the curse of pauperism — that rut of perennial poverty. In great cities businessmen and ordinary citizens took on projects of municipal improvement in their odd hours. For example, Peter Cooper of New York City built the Cooper Union, which provided instruction and training for that city's poor. Abraham Lincoln's 1860 public lecture in the Great Hall of the Cooper Union might have been the most important one of his election campaign. The Cooper Union, Reed emphasized, had benefited thousands. Reed felt that Denver had citizens like Peter Cooper, and he urged them to set aside time to shape their city so that future generations could avoid the burden of pauperism. With the proper foresight, future Denverites could enjoy public libraries, Cooper Unions, and other projects that would make up a distinctive quality of life in a community that worked together.[9]

What about the workingman? Would he have time to devote to benevolent projects, or must he continue working long hours with only a hope to earn money for bare living expenses? No, said Reed, long working hours were not acceptable. The worker and his family deserved better than exhaustion from ten- to fourteen-hour days, seven days a week. Modern society required that some people work on Sunday — employees of streetcar companies, railroad workers, and newspapermen, for example — but everyone needed one day for rest and recreation. Reed described this day as one in which men rested and had time for family and books, a chance for recreation in whatever form the individual chose. Reed reminded his listeners: "An overworked man is not the ideal citizen. He has no opportunity to be public spirited." Man must do more than just live; he must grow in mind and spirit. Reed asked his audiences to use their brainpower and experience to find solutions for these problems. A new public spirit could make Denver a great city.[10]

What did workingmen think about the church? The common view in the 1880s and 1890s was that the rich and powerful had made the churches the instruments of a gospel of wealth that promoted the ideal of the self-made man and considered poverty the inevitable result of slothful and immoral living. Russell Conwell, founder of the Philadelphia Temple and author of the popular lecture *Acres of Diamonds*, exhorted his audiences to seek riches. He declared that anyone could get rich with whatever resources were available: "Unless some of you get richer for what I am saying to-night my time is wasted. . . . I say that you ought to get rich, and it is your duty to get rich." Conwell also thought that the poor were punished for their sins, and that was the reason for their lack of riches. Most laborers did not consider wealth a plausible objective when they could hardly earn enough money to feed their families. When they turned to the churches with their claims of economic injustices by the capitalists, most laborers felt that the churches did not support them.[11] Washington Gladden, the Christian Social Gospeler, summed it up this way:

> The wage-worker regards the church as capitalistic. He stays away from the church, which does not belong to him, which does belong to his employer. The separation of the wage-workers from our churches is part of the general separation of the working from the capitalistic classes.[12]

In Reed's mind, the church existed for both the rich and the poor. In a sermon entitled "Why the Church Doesn't Reach the Masses," he asserted that people did not go to church "because of some inward feeling." American churches had created this inward feeling of hostility toward the church by neglecting the example of Jesus Christ. Reed remarked that the masses gladly heard Jesus because they identified with his language and conduct. He lived among them and shared their pain and anxieties; Jesus, Reed observed, was the consummate democrat. Reed concluded that churches in the 1880s lacked the spirit and mind of Jesus. It would take a great deal of patience for religious leaders and ministers to regain the confidence of the common people. The masses would not return to the church because of a preacher's words; the church must demonstrate that it stood for freedom and justice for rich or poor, and then the common people might consider returning.[13]

Could anyone from the working class attend Reed's church? Yes, Reed testified, he believed in an open church where all people could meet for spiritual and personal development. He had had an open-door church in Indianapolis, and he followed the same policy at the First Congregational Church. Attendance did not require a pew rental, nor were there any restrictions based on one's wealth or social standing. The church's institutional ministry opened its doors seven days a week for meetings, entertainment, and various classes. These activities encouraged any citizen to consider the First Congregational Church as a possible worship center on Sundays and as a resource through the week. The *Rocky Mountain News* commented that Denver's churchgoers selected a church largely because of its minister. A description of Reed's Sunday evening audiences reported that "[the] poor, street beggars, blind men and others can frequently be seen in the congregation on a Sunday evening." Workers came, too, because of Reed's defense of their rights.[14]

To Reed, the Knights of Labor replicated his own commitment to laborers' struggles for better wages and more humane working conditions. When Reed arrived in Denver, Buchanan, the local organizer for the Knights, had already gained a reputation as a "lung worker," one who did not work but rather stirred up the workers with promises. A strong promoter of the worker's right to organize, Buchanan published the *Labor Enquirer*, a weekly newspaper for laborers, which circulated throughout the Rocky Mountain region. He acquired some notoriety as a militant agitator who promoted the use of dynamite in labor disputes. Buchanan denied that charge, but he did print the price of dynamite in the *Labor Enquirer*, for informational purposes, he said. The local newspapers looked with little favor on Buchanan's efforts; the *News* described him as a liar, a loudmouth, and a professional workman who gave bad advice to workers. The churches did not publicly criticize Buchanan, but he expected little or nothing from them. When Reed and the Reverend Gilbert De La Matyr, pastor of the Evans Chapel Methodist Church, endorsed a labor parade that drew the disapproval of some ministers and the press, their gesture softened the attitudes of Denver's workers toward churchmen.[15]

Buchanan organized the labor parade to honor the birthday of George Washington, which fell on a Sunday. Because employers would not let workers off on Saturday or Monday, Buchanan was forced to schedule the parade on the Sabbath. Some ministers objected, and workers expected more deleterious criticism from the press and the pulpit. Buchanan suggested that he would be willing to invite a prominent clergyman of the city to pray before the mass meeting, and De La Matyr accepted the invitation, jokingly remarked: "If half that my brothers of the clergy and the newspapers say of you fellows is true, you are a very sinful lot, and are sorely in need of prayer. I am not afraid to pray in the presence of sinners." By involving the minister, the laborers believed they had defused the issue. Reed and De La Matyr both preached "labor sermons" in their churches without any more significant public criticism. From that day forward, Buchanan and many workers looked more kindly toward the church because the two ministers had sympathized with their cause.[16]

Local issues dominated the parade's theme. It was intended to demonstrate labor's importance to Colorado's industries and its interest in a number of bills before the state legislature. It was also hoped that the parade would be a recruiting event; indeed, Buchanan commented later that he had recruited enough new members to organize four new Knights of Labor assemblies. The *News* described the parade as an orderly expression of labors' interests in the upcoming legislative session and on its position on the issue of fair wages. The *News* approved of these objectives and called for impartial consideration of the labor bills and for patience by the workers to allow the political system to work in their behalf. As a result, the parade did not harm labor's activities in Colorado nor did it spur any effort to restrict their public demonstrations.[17]

In his sermon that Sunday, Reed stressed two items for serious consideration by Denver's citizens. First, he said that he did not believe the labor parade was intended to dishonor the Sabbath, for if parade participants could not get released from work on Saturday or Monday, then Buchanan had had no other option than to choose Sunday. The parade represented a legal way for labor to impress upon the legislature the strength of its organization and the importance of the labor bills, Reed noted. That free expression presented some danger, but a greater danger would arise from its restriction. Free speech made violence unnecessary.[18]

Second, Reed preached that cooperation between labor and capitalism still remained a possibility. Two important groups from the community, organized workers and businessmen, had attended an event that could spark a useful exchange of ideas. Most wealthy men had done manual labor and knew the hardships of long hours. This common experience would keep sympathy alive. If men would use their imagination and intelligence, they might find a solution. The *News* agreed with Reed's suggestion that legislators should examine the application of equal justice for capitalists and labor.[19]

That Sunday evening De La Matyr preached on the "Source of the Peril of Dynamite" to a congregation largely made up of workingmen. He claimed that wealth centralized by means of governmental assistance had caused the destruction of several of the world's greatest empires. He noted that in the previous twenty-four years, millionaires in the United States had increased from ten to more than five hundred, and that legislation had assisted this growth. If labor and capitalism could reach no agreement, if their disputes degenerated into a war of dynamite, then such a war would confront Christian civilization with its most deadly peril — devastation. De La Matyr argued that the highest priority was a solution to the problem of the just distribution of labor.[20]

How could the workers effect this just distribution? De La Matyr offered no immediate solution, but he certainly wanted to avoid violence and so did Reed. In the 1880s capitalists and their political allies were dominating economic policy in the United States, and organized labor had little political power. The federal government followed a passive policy toward labor and its battles; federal or state interventions usually were in behalf of the companies. Given these circumstances, Reed thought that the ballot was the correct way for workers to express their desires for just legislation and governmental policy. By voting, they could remove from office those politicians who would not right the wrongs that had been inflicted on the average workingman. To protest by voting was preferable to violence. Reed did not, however, excuse the federal government from its duty to protect the ordinary American from high prices and capricious wage reductions by the monied power.[21]

For many Americans the Russian czar symbolized the tyrannical ruler who wielded unchecked, harsh authority over his subjects. Reed defined a class of people in America who possessed power comparable to the czar's, and who had wielded enough control over people's livelihood that they, not the poor below them, had become the dangerous classes. These tyrants formed combinations that regulated wheat, pork, and coal markets to the extent that laborers lost essential income and investors reaped windfall profits. These men had few moral scruples and used their positions for their own gain while handicapping innocent workers. When Reed compared these powerful few with professional gamblers, the gamblers came out on top. At least one could choose to lose his money with a gambler, but wage laborers had no choice in market manipulation.[22]

For the worker, the ballot represented the best option for any political voice in Congress. In the 1884 fall election, Reed made the monied power's morality, not the tariff question, the critical topic for debate:

By the power of money [they] have set aside the natural and beneficent laws. It is entirely in their power to-day to buy honest labor to naught — to make industry of no effect, to utterly discourage both farmer and weaver. Has the state any power to protect men from criminals? How long will people listen to discussions of tariff, high tariff, low tariff, no tariff? That is not the question of the day.[23]

Protection from foreign products paled beside this problem of protection from those rich, insolent Americans who had banded together to make their neighbors poor. Reed lamented, "When working men come together that is a mob, when these robbers meet together that is a 'syndicate.'" In the coming elections, the workers would have the power to disarm these dangerous classes. Reed counseled against any hasty action other than the voting process: workers must try the ballot several times before they conceded defeat:

> Labor has not exhausted the power of the ballot. Why not once try the ballot for all it is worth; try it twice, try it three times. Fully and finally exhaust the power of it and then, and not till then, clamor for something else. We will have a better world just so soon and no sooner as a majority of the people of the world are in the right thoughts and in dead earnest prepared for a better world.[24]

In 1884 two labor disputes pitted Buchanan's union against the monied power in Denver: the Union Pacific strike and the coal miners' strike in New Mexico and Colorado. In the case of the Union Pacific strike, the railroad agreed to the workers' demands and ended the strike on 18 August 1884. In the case of the coal miners, the strike lasted longer and caught Reed's attention. The dispute provided Reed with a telling example of a large monied interest who attempted to control the just distribution of labor entirely for its own advantage. Again Reed reminded his congregation that laborers required protection from combinations who refused to pay an honest wage for an honest day's work.[25]

Combinations prevented one from dealing with the individual directly responsible for the company's actions, Reed complained. Oftentimes, the decision-makers even lived outside the affected community, which limited their availability to workers. With this buffer between the public and the monied interests, managers were free to carry out the monied interests' policies with little accountability or guilt. Reed cited the example of the character St. Clair in *Uncle Tom's Cabin*, who absented himself from his plantation while his overseer abused the slaves. Distance blurred their responsibility and eased the capitalists' consciences when they took their profits.[26]

Reed noted that "if you cannot trust a man much[,] you can trust a corporation still less." It appeared unlikely that the laborer would find justice under these conditions. Thus, no one could dispute the right to strike. When the workers exercised this right, capitalists hired imported Hungarian laborers — at cheaper rates — to take their places. To Reed, this was the sin of "assisted labor"; companies imported immigrants who had no desire to become citizens at the expense of American workers. The mine owners had forced the miners to sign a contract that spread "over more space than the Sermon on the Mount." The contract allowed the owners to close the mine or discharge the workers at any time, but if the workers struck, then they forfeited any claim against the company. Reed declared that if society accepted the legality of the moneyed power's combinations, then how could anyone question the urgent need for unions. The church had a responsibility to point to this wrong and to embrace those who had been wronged. Moreover, these confrontations between workers and management always had the potential for violence, and such a possibility boded ill for communities. The workers' complaints in Colorado and New Mexico required sensible solutions. Again, Reed emphasized that the volatile relationship between capitalism and labor demanded everyone's attention: "This question of wages and labor must be settled. I want some way out of this that has no fire in it, some path that has no blood on it."[27]

In Reed's opinion, the worker had become enmeshed in a dilemma: he had little political or economic power, but he faced a sizable opponent that dominated his everyday life. A lone worker had no firm footing in this push-and-shove match with the moneyed power. Reed defended labor's right to use any power generated by its organizing successes to negotiate a solution that would be satisfactory to all concerned parties. Reed thought it was important to recognize that although the unemployed were often viewed as tramps, they would work if given an opportunity. It was the industrial process and its heartless management that had made them victims of a system that condoned profit without a conscience.

The Evolution of the Tramp

In the year 1886 America dedicated the Statue of Liberty, a symbol of justice and equality. In that same year, the nation experienced the violence of the Haymarket Affair, the peak of the Knights of Labor, and the May 1st strike for the eight-hour day. Labor discontent seemed to permeate all parts of the country. The economic slump of the early 1880s dumped more

jobless men into the nation's labor pool, and as unemployment increased
tramps roamed the countryside. Reed acknowledged that some people
would always live on society's economic margin, but his faith in humanity's
steady push toward a better life made him conclude that most people were
not content with such a bare existence. In 1886 he challenged Denver with
this question: Is the pauperism of the Old World to be made an American
Institution? [28]

For a young, successful city, recently removed from a rough-and-tumble
frontier, this was a provocative and unsettling question. Denver's aristocrats
wondered how pauperism could exist in their land of opportunity. Colorado had acreage available for new farmers, Denver offered room for migrants and immigrants alike, and those without means could get wage labor.
The *News* commented that "individual push and thrift are the best as-
surances of general progress and prosperity." If we were to apply Frederick
Jackson Turner's 1893 interpretation of the frontier to Colorado, then we
could say that the state in 1886 had emerged from chaos with opportunity,
democratic institutions, and more than two people per square mile. Denver
and the Rocky Mountain region symbolized *la frontera*, charged with both
promise and possible conflict. [29]

The public viewed the tramp as a major threat to property and social
order in the ongoing drama between promise and possible conflict on *la
frontera*. Some thought that his predicament resulted from his own immorality or from too much well-intentioned assistance. Almost no one considered the influence of economic upheaval upon his income or industry's
power to enslave him within a system that used his labor, but cast him aside
when the return on investment dictated such a move. And few drew any distinction between the professional tramp and the unemployed who had lost
their jobs because of circumstances beyond their control and now looked
for work. Moralists in the 1870s counted these men among the "dangerous
classes." In the mid–1880s, in his book *Our Country*, Social Gospeler Josiah
Strong warned that when the land had been exhausted, when the cities
filled with idle workmen and militant socialists, then America's institutions
would confront the foreboding possibility of destruction. Strong preached
that regeneration would be America's only hope for survival. [30]

Destruction need not happen, Reed believed. He saw opportunity for
change: it might involve conflict, but it could also improve the community.
It would require church members and citizens alike to alter their attitudes
toward the unemployed. Christians had to practice a form of assistance that
went beyond the hand of friendship, that accepted the predicament of the
unemployed as beyond their control and undeserved. With changed atti-

tudes and a willingness to serve, the church could cooperate with public agencies to initiate a plan that would include money for groceries, housing, and clothing as well as job programs to help men and women regain their dignity through useful work.

Denver had fewer factories than the larger industrial cities; its economy depended upon railroads, mining, and agriculture. These industries had all been influenced significantly by the boom-and-bust cycles of the 1880s, and Denver's and Colorado's growth had fluctuated with the cycles. For example, the years 1878–83 had seen economic expansion; but in the years 1884–86 the economy had become stagnant; then, from 1887 to 1892 Denver's economy expanded yet again; but four years of depression from 1893 to 1897 once again seriously damaged Colorado's economy.[31]

These cycles brought opportunities on the one hand, and disastrous wage reductions and job losses on the other. The unemployed eventually became the poor, symbols of failure and an undesirable economic burden. For many Americans, these tramps presented a threat to the social order. William Graham Sumner, a Yale professor whose Social Darwinist philosophy held great influence, believed that "a drunkard in the gutter is just where he ought to be. Nature is working away at him to get him out of the way, just as she sets up her processes of dissolution to remove whatever is a failure in its line." Perhaps charity organizations were unnecessary, if the poor's decline was inevitable. Yet charity organizations endeavored to provide a measure of "sympathy, encouragement, and hopefulness"; often they combined sentimentality with callousness. Because charity workers believed that idleness was the result of the poor's drinking or their dependence on assistance, they struggled to avoid any action that might encourage their charges not to work. One charity worker argued that to give a man food he had not earned destroyed whatever morality he had, or, if he were already bad, pushed him farther down the road to damnation.[32]

The fascination and fear of the moralists focused on the tramp: he was the one who rebelled against all work and seemed blatantly happy. The perceived large numbers of tramps bred fear, and people searched for effective methods of dealing with these "willful poor." These methods included suppression, arrests, and screening tests to discover who would work. In the 1890s the moralists considered a new method: the creation of work colonies for idle European immigrants. The hope was that the colonies would keep the "laggards" in one place and teach them to work for their bread.[33]

The Queen City had its share of suffering in the 1880s. Citizens were exposed to the suffering of the poor throughout the city. Homeless children and unemployed men and women populated the streets, while immigrants subsisted in shanties — and all begged for food and clothing. Tramps haunted Denver's neighborhoods with an intimidating presence. What could be done about the tramps?[34]

In "The Evolution of the Tramp," a series of four sermons preached in January and February of 1886, Reed attempted an answer.[35] These sermons presented Reed's views about the unlucky individuals who were caught in the expanding, industrial society that was now the West. They identified the two vital issues raised by the ubiquitous tramps: (1) why did tramps choose idleness instead of work; and (2) how could the church and the community redress the underlying causes that produced tramps?[36]

In the first two sermons in the series, "Trials of Tramps" and "Talking of Tramps," Reed spoke to the factors that influenced the transition from working person to wanderer. He told his congregation that becoming a tramp was a process, a progression from one with work to one without any hope of work. One must consider the tramp in his own environment with its own possibilities — not as one who lived in affluent society. He illustrated the tramp's world by telling a story: A tramp had come to his door and his appearance marked him as a "ne'er do well"; he had shabby and unclean apparel and an emaciated look. His shabbiness affected his behavior — when he moved he slouched and shuffled — but he voiced a clear request for help. The tramp was from a New Hampshire factory town and had "smelt oil and breathed cotton fuzz since he was 8 years old. . . . He wants work . . . [but] his muscles are paper twine, . . . not good enough for a pick." Reed then revealed the moral of this story: "Division of labor has fitted him to do one thing well and unfitted him for anything else."[37]

Industrialization had made man's labor worthwhile only in combination with other men. The old master mechanic who made all the parts of a product, such as a wagon, had faded away. In modern manufacturing, different men made different parts, which were then fitted together to make the complete product. A man who learned to make one part could not succeed in a world that had reduced labor to specialized tasks. In nine days — the time it might take to learn a new trade — a man could die from starvation. A man might ask, why train for a new trade when the machines had reduced the demand for his skills? Reed applauded manufacturing's advances and argued that they truly benefited the public, but he abhorred the processes of industrialization that generated helpless and lonely workers.[38]

Without suitable clothing, without work, without any human consideration, such treatment would surely move a lonely man to anger. Reed reasoned, "With dirt and rags and cold victuals come rudeness of manner, coarseness of speech. Let anger in and how long will civility and urbanity last? . . . When hope goes out of a man, fear goes out." The do-gooders criticized those who visited the saloon, but at least the saloon offered a kind word. Reed contended, "If you wish men to be better you must make them happier." Tramps were not saints — and what if they had stolen a little food? Two years later, Reed approvingly quoted Cardinal Henry Edward Manning, the Roman Catholic activist who had interceded for the London dock workers and said, "Necessity has no law, and a starving man has a natural right to his neighbor's bread." How could the theft of bread to feed one's family compare with the tycoons who had stolen not a morsel, but a railroad?[39]

Reed did not believe that immorality caused poverty, or that poverty was a crime. Men and women wanted to work and if they would not work, let them suffer. But where was work? He warned, "A neglected class soon get to be out of all sympathy with society." He recommended a "Friendly Inn" for Denver, where tramps could work for food and shelter. Whereas pauperism was widespread in Europe, "American rags are not so ancient as those of London."[40]

Reed then compared America and England, showing that the English tolerated pauperism as a consequence of their natural social order. He attributed royalty's insensitivity to such destitution to an inbred trait in their ancestry: "Anybody who has this strain of blood in them has the king's evil raised to at least the sixteenth power." But where could hungry and hopeless people go? Reed answered, "When God said, 'I am tired of kings,' America was discovered." Americans believed that people were born with the right to life, liberty, and the pursuit of happiness. It was a disgrace that this country tolerated a system which created a Vanderbilt and a tramp at the same time: "But that one man can acquire many millions of dollars and that another man equally industrious can not earn a living makes me think that something is rotten . . . in America and in my time." A natural process had not caused the discrepancy between wealth and the common laborer; it had originated in the greed of the monopolists.[41]

Some charity workers suggested sending the tramp back to the land — let him homestead. Reed dismissed this solution:

I will call back my tramp and tell him to be a farmer, go out anywhere, settle on the public land and grow up with the country. . . . But I have discovered that the thing is not so easy. . . . I cannot go anywhere

without running into a 'wire fence.' . . . My tramp is not exactly the
man to assist in the beginning of agriculture in the West. . . . The per
cent of farmers who succeed is not heavy.[42]

Agriculture could not solve the problem of the tramp. Instead, Reed emphasized the need to prepare for a crowded country. The question was how
to live and let live. With plentiful space and American cleverness, this
society could design an economy that would contain equal opportunity for
all who wanted to work. He insisted, "This nation is wise enough to devise a
more excellent way. [If] we are wise enough to prevent something, we
ought to be wise enough to prevent pauperism. . . . There need not be
pauperism."[43]

In the final two sermons in this series, Reed explained that conditions in
the 1880s differed from those of the early 1800s. The golden days of the
first settlers had passed, and subsequent generations faced different circumstances and different problems. Society could not stop progress, nor should
it regress into a world of natural forces, as the English art critic John Ruskin
had suggested. The community ought to profit from its progress, accept
that it was an organic unit, and function as one. If society properly planned
its economic structure, the resulting fairness for all citizens would contribute to taxes, spending, the establishment of homes, and happier people:
"There is earth enough, food enough, there is not kindness enough." A
community with mutual concern was the correct foundation for society, not
the money-hunger of the commercial society. Nature provided some men
with intelligence to lead, others with manual skills, and some with little
initiative, but in the cooperative community, "Justice, kindness, [will] pay in
cash and comfort."[44]

Reed rejected the popular view that the tramp's laziness and immoral
behavior resulted in his wanderings. It was the lack of choice that put
hungry men on the road in search of work; industrialization and society's
attitude had cast them in the role of vagabonds. Robert Burns, Reed's
favorite poet, said it clearly: "Man's inhumanity to man / Makes countless
thousands mourn."[45] Such misery in the midst of the land of opportunity
could compel even vagabonds to a savage uprising. Reed feared that if their
cries were ignored, the possibility of rebellion would increase. Most political economies were inhumane and by necessity needed some mechanism to
balance greed and fairness. William Graham Sumner's laissez-faire economy would only enlarge the monopolists' power and further limit justice
for the poor. Reed emphatically rejected the laissez-faire philosophy; society could not depend on a natural process to sort things out. Unless

society committed to a method of relief that addressed the causes instead of the symptoms of poverty, it would face the danger described by Strong. This was not a cyclical, temporary condition but an ongoing probability, one that demanded more than the occasional dollar or used overcoat. The tramp's predicament required the participation of everyone to find a workable solution that would last beyond any depression. Reed stressed:

The welfare of each man is the concern of every man. What is bad for the bad is bad for the true. The strength expended of class against class must now be conserved for the good of all.[46]

A solution that came from the majority would make a positive contribution to the whole. First, resources and humankind's energy would be directed toward the uplifting of the poor,, and then the poor's pent-up anger and frustration would be neutralized. Disregarding their circumstances could create conditions like those that caused the French Revolution. America's masses were not aware of their power, but knowledge learned in the public schools could change that. Like the quiet rain that eventually wore away the rocks of the mountains, an awareness of injustice would grow until it erupted in conflict. One could expect that with modern weapons, the havoc would be more widespread and destructive. Society had to respond before the right conditions spawned a rebellion.[47] Americans enjoyed free speech, which was an effective antidote to senseless violence. Reed believed:

The press is free and to resort to violence to mend matters simply shows that man has lost confidence in the power of reason; that he has lost confidence in the educated will of the people. . . . If an intelligent nation like this, with the measure of freedom we have, cannot settle our social questions without burning powder we are not worth saving.[48]

If the safety valve of free speech were closed, then one could expect an outburst somewhere. To wait for deliverance by a miracle was to avoid the problem at hand; instead, Reed wanted citizens who were unafraid to work for "a friendly island in a Pacific sea."[49]

Reed's description of tramps as victims of industrialization ran counter to the majority's view that tramps were immoral and indolent. The tramp as a victim of the industrial process was a matter of interpretation for many, not necessarily a fact. Historian Paul Ringenbach has argued that a distinction between professional tramps and the involuntary unemployed was not made until the 1890s. Perhaps we can say that the distinction might have been an operating principle for some social workers, but it was not functional for most middle-class Americans.[50]

An out-of-step visionary in a successful, entrepreneurial society, Reed recognized that urbanization and industrialization characterized the modern world, and performed like immutable forces. Wage labor certainly constituted an integral part of late nineteenth-century life, and to Reed it was obvious that western agriculture could no longer serve as a "safety valve" for discontented urbanized masses. But his plea that both church and community had a stake in the future rehabilitation of the tramp conflicted with the laissez-faire economics of Colorado and the nation. One year after delivering these sermons, Reed co-founded Denver's Charity Organization Society to combine local charities and make collection and dispersal of aid more efficient. He thought such a combined effort could more effectively relieve the suffering of the poor. Although he implored church members to give tramps the benefit of the doubt, organized charity effected no evidence of behavioral change in these Christians. There was no war on poverty in Denver.[51]

In his sermons, Reed made four points that illustrated his beliefs about unemployment and tramps. First, the industrial process victimized the tramp — the machine age had rendered him helpless and lonely. As a product of America's social system, the tramp symbolized that system's failure. Second, the frontier no longer offered the tramp an equal opportunity to prosper. If land were available, could the average tramp farm successfully? Reed emphatically answered no. The average tramp had no farming skills. Third, the French Revolution's example clearly demonstrated that the masses' suppressed rage could erupt into a violent rebellion. Why had no rebellion occurred? Because the people did not yet know how or when to use their power. Like the slow return of Samson's strength, they would slowly discover their latent power and rise up against their oppressor. Finally, although the problem of the tramp appeared unsolvable, America had the capacity to provide jobs for those who wanted work and who deserved a chance because they belonged to a republic that promised equal opportunity.

These sermons on the victimization of the tramp aroused some citizens, and the *News*, by printing interviews with tramps, showed how the industrial process could produce a tramp. The tramp's fate hinged on the uncertain cycles of the job market, and Reed warned that danger lurked if the country did not address the problem in some material way. Still, no public works plan or businessmen's program to hire and train the unemployed ensued. During the Panic of 1893, when tramps once again roamed the countryside, the *News* published articles that recommended creating opportunity for willing workers in a fading frontier. Perhaps Reed had made a small dent in the laissez-faire armor of a few elites, but *la frontera* between capitalism and labor remained, with its persistent possibilities for change and conflict.[52]

Strikes, Haymarket, and Socialism

In an address to Denver barbers on the occasion of their efforts to organize a union, Reed contended that the labor question required a three-part answer: profit-sharing, arbitration, and shorter work hours. This statement aligned Reed with reformers like Lyman Abbott, Edward Bellamy, W. D. P. Bliss, and Henry Demarest Lloyd. During a trip through the West, Lyman Abbott, editor of the *Christian Union*, visited Denver and expressed some interest in the views outlined in "The Evolution of the Tramp," especially as they related to the labor question. Abbott agreed with Reed that the labor problem was the most pressing issue of the day, and noted that there had been changes in the relationship between labor and capitalists. He observed that workers were now better educated and more capable of interacting with capitalists on an equal footing; the description of a "mistress and servant" relationship no longer fit. He speculated that the country was moving closer to real, practical democracy than at any time in its past. For the worker to get what he deserved, Abbott proposed that labor and capitalists consider the methods of profit-sharing and cooperation as possible solutions.[53]

With Abbott's comments on profit-sharing fresh in his mind, Reed examined a similar plan while on a summer trip to New England in 1887. He visited a factory in Willimantic, Connecticut, that had adopted a form of profit-sharing. Generally, he thought that it functioned well enough for worker and employer, but that it was not wholly cooperative. The men were paid wages and had a written agreement with the employer that specified how much of the profit they would receive if the company's earnings exceeded a minimum amount of profit. But Reed wanted a system in which workers and employers shared in the profits equally, with no required minimums.[54] Reed viewed profit-sharing as a way to improve the worker's wages, but with the advent of the eight-hour movement, he faced another challenge.

When the eight-hour movement planned a national demonstration on

1 May 1886, the *News* halfheartedly called for a calm, reasoned approach to the problem. Its editors noted that Colorado did not wish to oppress wage-earners, but the enforced leisure that an eight-hour day would bring would not necessarily equate to improvement for workers or employers. Still, Reed fervently promoted an eight-hour day.[55]

The Haymarket Affair introduced a different outlook on the issue. Many churchmen were among those who regarded the Haymarket bombing on 4 May 1886 as an unmistakable attack on property, order, and the state. No matter how much information circulated among the public, they considered the accused bombers as anarchists and socialists. The Haymarket Affair created a hostility toward unions whose aftermath would last until the end of the century; it also marked the end of the Knights of Labor and unleashed an avalanche of unfavorable publicity about socialism and "revolutionary" immigrants. The Sunday following the bombing, Reed preached against the kind of socialism that endorsed violence as the agent of change. Reed wanted change through arbitration, not by mobs and bombs. He especially did not want this tragedy to disgrace the idea of cooperation contained within his more reasonable definition of socialism. Reed interpreted socialism as a desire for a better social order than the existing one, and he expected these changes would be accomplished gradually, using education, the ballot, and negotiation.[56]

The wave of nativism that swept the country after Haymarket affected many reformers' attitudes toward any riotous immigrant workers. For example, Edward Bellamy recoiled from the Haymarket violence; he felt that one need not employ radical socialism to form a new collectivist social order. Bellamy's alternative included a benign ruling elite that would impose military discipline on unruly laborers. Reed took an equally strong stand against the recent influx of Polish, Hungarian, and Bavarian immigrants. He argued that these immigrants came to America because their own countries had pushed them out. He opined that these civilizations had declined, and that obvious weaknesses had tarnished their national characters. He used the Poles as an example: Reed remembered that in Milwaukee the Poles had been "gatherers of swill and makers of noise." On election day Poles had sold their votes. The Americans had despised them, not for selling their votes, but because they sold them so cheaply. Reed most strenuously objected to those immigrants who came not by choice but with assistance — these were people who took jobs from Americans at lower wages. Those who chose to come and who participated in America's democratic system usually became good citizens, Reed believed. But "assisted immigrants" came with anger and the idea that change came by violence — they knew no other way. Such foreigners distorted the meaning of socialism and confused the public; they could never induce Americans to follow them.[57]

Reed acknowledged that different views of socialism circulated around the country — some encouraged violence; others a gradual, more reasonable approach. Reed abhorred a socialism that promoted the violent overthrow of the American government. He understood that those who would denounce the eight-hour movement would certainly connect the "red flag" to the actions of the mob in Chicago and Milwaukee. But he believed one could find a more accurate meaning of socialism and its application to the United States in the writings of Professor Richard Ely of Johns Hopkins University. For example, Ely argued for a peaceful transformation of society through a cooperative union of capitalism and labor — not for revolution by dynamite. The socialism that Reed preferred taught that the world would evolve into a better place, and that each individual could contribute to this process. This type of socialism was grounded in justice and cooperation, not in anarchy, communism, or nihilism. Reed avowed: "Such a doctrine is very much to be desired, and the practice of it also very much to be desired. A little obedience to the plain commandments of Jesus Christ would help a great deal and would not be 'un-American.' "[58]

While Denver socialists likely applauded these sermons, the *News* column, "Curbstone Comments," showed that not all Denverites agreed with Reed's thoughts about socialism. One citizen remarked that limitations on the freedom of speech seemed proper for those who promoted assassination and the wholesale confiscation of public property. Reed responded by pointing out that a misunderstanding of the labor question and socialism prevailed in America. People did not read both sides of the question and reasoned from the wrong premises. Reed believed his fellow citizens were reacting emotionally and needed to become better informed about socialism, but he could not see that his own nativistic stance also depended more on emotion than on reason. He never wavered in his opinion that immigrants ought to assimilate the American republican way — if not, then let them leave quickly.[59]

The Democratic party nominated Reed as its candidate for U.S. representative in the 1886 election. Before election day, Reed again dealt with the labor question by discussing the definition and application of socialism. To speak in support of socialism as a candidate probably did not endear him to Colorado voters, no matter what definition he used. Nonetheless, Reed stubbornly barreled ahead with a definition of socialism as "a better arrangement of the social relations of mankind than that which has hitherto prevailed." All rational souls would admit that with social relations as they were, the world needed redemption. How to bring about that redemption remained the troubling question. Cooperation, a principle prominent in Jesus' teachings, presented a way to reform the earth. Individualism had no place in this concept—which instead stressed "the greatest good to the greatest number." Thus, each person would work for the interests of the entire community as competition receded. This hurrah for socialism did not figure significantly in his loss, probably due to the heavy labor vote.[60]

In 1888 the Burlington Railroad strike in Chicago provided Reed with another example of the unjust use of power by corporations and the intrinsic inequity in the labor unions' struggle for justice. He lamented that a man such as the railroad tycoon Jay Gould could purchase justice through the courts, whereas the working men had neither the means nor the political influence to do the same. If monopolists like Gould could hire mercenaries to protect their interests, then why deny labor the right to organize and to demand some redress for arbitrary wage reductions. Reed believed that the use of armed Pinkerton men as strikebreakers was an unconscionable act, and he strongly denounced it. Such tactics had no rightful place in the American republic. Even the tactic of excessive generosity required a cynical eye. The philanthropy of a John D. Rockefeller or an Andrew Carnegie might tempt one to reevaluate one's views, but Reed thought not. He did not accept the notion that a single act of generosity could bring about systemic change. Labor demanded justice, not the unreliable generosity of the tycoons.[61]

The ineffectiveness of strikes to rectify the wrongs suffered by labor, particularly as exemplified in the 1892 Homestead strike, caused Reed to push harder for arbitration as the civilized way to reach agreements between labor and capitalism. While some Christian socialists rejected strikes outright, others like W. D. P. Bliss argued that laborers had to strike to gain their rights. Reed understood that strikes sometimes became the last resort for the harried workers, but he preferred arbitration whenever possible. Reed proposed: "Let workmen and capitalists talk across the table—talk until there is no misunderstanding. I have great confidence in freedom of speech." Capitalism's insolence had created the chasm between workers and employers, but arbitration could bridge that chasm and save both parties money and effort. Eight-hour days and an acceptable form of profit-sharing should occupy the highest priority on this agenda. Against skeptics,

Reed argued that arbitration advanced more hope than prolonged industrial war.[62]

Cripple Creek, 1894

The 1894 Cripple Creek strike caused Reed to look more favorably upon strikes as labor's weapon to use in its struggle against capitalism, and it provoked his resignation from the First Congregational Church. In mid-January, Cripple Creek mine owners decided to take advantage of the economic uncertainty brought about by the Panic of 1893. They increased the miners' shifts from eight hours a day to ten hours, but without also increasing the $3.00 per day minimum wage. John Calderwood, president of the local union, which was associated with the Western Federation of Miners, called for a strike. The miners and owners then engaged in several violent confrontations over a period of months. Finally, the owners enlisted the aid of the sheriff of El Paso County, who hired his own "deputies" to end the strike by whatever force necessary.[63]

At this point Davis Waite, the Populist governor and a strong supporter of labor, decided to intervene. Governor Waite succeeded in arranging a meeting with the miners in Cripple Creek to assure them that the "deputies" would do them no harm. The union then appointed the governor as their sole arbitrator to negotiate a settlement with the mine owners. Governor Waite met with the owners' representatives, J. J. Hagerman and David Moffat, and reached an agreement on 4 June. The miners would work eight hours and receive $3.00 per shift, and the employers agreed not to discriminate between union and nonunion men. With the strike ended and both sides still armed, Governor Waite dispatched the state militia to maintain the peace and to enforce the agreement.[64]

On 3 June 1894, as strikers and deputies taunted each other across barricades on Bull Hill, Reed preached the sermon, entitled "Laws Favor Wealth," that would cost him his pulpit. In it, he pointed out that previous decisions by American employers to import cheap labor from abroad to reduce wages had created volatile situations. Such immigrants, "70 cents a day men, from over the sea, men who can live in holes in the earth on dog meat or garbage," eventually demanded more once they had experienced the plenteous bounty of America. But in Cripple Creek, the capitalists who had concocted this contemptible mess now whined about labor unrest. If mine owners and citizens wanted a productive and peaceful society, then

American workers warranted better treatment than had been evidenced in the Cripple Creek tragedy. Reed lamented: "Is life worth living when it means to work, eat and sleep? Ought there not to be a little comfort in life? . . . Is there any real economy in forcing wages down to the living limit?"[65]

The moneyed power had the advantage over the worker, but the workers' rights also needed leverage. As citizens of the republic, they too deserved protection:

> There is a capital of money: there is another of muscle, raw or trained. That is all many men have, simply power to work under direction. Ought not that to be protected? . . . Our laws come down from Rome, from a time when the individual was not of much account. Conditions have changed. These laws should be amended to fit a republic. The poor have too little to do in making the laws that govern them. The deputy sheriff who, through poverty or politics, has enlisted at $5 a day does not quite know what he is doing. The miner up there on the barricaded hill has a deep sense that he was there first. My heart goes out to him. It is a time for a heart and reason. . . . I long to see a world in which a man because he is rich will not be insolent, and I long to see a world in which a man because he is poor will not be mutinous.[66]

Powerful members of his congregation objected to these sentiments, and Reed abruptly resigned on the afternoon of 6 June 1894.[67]

On that same evening, Reed spoke to Denver's Union League Number 65. At that meeting he had sarcastically observed that when seven or eight gentlemen gathered to fix the price of coal, they called it business; but when a few hundred laboring men took action to help themselves and their families, these same gentlemen labeled it anarchy. Reed then made a statement that received wide publicity and elicited bitter criticism from Denverites and churchmen nationwide. He said, "Jesus Christ was the greatest anarchist in the world. He was the greatest socialist in the world." A true anarchist had the law within himself, Reed explained, and needed no legal structure to guarantee proper behavior toward his fellow man. If society adopted a socialism based on cooperation, as outlined in Jesus' teachings, it would introduce an effort in the production and circulation of goods that would benefit everybody.[68]

To label Jesus a socialist sounded blasphemous to many Denver Christians, but to equate him with an anarchist was too much for any churchman to bear silently. In the weeks that followed churchmen from Colorado and beyond indignantly sermonized to show that Jesus would have had nothing to do with anarchy in any form. The Reverend Robert McIntyre of Denver's Trinity Methodist Church made it clear that linking Christ to anarchy was like the linking of light to darkness. The devil represented anarchy (darkness) and confusion, but Christ came to bring order and light. McIntyre said, "I now read with hushed tones and crimsoned face and in deep sorrow that Christ was an anarchist." A Presbyterian minister from Carthage, Missouri, solemnly doubted that Reed could get forgiveness for this sin. The most far-reaching, hideous effect of Reed's utterance, according to one New Mexico Republican, was the assassination of French President Sadi Carnot. She claimed that Carnot had been assassinated by an anarchist on 22 June 1894, as a result of Reed's infamous remark, which had reached Europe via transatlantic cable, . In Reed's defense, one admirer wrote that his remarks were "Myronisms," typical of the epigrammatic preacher. If Reed had intended merely to shock the public — assuming that he had a purpose and this was not just his impetuous temper in motion — so as to make them think about the problems of labor and capitalism, then his action backfired because he brought more attention to himself than to the issue.[69]

Reed saw in the Cripple Creek crisis the chronic motivation for the laborer's struggle. The corporate system that forced miners to spend their scrip at the company's store, and unilaterally reduced wages and lengthened hours — all indicated the rightness of the miners' grievances. This despotic behavior by mine owners would unite workers, and Reed gave them a special rallying cry: "Special advantages to none, equal opportunities to all. Under this banner we fight this fight." Reed placed himself in the center of the battle between labor and capitalism, and defiantly vowed to continue discussing the issues publicly, regardless of the consequences.[70]

The *News* deplored Reed's resignation. In the midst of a depression that could precipitate a conflict between labor and capitalism, Colorado needed a man like Reed. The masses believed in him, and the labor unions trusted him and respected his judgment. If the situation turned violent, he could mediate between capitalism and labor. The public identified Reed with sensible negotiation, and they believed he could mitigate the common people's reaction more than any of the extremists. Letters to the editor confirmed this conclusion. The *News* expressed a strong concern for the city's investments, and affirmed that Reed "is a good, bold and independent man and the people will stand by him."[71]

The masses recognized Reed as their champion, but he often hobnobbed with the wealthy and never perceived them as enemies because of their money. He did question their use of money, for money meant power. In a world that needed relief from an abundance of unnecessary suffering, he tried to persuade the wealthy to wield their power in ways to relieve that suffering. Reed understood that powerful comrades could unknowingly contribute to God's coming kingdom, and so he cultivated these friendships. At the same time, he believed that the masses could function as a balance against destructive greed if they became more involved in a cooperative society. Edward Bellamy, however, looked more to the educated middle class to fill the critical functions in the new industrial system. Reed held, however, that as the masses moved upward into the middle class, they could serve as catalysts to accelerate the creation of the cooperative society.[72]

Reed's Cripple Creek remarks and his subsequent resignation propelled him into the spotlight of political and labor issues. The Populists considered him for governor, but Waite again won the nomination. When offered the lieutenant governor's slot, Reed did not send his acceptance in time for the convention to approve it. Despite losing these nominations, he campaigned tirelessly for the declining Populists. The Republicans attacked Reed's character, hoping to neutralize his campaign efforts, but the *News* condemned these diatribes by "the beer-guzzling pot-house politicians of the Republican party." Meanwhile, Samuel Gompers, president of the American Federation of Labor, invited Reed and Tom Patterson to speak at the winter AFL Convention in Denver and both men accepted.[73]

When Eugene Debs's American Railway Union held a meeting on 15 July 1894 in Denver, Reed spoke in support of their sympathy strike for the Pullman strikers in Chicago. By this time, he had assumed a more militant posture. He said he supported the peaceable removal of strikebreakers if such action was necessary to protect the strikers' jobs. He repeated that Jesus Christ was an anarchist, and "was killed by the representatives of the law, the church and state, for daring to practice humanity." Reed assured his audience that the world's oppressed had God on their side and that they would win this fight. Even Jesus Christ acted militantly when he drove the money changers out of the temple, and he would drive them out again. He praised Henry George's theory of land and taxation, and asserted: "The only title to land on earth is occupancy and use. The land belongs to the people of the nation." Denver had vacant lots that homeless men could claim, and if they improved them with gardens and homes, let them stay. Finally, Reed confessed that he embraced the description of socialist; he boasted that some of the world's foremost men had accepted that label. The evening ended with the reading of a telegram from Debs at the Pullman strike in Chicago that encouraged the Denver supporters: "All forces stand like a stone wall. Victory certainly ours if we stand firm." The Pullman strike ended in defeat, but the struggle continued.[74]

The labor question continued to be Denver's major concern during the Panic of 1893. When the state finally emerged from the depression in 1898, the unskilled workers' situation had not changed. The state legislature made eight hours the legal limit for public work in Colorado, but mining and limitations for women's hours would have to wait until 1913. In March 1895 Reed preached on the issue of workers' hours and wages. He strongly endorsed eight hours as the maximum for the average worker — eight hours made up enough work for anyone regardless of the occupation.[75] William Morris, the British poet and socialist, provided the theme for Reed's sermon:

It is right and necessary that all men should have work to do which shall be worth doing, and be of itself pleasant to do, and which should be done under such conditions as would make it neither over wearisome nor anxious.[76]

Now it was up to the state to prevent overwork for factory laborers and for children, so that families could come together and improve their souls. The following Sunday Reed argued that labor was not a commodity. The relationship between an employer and a worker ought to have some sentiment and mutual respect — it was more than a product for sale. All laborers deserved wages sufficient for the needs of their families and for a life beyond their labor.[77]

Friends had urged Reed to continue preaching after his resignation and invited him to open an independent church. Beginning on 3 February 1895, the Broadway Theater became transformed every Sunday into the Broadway Temple. The Temple's doors opened for all people, without regard to social status, and required no pew rentals. Reed saw a society developing in which churches would concern themselves more with the present life and less with needless dogma or preparation for an afterlife. Reed believed that life progressed toward justice for all people in God's kingdom on earth, although he did not expect its full arrival in his lifetime. From his new pulpit he openly declared his support for socialism, and his activities in the Rocky Mountain West demonstrated his commitment to use socialism in creating "the comfortable life."[78]

SIX

Christian Socialism:

A More Comfortable Way

"We cannot stop invention, but I believe we can slowly arrange our social affairs so that the profit of invention will be distributed," proclaimed
Myron Reed in 1896. But this objective had to address what methods or
agencies to use in establishing a cooperative community. An industrial and
urban nation confronted post-Civil War America with the perennial issue
of how to define government's role in this dynamic society. And this new
America presented a challenge to religious organizations — what adjust-
ments, if any, would be required in their theologies and social programs?
Would the emphasis on individual salvation remain, and/or would the
church become more involved in political and social issues?[1]

Some churches responded with the Social Gospel, which grew out of
reactions to industrial growth and the rise of the New Theology, according
to historian Paul Carter. Horace Bushnell contributed the key idea that
provided the impetus to the New Theology: the gradualistic concept of
salvation. The Social Gospel taught that humanity's collective institutions
and society's organization both stood under religious judgment. Taking
these judgments seriously, the Christian then had the responsibility to work
toward society's reconstruction. Christian Socialists accepted these premises but went a step further by favoring socialism as the political method to
reform society. Reed accepted the concept of God's judgment of society and
its institutions, and the obligation of Christian churches to proclaim that
judgment and agitate for reform.[2]

Washington Gladden, Congregationalist and Social Gospeler, viewed
socialism as a preferable alternative to traditional individualism. In one
speech, he said:

If I were shut up to the alternatives of Individualism with its fierce survival of the strongest and Socialism with its leveling tendencies, I should take my stand with the Socialists. . . . We ought to favor state action whose purpose it is to improve the condition of the poorest and least fortunate classes . . . the real motive of socialism.[3]

Reed, too, rejected extreme individualism as it was articulated in popular Spencerian ideas. Reed believed that individuals assumed an importance in the community because they were God's creation and his children. God's community was an organic one and its members would be redeemed as a community — not one by one. Reed gradually came to embrace a universalist view of salvation, and he often highlighted this child-of-God relationship as constituting in itself the certainty of an individual's salvation.

Edward Bellamy's novel *Looking Backward* (1888) caused as much excitement in Denver as it did in the rest of the nation. Reed used it as a sermon topic, stressing that to live in Bellamy's world, human nature would have to change. Reed argued that the coming kingdom of God required human nature to change from selfishness and insensitivity to caring for one another. He believed that environment fashioned human nature from childhood to maturity, that values and behavioral patterns made indelible impressions on human nature, and that these could not be changed even in extremely stressful circumstances. Where and with whom people lived, how they learned, what they read, what they ate — all determined character. Sometimes Reed wondered what kinds of essays Ralph Waldo Emerson might have written if he had grown up in New Orleans on a diet of creole food? The essential question for Reed was how to accomplish this infusion of caring. Changing people's behavior must depend upon education and a growing awareness of God. According to Reed, attempts to contribute to society and to generate good works defined one's capacity for caring — even if these attempts failed.[4] For Reed, *Looking Backward*'s strongest message was that gradually such change could bring about the comfortable world he envisioned.

The Rocky Mountain Social League

Socialism appealed to Reed as one method to realize the cooperative society. His favorite epigram for Christian socialism was: "From a man according to his power, to a man according to his needs." Because the community formed the basis for one's identity and security, Reed agreed with

Bellamy that belonging to the community reduced the anxiety of the individual. Reed saw society as an organic whole, or as he described it: "The welfare of each man is the concern of every man." He had implicit faith in the people and taught that community decisions outweighed those of individuals. The organic whole had an innate sense, no doubt a God-given one, for while they may stumble from time to time, they will stumble in the right direction. The process was not neat and tidy, but eventually the people made the right choice. For Reed, socialism was merely the method by which to attain the kingdom of God on earth: it was never an end in itself.[5]

The Denver socialists had a rough year in 1886. The Chicago Haymarket Affair brought a widespread apprehension that armed anarchists might stage rebellions across the nation. Tension in Denver reached a high level of intensity, as local socialist groups remained vocal and defensive throughout this emotionally charged period. The *News* regularly published prejudicial articles denigrating the German anarchists, and agreeing that they had gotten what they deserved. But when it finally appeared that no uprising would occur in Denver, the *News* acknowledged that freedom of speech without persecution had made the largest contribution to keeping the local peace.[6]

Expressions of support for the arrested Chicago anarchists by local socialists further alienated them from Denver's civic leaders, however. The newly organized Rocky Mountain Social League, while not a promoter of anarchism, became identified with the Haymarket anarchists. In 1886 Joseph Buchanan of the Knights of Labor had gathered together a group of like-minded souls to establish the League. Its objective was to distribute literature expressing radical views on social and economic questions. The League met on Sunday evenings, which caused some to describe it as a socialistic church. Speakers addressed a variety of subjects at each meeting. Among the guest speakers were ministers Gilbert De La Matyr of Evans Chapel Methodist Church, Myron W. Reed of the First Congregational Church, Thomas Van Ness of Unity Church (Unitarian), and Henry Stauffer of the United Brethren Church. The format allowed for questions and discussion from the audience. The meeting often included such songs as "Labor Free For All," "Our Cause," and the "Marseillaise." Buchanan claimed that the League did more to enlighten the community than any similar organization. The press reacted adversely to the League, and one can only wonder what the community thought of Reed's irregular attendance.[7]

Reed had begun preaching about socialism in 1886, more in defense of what he understood to be its true meaning than as an evangelist. The Haymarket Affair had focused the public's attention on the evils of anarchy, however, which now became an evil word. After Haymarket, Reed preached several sermons in which he defended his interpretation of socialism as the nonviolent agitation for a new and better social order. The League's existence in Denver probably encouraged Reed to think more deeply about socialism, and it also bore the brunt of the public criticism of anarchy and socialism. At best, Buchanan had a tenuous relationship with the press, and the newspapers never failed to point out that he had previously recommended the use of dynamite to solve labor conflicts. Yet the *News* never attacked Reed for his socialistic leanings. John Arkins, Reed's close friend and the *News*'s editor, never named Reed in any article that criticized the issues Reed supported. When Arkins died in August 1894, Reed preached the funeral sermon and said, "When I came down the street this morning, I felt as if the world was mighty thinly populated." Many times Reed publicly thanked the *News* for its backing. He knew that having the newspaper on his side certainly made his public life more tolerable.[8]

Some of Reed's peers shared his socialist views. Thomas Van Ness of Unity Church served in Denver during the latter 1880s and became well acquainted with Reed. No doubt they found time to discuss topics of mutual interest; a friend who shared Reed's ideas, particularly in 1886, soothed the feelings of intellectual loneliness. Although general reaction to socialist activities was focused on the League and the *Labor Enquirer*, neither entity ever became more than a source of propaganda for socialism.[9]

Christian Socialism

Reed admired two British Christian Socialists, Charles Kingsley (1819–1875) and Frederick W. Robertson (1816–1853), and he spoke of their influence on his preaching and on the development of his ideas about Christians' tasks in a growing industrial world. Kingsley, especially, inspired Reed because he had gone willingly to a parish whose members were illiterate, poor people whose community had been infested with typhoid and diphtheria. Kingsley's efforts brought a library and a school to the community, and he introduced sanitation and personal hygiene procedures that soon eliminated the diseases. Kingsley's church had overflowed, as the people came to hear his plain and simple sermons.[10] Reed quoted from a Kingsley sermon:

I assert that the business for which God sends a priest is to preach freedom, equality, brotherhood, in the fullest, deepest, widest meaning of
those great words; that in so far as he does this he is a true priest; that in
so far as he does not he is no priest at all. The church has three special
possessions and treasures — the Bible, which proclaims man's freedom,
baptism his equality, and the Lord's supper his brotherhood.[11]

The newspapers had labeled Kingsley a socialist, but he continued to advocate for the poor and to make their life more comfortable.[12] Ministers who
acted out servanthood to this degree earned Reed's unqualified respect.

Reed's other champion, Frederick W. Robertson, displayed the same
simplicity and courage in his ministry as did Kingsley. Robertson's theology complemented Reed's and is summarized by the following statement:
"This, then is the Christian revelation — man is God's child and the sin of
man consists in perpetually living as if it were false." Reed knew the story of
how Robertson had responded to a parishioner's rebuke with the words "I
don't care", and he often invoked these same words with his detractors. In
the Robertson story, the parishioner had been alarmed by Robinson's public support for the Sunday opening of the Crystal Theater to allow laborers
who worked six days a week to attend performances. The lady had pressed
Robinson, "Do you know where 'I don't care' leads to," to which he had
answered, "Yes, it leads to Calvary." Robertson's unqualified commitment
to the example of Christ without regard to social pressure stirred Reed; he
hoped that he could equally inspire others.[13]

For Reed, Christians who entered servanthood as did Kingsley and Robertson, regardless of their denominational affiliation, obligated themselves
to bring about the kingdom of God on earth. Reed pondered how to persuade people to do this in a modern industrial state. Kingsley, Robertson,
Horace Bushnell, and Matthew Arnold all contributed to Reed's formula-
tion of general principles, from which he drafted his responses to this
question. Christian socialism appealed to Reed as one method of reform
that could attract people and establish an ethical basis for the emerging
kingdom of God. Its philosophy included the principle of cooperation, the
solidarity of humanity, and the projection of a better society — and God
through Jesus Christ constituted its energy.

In an 1892 sermon entitled "Socialism," Reed defined what he meant by
Christian socialism. The summer labor wars had brought no lasting solution to the conflict between labor and capitalism. Reed enumerated these
conflicts: the strife at Homestead; the strike of miners at Coeur d'Alene,
Idaho; the strike of coal miners in Tennessee; and the strike of switchmen in

Buffalo, New York. In each case, workers had left their jobs in defiance of management, and at each place state militias had been brought in to forcibly break the strikes. These incidents solved nothing and cost millions of dollars. But it was the corporations, exerting their political influence, who had pushed state governments to intervene violently. People cried out for a new order, and Reed affirmed that one was coming: "There ought to be a new earth, and what ought to be will be. No one will assert that this is the ideal social system — this one that we are living under." Socialists, Reed explained, simply desired something better than what existed, something more humane and responsive to human need. Most of the public supported the cooperation between the state militia and corporations to break strikes and to protect property; therefore, a transformation in attitude and behavior must happen for the sake of the masses. The nineteenth-century idea of an uplifting and inevitable progress colored Reed's view of the future. Persuasion, not force, would form God's new earth.[14]

Reed perceived a "righteous discontent" that broadcast its unhappiness with the present order through newspapers, speeches, and books. America now had available a large literature of discontent; many novels addressed contemporary social questions. Reed cited Hamlin Garland's narratives of rural America, Ignatius Donnelly's provocative book, *Caesar's Column*, Edward Bellamy's *Looking Backward*, and the British socialist William Morris's book, *News from Nowhere*. Reed thought that Morris's book painted a good picture of the coming new earth. These books confirmed that many literary men had turned to socialism.[15]

Reed looked at the nation and described examples of socialism already established as proof that it worked. The government founded public schools, post offices, and the telegraph for the public's benefit. Schools insured that future citizens would understand their government and preserve it. Cheap postal rates with reliable service, telegrams at prices common people could afford, and state asylums, prisons, and homes for the physically challenged — all heralded a new socialistic age. The public could profit from the state management of railroads, and Denver could advance socialism by furnishing citizens with heat, light, water, transportation, and telephone service. If the government provided these services at a reasonable cost, then citizens could contribute to the larger society.[16]

Reed found no merit in the complaint that socialism destroyed competition, especially in a country where monopolistic railroads and corporations reigned supreme. Likewise, socialism did not stifle creativity: geniuses like John Milton, Robert Burns, or Shakespeare wrote not to accrue wealth, but to explore questions about the human condition. Reed surmised that Milton "was looking at Satan and Michael and such people, and not for a book seller." The possibility of economic gain did not drive creative people, but the urge for self-expression and contributing to society did.[17]

Reed identified the chief objection to socialism as the fear of losing individuality. In a free enterprise system, individuals were rewarded for inventiveness, and great risk promised great rewards. But, Reed believed, limited individuality did not require that creativity be scrapped. One could set the limits of individuality and incorporate those limits into socialism. Reed did not define what those limits should be, but he did place the community's well being ahead of individual expression. For example, he believed that one person's individual liberty ended where another person's began. The problem was how to apply this idea when society found it difficult to even define the term "individual liberty." For Reed, individual liberty meant the freedom to choose such things as food, books, music, and this kind of freedom could exist within the kingdom on earth. Reed's definition was ambiguous in other areas, suggesting that the emerging community should define individuality more clearly, and that each community's definition would be qualified by it own unique circumstances.[18]

Christian socialism had two aspects that possibly led Reed to embrace this school of thought. When Reed spoke of socialism, he often quoted: "The motto of this kind of socialist suits me very well, 'From a man according to his powers [abilities] to a man according to his needs.' That is Christian." He explained that God gave to each individual some special ability, an outstanding singing voice, for example, and that each individual had a responsibility to share his or her gift with the community. "Your genius is a gift from God for you to give to his children and die famous and beloved." Socialism should provide for each person's basic needs and more, but to employ one's gift to amass a fortune smacked more of heathenism than of Christianity.[19]

The second half of the socialist creed referred to people without gifts, ability, or opportunity. What would happen to them in the socialist community? Reed's answer: "Feed him, clothe him, shelter him. He needs more than any genius; compensate him if possible for his lack of faculty, of opportunity. That is my kind of socialism, and also the only kind of Christianity." Reed hoped to fashion all humanity into one productive citizenry, but he knew that not all people would or could achieve an equal level of development at the same time.[20]

The Charity Organization Society functioned as a safety net for those who were incapable of reaching a higher level of responsibility in the community. Reed's positions created tension between him and those who had traditionally distinguished between the worthy and the unworthy poor. To Reed, charitable organizations were obliged to provide life's necessities to any person, based solely on need and, if possible, to help that person reach a level of self-support. It was reported that Reed never refused help for anyone who asked, and he tried to introduce into the Society as much compassion as possible. Reed's socialism reflected his belief that servanthood as revealed by Jesus called all Christians to learn the way of service. But learning how to serve in circumstances that imposed limitations involved a process of success and failure. Therefore, the community had to nurture and demonstrate consistently Jesus' example in faith and works.[21]

In 1892 the Populist party had gained enough strength in Colorado to defeat the Republicans for only the second time in sixteen years. Victory and an impetus for reform prevailed in Denver, and no doubt it buoyed Reed's hopes for change. The Populists aimed to revive the forgotten republican ideology, "government of the people, by the people, and for the people." Colorado politics had been long dominated by the Republicans, but now the Populists would get their chance. Perhaps Reed was affected by the heady atmosphere of political victory, for he now assumed an even stronger posture when presenting his socialistic ideas.[22]

In January 1893 Reed preached two sermons, "Competition" and "Cooperation," in which he spelled out probabilities for success and the advantage of cooperation as basic organizing principles for a new community. Vanity so consumed the human race that people used any means to maintain a status equal to their neighbor's. Reed argued that competition fed this basic impulse, threatened cooperation, and thereby worsened the human condition. Today's enlightened citizen must recognize that not all people had the same ability, but every person should have an opportunity: "We cannot all excel in the same line, but there must be in a well ordered world a path for every pair of feet. If there is not an unhindered path, then the world is not well ordered." A competitive world did not provide opportunity for everyone. Businessmen imported "discontented immigrants" to work for pennies and uproot Americans from their jobs. Reed suggested that one who viewed this country as great and glorious should read Jacob Riis's book, *How the Other Half Lives*. Riis's depiction of life in the city for the poor immigrant revealed the harsh and diseased environment that engulfed adults and children. Children labored in urban factories sustained by competition, and as much as church members discussed possible remedies, the government remained the best possible agent to effect a solution. Riis truly described a world of survival of the fittest. But survival for what, asked Reed? Wealth, derived from competition, justified itself at the expense of

the powerless, and that did not equal greatness. Anticipating Charles Sheldon's classic question, "What would Jesus do?," Reed asked, " 'Bear ye one
another's burdens.' How would that work in mercantile life?"[23]

Competition made it impossible to obey Jesus' commandment, "Thou
shalt love thy neighbor as thyself." If the neighbor represented competition
for position or wages, then how could one practice any love for the neighbor? Competition compels individuals to place their own interests ahead of
others' in order to succeed. Along with Henry Demarest Lloyd and Edward
Bellamy, Reed saw competition as dehumanizing. As an alternative, Reed
suggested cooperation. The bees, ants, and wolves illustrated cooperation
in the animal kingdom. Each had duties in their respective communities,
and if these were not fulfilled, then the community suffered. The early
American pioneers had depended upon one another to survive. even the
utopian communities, Brook Farm and New Harmony, had provided a bea-
con of hope despite their failures. Brook Farm had too many prima donnas
who would not contribute to the community: "Margaret Fuller talked too
much. Hawthorn [sic] was too shy. He lived two years in Concord and there
was no sign of life about the house except on Monday when the washing was
hung out." New Harmony had had no "worldly talent." These settlements
had lacked the practical knowledge required to achieve their objectives.[24]

Yet these communities illustrated that the principle of cooperation was
not the source of their failures. The Shakers had succeeded (although Reed
did not endorse their way of life) because they had understood the importance of cooperation. Reed mentioned several interesting experiments in
Denver that he had not investigated. The People's Union, for example, was
purported to be a model city that would provide work for all men and
women in need. Its planners proposed a community large enough for one
million people, funded by stock shares that could be purchased in installments. Its aim was to "demonstrate that cooperation and reciprocity naturally translates idealism into the nearest realism and simplest forms of
active good borne right into the common lives of the people." Reed expressed no particular preference for this plan. His purpose was merely to
emphasize that cooperation was preferable to competition, and it would
win out if people committed themselves to it. "The nation is co-operative
in some things. Why not in all things? Then comes the death of envy and
jealousy and strife. All we need in this world is intelligence and a good
disposition." Persuasion powered by intelligent action and sensitivity to
others' limitations would enable the development of a reasonable plan for
cooperation.[25]

Reed agreed that cooperation under any circumstance would not proceed smoothly, least of all in the arena of politics. Just prior to the 1893 fall election, Reed earnestly urged the people to vote. The depression had pushed many citizens to despair, and Reed tried to encourage them by pointing out that the state's resources could provide food for all its citizens. If they hoped to restore government by the people, then the voters must take government away from the monied power. The political questions facing Coloradans focused on land, labor, and monetary policy; Reed held that all were ripe for solutions. Each voter should make his voice heard in these deliberations. Reed noted that "the dirty pool of politics" had a bad reputation, and he warned that unless "the best people of the county exercise their rights there will soon be a county not worth living in." Reed's political philosophy taught that intelligent action could prevent most of the evil in life, but most native-born Americans seemed apathetic. Reed suggested that a good scourging by an American counterpart to William M. Thackeray, the English novelist and social satirist, would help them.[26]

The "dirty pool of politics" went from bad to worse in Reed's view when the American Protective Association (APA) gained some influence in the Colorado Republican party. The APA denounced the Catholic church as un-American, noting that under the leadership of the pope, the church had conspired to undermine "true Americanism." As an anti-APA voice, the *News* argued that "American institutions could survive without their [the APA's] 'protection'." Reed opposed the APA because of its anti-Catholicism, but also because he opposed any organization that set itself apart from the larger community. Reed believed that American Catholics already exercised their duties as citizens. When a reporter caught him after a vacation to New Orleans and asked him about the APA, Reed responded "Take this A.P.A. agitation now; is there anybody that really believes its twaddle about the Catholic church?" When he urged people to vote, Reed asked for tolerance and consideration of candidates irrespective of their religion. He appealed to all voters: "Dirty or clean, the pool of politics is the place for the people — all of them. Most people wish their country well, but wishing is weak. They must wade right in and do something."[27]

Activism came naturally to Reed, and before long he had stepped right into the middle of the 1894 Cripple Creek miner's strike. The miners struck when mine operators reduced wages and increased the work day. In Reed's sermon on 3 June he clearly identified with the miners on Bull Hill: "The miner up there on the barricaded hill has a deep sense that he was there first. My heart goes out to him." This sentiment compared well with Robertson's motto, "I don't care," but it resulted in Reed's resignation as pastor of the First Congregational Church.[28]

Reed's primary motivation for his work in politics, charity, and labor was to build humanitarian institutions to respond to people's needs. When he evaluated his accomplishments in June 1894, he could easily have become disillusioned. Instead, he looked to the Populist party for hope, and he looked for ways to help the party. Soon after his resignation, a *News* reporter asked him about his future plans. At that time, Reed did not rule out running for office, but he would not name any office or party affiliation.[29] He did, however, volunteer these comments about his amicable separation from his former church:

> There is no one in the church that does not wish me well; but at the same time my ideas do not coincide with theirs, and I don't blame them for not wanting to pay a minister to tell them things they do not want to hear. I am a semi-socialist and have been for years, as you of course must know if you have heard my sermons. My ideas on capital and labor, which is the leading, the only question to-day, are not suited to my congregation.[30]

Finally, his friends persuaded him to begin an independent church where he could preach his convictions without any intrusion from the ecclesiastical machine or unfriendly trustees. The *News* estimated that in an independent church Reed would attract an audience as large as three thousand each Sunday, and it also claimed that nearly one thousand Denverites regarded Reed "as the greatest philosopher in America." Reed, who had never been wedded to an ecclesiastical machine, began looking for a suitable location in which to house this anticipated congregation.[31]

The Broadway Temple

After returning to Denver from a long vacation in January 1895, Reed learned that the state Senate had appointed him its chaplain for the coming legislative year. When he discussed his future plans with a *News* reporter, he told the reporter that his new organization would not qualify as a church. It would resemble the late David Swing's independent Chicago Central Music Hall. Reed said emphatically: "But it isn't a church. If it was I should not have anything to do with it. I do not want to encroach on the territory of any of the churches." He proposed a ministry directed to a large and populous group of non-churchgoers, who for one reason or another identified with no particular denomination.[32]

The new association engaged the Broadway Theater and renamed it the Broadway Temple for each Sunday evening service. It opened on 3 February 1895 with the following statement:

> The organization is non-sectarian, having no ecclesiastical connections whatever. The membership is open to all who believe in the "Fatherhood of God and the Brotherhood of man." The association has no constitution, by-laws or creed.[33]

When Reed greeted the congregation on that first Sunday, he said that he came with profound sympathy for the poor because of his own poverty. He came from a poor family and never knew any relative that had wealth. He would avoid any ecclesiastical machinery that appeared to be against labor or the poor. For this one day in the week, Reed announced, there would be no difference among people; the Broadway Temple would welcome all people, regardless of their financial status. The *News* described a congregation that included state legislators, state officials, infrequent church attendees, and representatives from every profession and vocation in Denver.[34]

Reed's first sermon, "An American Gospel," was delivered to a partisan audience. He drew warm applause when he said: "I shall continue to speak, if permitted, as I was speaking when interrupted on the 3rd of June last." In this sermon, Reed emphasized two of his favorite themes: God's work through individuals to establish a new community, and the opportunities available to make the earth more comfortable. He stressed that the way in which Americans used their opportunities would be critical to the building of a comfortable world.[35]

Reed characterized Moses as a leader who used available materials and his opportunities to build a nation that made Abraham, the father of Israel, proud. Moses led his people out of slavery to the border of the promised land. Reed admonished his listeners to remember that time and location conditioned all Biblical teaching, and he told them that they should peel away yesterday's leaves of polygamy and slavery and look for today's kernel of truth. Slave labor's injustices provoked Moses to inspire his people to follow him. He then exercised the right of revolution and led a successful strike against the Egyptian pharaoh. It took forty years for Moses to lead the Israelites across the desert, but this journey provided the necessary time to teach and develop leaders for the emerging community. The Israelites needed this preparation before they could organize to govern the new nation.[36]

How well had Americans used their resources to build a great nation, to increase justice, to give the masses ways to help themselves, Reed asked rhetorically. And then, with some frustration, Reed remarked:

> But to-day I hear many discouraging words. At times it requires quite an effort to be optimistic. . . . The men of the past who tried to shake off the grip of kings were very hopeful. They said that the people did not need kings. They were capable of self-government. . . . In theory we now have every outward advantage. But in fact we are not doing all we can. We are a disappointment.[37]

America, Colorado particularly, had failed to provide jobs for those people who wanted work; instead, they had been forced to steal coal. In Denver an unemployed man had stolen a sack of coal to keep his family warm and was killed. Death seemed a heavy penalty for taking coal in a state so "well furnished with coal as Colorado." Reed solemnly said, "It is not the will of God that men should be out of work and that children should freeze and that men should be shot to death for stealing a sack of coal." Where were the voices of outrage, he asked. Reed recalled that many sermons had been preached on the sins of dancing and gambling, but he had heard none about usury or gambling with grain commodities or life's necessities.[38]

America stood at the threshold of possibility, but would it take advantage of its promise? Reed contended, "No good things that I can think of need be postponed." But he admitted that two things were required to accomplish anything — a willing listener and a dutiful doer. Just as the Israelites took forty years before acting on Moses' truths about the promised land, many American listeners needed time to hear the truth of a better life and to make it their own: "You cannot build a tree — it will grow."[39] The kingdom of God on earth would grow like a plant. Socialism offered a means to create more justice and to realize a more comfortable life.

Reed continued to preach on a wide range of topics, but he never abandoned the theme of Christian socialism. The topics of competition, evidences of socialism in society, and the remedy of a maturing American republic that held the promise of a more comfortable life energized him. Repeating themes from his 1892 socialist sermon, Reed held the Standard Oil Corporation up as a model for the national scandal of competition. This sermon was probably suggested to him by the 1894 publication of Henry Demarest Lloyd's treatise, *Wealth Against Commonwealth*.[40] Reed pointed to the trusts as examples of the decline of competition. He defined trusts as the "unconscious forerunner and incipient form of socialism."

Why? Because they taught cooperation. The Standard Oil corporate leadership realized that competition in the oil business meant waste. To prevent waste and to make more profit, they bought or forced out competitive companies and consolidated the oil business into one central operation. The state could have introduced the same efficiency and distributed the profits, as jobs or public projects, to deserving citizens. John D. Rockefeller could have been a more effective Christian in the federal cabinet as secretary of the oil business. In Reed's eyes, Rockefeller appeared more despicable because he professed Christianity, yet his actions belied his commitment. Reed declared: "But the man who believes that the theory of Christ is workable and who wishes to be his disciple must go on and try to make that theory practical in himself and in the neighborhood and in the state."[41]

Reed looked for signs of the new community around the country. Anything that resembled his ideas of social justice or sentiment toward humanity lifted his spirits. After a California vacation in 1895, he reported signs of socialism on the move. Discontent made people look for remedies; it resulted from God's spirit active within each person and one's experience of everyday reality. Reed noted that California had its share of discontent because of the continuing depression. He made an observation that sounded like an approval of Marxian class struggle: "[California] is a well prepared ground for the sowing of socialistic grain. Nowhere is there such a gulf between the rich and the poor. In the coming battle between the predatory class and the serfs, San Francisco will be a center."[42]

Perhaps Reed made this remark to shock his readers, but it did not reflect the ideas expressed in his sermons or the causes in which he participated. Reed's socialism most closely resembled that championed by W. D. P. Bliss. Bliss, a Christian Socialist minister and organizer, sought to educate the reading public through his magazine, the *American Fabian*. Without confirmation of Reed's participation in Fabianism, we can say he believed that socialism "simply needs a knowledge to be accepted." Reed's emphasis on the gradual coming of God's kingdom, his teaching ministry, the stress on good books and education, his plea for the involvement of ordinary people in reform — all testified to his belief that socialism grew to maturity through the efforts of enlightened citizens who learned while doing. Reed had confidence that it would happen in this manner because of the public's general discontent and the receptivity to socialistic ideas among his audiences.[43]

The right of revolution remained for Reed a cardinal principle in the American republic, but one to be used only as the last option, should the institutions and the ballot fail. In Reed's reading of history, he interpreted all governments as somewhat oppressive. But the people gained their rights in spite of kings or tyrants. The few people who pushed the world toward light and life found no favor with "the powers that be." The hope for Reed's new community resided in the redeeming potential of the American republic: "With the recognition of the rights of man came a recognition of God." This republic represented the last fair trial to determine whether the "common sense of most" could govern. The present discontent worked as a positive force to move the people toward a better understanding of the cooperative community, and they embodied the last hope for salvation.[44] Reed had faith in the common people:

> Our salvation depends on natural people. . . . The heart of the people is right. I do not place much emphasis on what they do when they are scared, when they are on the edge of winter. But in the spring the people are free. Anybody can live somehow in summertime. I wish the general election occurred, not in November, when the grass is dead, but in May, after the resurrection.[45]

Socialism continued to disturb many concerned Denver citizens, and the newspapers covered any significant event related to socialist organizations or speakers. On 23 January 1896 Reed and Dean Henry Martyn Hart of St. John's Episcopal Cathedral, entertained one hundred fifty men at the exclusive Candlelight Club with a debate about the promise and errors of socialism. Dean Hart argued that all reforms through the centuries, from New Testament days forward, had come about through the doctrine of altruism introduced by Jesus. Nonetheless, discontent dominated the majority of people. If uprisings against the law, like the recent railroad strike in Chicago, achieved success, then they endangered the general welfare. The laws of the republic governed all citizens, rich and poor, and endeavored to distribute justice evenly among them. Dean Hart raised the common criticism that socialism limited individual initiative and creativity. Instead, he proposed a one-tenth tithe paid to a public fund, similar to the Mormon practice. All citizens could benefit from the public programs generated from this fund. When Dean Hart finished, the club members sang "The Star Spangled Banner" although it was not yet the national anthem.[46]

Warming to these sounds of patriotism, Reed countered by stressing that socialism asked for a better arrangement of social relations than presently existed. He admitted that socialism offended "the uncomfortable pot-bellied people." Concentrated wealth had exploited the people and produced the tramp by replacing skilled labor with machines. Reed, like many others, looked "for a new earth." The present system, even with reform efforts through the centuries, had produced a great deal of dissatisfaction among the common folk. The unemployed wanted jobs and they had a right to work. Labor unions struggled to keep up wages and to shorten hours. All men should have worthwhile labor and the right to perform that labor under healthy and safe conditions. Some people objected to socialism because they believed it would inhibit private enterprise and violate human nature. Reed's rebuttal referred to the extremes of private enterprise, which had damaged the quality of living, whereas socialism, exemplified by the carpenter's son, would make life worth living. He reminded his listeners that the socialist demanded not equality of possessions or intellect, but "equality of opportunity. And if you think you have got equality of opportunity, just go into the oil business."[47]

For Reed, the common people still offered the best hope to reform the present social order and introduce a new community. One Sunday, Reed chronicled the noble deeds of historical figures, noting that most folks admire courage. "But there is an inconsistency in human nature. We admire a noble action, love a hero, read his legend with tears. Why do we not become what we admire? It is difficult." One had to accept the ordeals in many people's lives, but at the same time, try to find ways to relieve them of whatever kept them from becoming productive and comfortable citizens. Reed commented: "I take the best possible view of the life of our day. I believe that men are naturally honest and noble if they have a chance. But we are born into a world of competition and a world of can't." If the masses were to have any worthwhile chance, then a reformed societal order was required. "A very rich man is not only dangerous to society, but he is dangerous to himself. . . . In this kind of world it is not possible for a New Testament man to become very rich." To stand before God's judgment with inactive dollars would put one's soul in danger; one had the responsibility to contribute to the social well-being of the less fortunate. Reed concluded: "All I ask of him is to make his inheritance not an oppression, but a blessing." Society had to demand opportunity for everyone.[48]

Again, Reed returned to the principle of cooperation, which represented good socialistic doctrine and the best way to create opportunities. The Shakers demonstrated a form of socialism in which Reed saw this socialist maxim operating: "From every man according to his powers, to every man according to his needs." After explaining how the Shaker community functioned and stressing their serenity, Reed surmised: "I am persuaded that this is true: that wherever man works with man and for man, where that is the rule of the community, there is comfort of mind, health of body and in due time wealth, and salvation of the soul." Cooperation delivered not only a more just society in human circumstances, but it created a spiritual peace. He pleaded for the people to try the cooperative principle, for it would produce a healthy and beneficent community.[49] Reed soon had the chance to do just that.

Cooperative Commonwealth

The communitarians enjoyed their last hurrah in the 1890s. Denver saw a number of cooperative communities founded and cooperative reform efforts undertaken in this decade. These included: the People's Union; Wage Earners, organized by Colorado union representatives; the Christian Church colony in Routt County; and the Brotherhood of the Co-operative Commonwealth, in which Reed participated.[50]

Norman Wallace Lermond, a Maine reformer, founded the Brotherhood of the Co-operative Commonwealth in 1895. It aimed to educate all Americans in the truths of socialism and to unite all U.S. cooperationists into one large fraternal organization. His first few efforts at colonization failed, but he kept writing to sympathetic activists. Soon after the 1896 St. Louis Populist party convention, the Brotherhood was organized and elected Henry Demarest Lloyd president, but Lloyd refused to serve so the Brotherhood turned to Reed. Lloyd did agree to put the organization in the black by donating ten dollars. Eugene Debs, the popular labor agitator and president of the American Railway Union, made his debut into socialism when he joined the Brotherhood and became the organizing secretary.[51]

Debs had embraced socialism in a speech on 1 January 1897. He envisioned socialism as a part of the political process, devoted to change in the interest of the working people. Debs believed that colonies based on the principles of socialism could benefit laborers economically and politically. Reed supported Debs's union activism and the development of colonies based on socialistic principles. At about the same time, Ed Boyce, president of Western Federation of Miners, had asked Debs to visit Denver to inspire the striking miners in Leadville and Cripple Creek.[52]

Debs arrived in Denver on 10 January and attended worship at the Broadway Temple. Reed spotted him in the audience and asked him to speak briefly. After Debs's general remarks on labor, Reed preached on "Both Sides." Using Frederick Robertson's idea that "the truth is the union of two seemingly contradictory propositions, not the via media between them," Reed agreed that every issue had two sides. On the issue of labor versus capital, Reed came down on the side of labor, "the side that has not capital but muscle and skill." The capitalists had newspapers and their politicians to lobby for them, but laborers needed a voice to explain their side. That voice of explanation, imperfect though it was, trumpeted from the Broadway Temple pulpit — so thought the laborers in the West.[53]

On Tuesday, 12 January, Denver's Turner Hall was packed with working men and women who anticipated an electrifying speech from Debs. They were not disappointed. The two speakers, Debs and Ed Boyce, asked Reed to join them on the platform. Debs's speech focused on the suppression of labor by government and capitalists alike.[54] He also honored Reed by describing him as "a modern Jesus Christ . . . who is preaching without fear the gospel of righteousness." Debs said that Reed symbolized the men by which the world has progressed and as long as he stood, he would preach the truth in defiance of public opinion. The audience called for Reed to come forth, and he then described Debs as an apostle of freedom.[55]

In 1897 Debs left the Brotherhood of Co-operative Commonwealth to devote more time to his new organization, the Social Democracy of America. Meanwhile, Reed attempted to establish a colony in Utah. In addition to the Brotherhood's objectives of education and the union of all existing cooperationists, Reed announced that the colonies would concentrate on socializing one state at a time. All ministers who joined must leave their creeds behind; minding one's own business formed the cornerstone of colony's philosophy: this was Reed's creed of "live and let live." He credited Debs and Lloyd as the moving spirits behind these efforts at "restoring man to his original state of happiness." Unfortunately, nothing lasting resulted.[56]

On 26 October 1896 the *News* printed a story entitled "Denver's New Religion." Some of Denver's civic leaders, Reed among them, had organized a new church society dedicated to educating the voting masses on municipal reform. The socialist maxim "From every one according to ability, to every one according to need," formed the Civic Church's working principle. If the colonies could not prove themselves as effective vehicles for change, then these socialists would attack from another flank. An institution devoted to teaching common folk how to bring about social and political reform in the cities fit perfectly with Reed's goals. Within a few months, W. D. P. Bliss was invited to preach a sermon at St. Mark's Church, in which he would advocate municipal reform. The Civic Church continued to invite notable speakers versed in municipal or social reform to address the society.[57]

In February 1897 the Reverend Ruth B. Ridges of Toledo, Ohio, was selected as the pastor of the Civic Church. Laurence Gronlund, a non-Marxist socialist had proposed the idea of a civic church. Gronlund explained that civic churches would supplement Christian churches by teaching people the proper organization of social and industrial life. These churches would prepare believers to implement the socialistic gospel. With Reed's non-Marxist orientation, he no doubt knew about Gronlund's *The Co-operative Commonwealth: An Exposition of Socialism* (1884), which Julius A. Wayland, publisher of the *Coming Nation* and the *Appeal to Reason*, widely distributed in Colorado. Also, Joseph Buchanan's *Labor Enquirer* printed reading lists, which included the Gronlund book. Reed read both the *Labor Enquirer* and the *Appeal to Reason*. Nevertheless, even with this publicity and distinctive leadership, neither the colonies nor the Civic Church endured in Colorado.[58]

Perhaps Reed's tenacious belief in the coming kingdom of God on earth sometimes blinded him to problems of persistent human greed and manipulation, but he pounded hard on socialistic themes, even repeating old sermons. He labored unceasingly for a new community, confident that God's spirit moved humanity toward that end regardless of individual or collective performance. Throughout the generations, the true Christian's obligation as God's servant demanded that one respond to society's possibilities for more justice, to the suffering with relief, and to create opportunities so that all people could participate in a more comfortable life. Reed pleaded for each one to remember: "An injury to one is an injury to all." In the American republic, which Reed believed God had inspired, the new community would finally emerge in the twentieth century. Reed drew from the New Theology and from the nineteenth-century's best minds to guide him through life, hoping to leave something others could build on.

Part Three

Legacy of a Crank

*"A crank . . . brings hidden obscure
values up and into the light."*

The Onward Trail

James Whitcomb Riley

(for Myron W. Reed, Denver, January 30, 1899)

Just as of old — with fearless foot
And placid face and resolute,
He takes the faint, mysterious trail
That leads beyond our earthly hail.

We would cry, as in last farewell,
But that his hand waves, and a spell,
Is laid upon our tongues; and thus
He takes unworded leave of us.

And it is fitting — as he fared
Here with us, so is he prepared
For any fortuning the night
May hold for him beyond our sight.

The moon and stars they still attend
His wandering footsteps to the end —
He did not question, nor will we,
Their guidance and security.

So, never parting word nor cry —
We feel, with him, that by-and-by
Our onward trails will meet, and then
Merge and be ever one again.

(Myron W. Reed, Recollections of Myron W. Reed, Minister of Broadway Temple, 1895–1899, manuscript, Western History Department, Denver Public Library, Denver, Colorado; also published in the Indianapolis Journal, 30 January 1899, p. 8)

SEVEN

Epilogue:

Friend of the Masses

During the 1880s and 1890s, Myron Reed achieved national recognition as a preacher–politician, an innovator in charity work, and a Christian Socialist. As a prominent religious figure in the Rocky Mountain region, he commanded a sizable audience wherever he spoke. But public memory of Reed faded within one generation after his death. He published no significant book that seized national attention, and he established no lasting organization that advanced his ideas. Without his personality and magnetism, the Glenarm Club, the institutional church, the Broadway Temple, all declined upon his departure. What, then, was his lasting contribution to the Gilded Age West?

Reed never lived to see a social structure that resembled the kingdom of God on earth. He continued trying to make it happen, but he was disillusioned by the constant examples of injustice he saw all around him — injustices that, he believed, should have been solved during humanity's advancement in the nineteenth century. The capitalists remained in power, and the poor's general situation showed no long-lasting improvement. Instead, charity still only provided temporary relief, emphasizing efficiency rather than sentiment, and no effective programs were developed to eradicate the causes of poverty. Reed believed socialism had the potential to model the principle of cooperation. But as time passed, socialism proved unable to ignite the changes Reed hoped to see. It failed to recruit the kind of dynamic leadership that could meld its followers into a powerful political phalanx, particularly in the West. In spite of all his individual accomplishments, Reed could not measure any significant progress in the amount of justice meted out or in the quality of America's mission as an example to the world of a cooperative republic.

The Spanish–American War troubled Reed, for he viewed it as harmful to America's world image. Reed shared the non-Marxist socialist position that America had a democratic mission to the world, but his opposition was even more strongly grounded in his belief that America was the global messianic example — the nation where the kingdom of God would finally emerge. He agreed that Cuba deserved its independence from Spain, and that perhaps America's intervention could be seen as a defense of democracy, but he thought war was unnecessary. He also thought that if America was going to intervene, then it should use its power to end the war quickly. But like most Americans, when the battleship *Maine* exploded in Havana's harbor, Reed was filled with an emotional patriotism. He proposed an immediate and decisive solution: the United States should recognize Cuba as an independent nation, extract payment from Spain for the battleship's market value, publicly hang the men who had destroyed the *Maine*, and complete all these actions within seven days. In such a crisis, Reed believed, America needed a forceful, decisive Andrew Jackson, not the cautious, plodding William McKinley.[1]

With leaders like McKinley, the "mortgaged president," Secretary of War Russell Alger, the "noted coward," and Secretary of State John Sherman, "some kind of thief" who earned millions while he was a U.S. Senator, Reed summarized: "We are at this time the gayety [sic] of the nations, the prize chump of the world." The conduct of the national leadership reflected negatively on America's reputation as a republic that merited imitation throughout the world. Reed strongly opposed the annexation of the Philippines, for to him they represented a prime example of a nation unprepared for American-style democracy. Reed blustered, "If God had wanted him [Filipino] an American, he would have made him an American." How could America export democracy when it had not learned how to make democracy work at home? Annexation would bring many more unfit immigrants into an already crowded country; America had enough. Ironically, Andrew Carnegie and Reed concurred on this anti-imperialistic stance. On the positive side, Reed saw war as a proving ground for new leadership and inspiring deeds. He would have agreed with Charlotte Perkins Gilman that war was the one great "socializer." Men learned to cooperate on the battlefield and to synthesize complex issues into simple, easily understood maxims. These heroes would produce the leadership that would guide the nation into a new twentieth-century community.[2]

When Reed looked forward to the twentieth century, he imagined that all things would surely come together to form the kingdom of God. The unlearned lessons for better human relationships would be learned, a greater approximation of justice would be realized, and humankind would practice a philosophy of "live and let live." What kept this hope alive was Reed's immutable belief that what ought to be will be as God had revealed in Jesus Christ.

What had begun as a compelling and passionate endeavor that promised a new earth turned to bitter disappointment for Reed in his last days; still, he never rejected the New Theology's emphasis on the centrality of Christ or God's benevolent push toward his kingdom on earth. During the fall of 1898, Reed's thoughts seemed to dwell on death and on questions about how much a person could accomplish in a lifetime. At the Broadway Temple's third anniversary, he reflected that he thought he had talked sense and felt appreciated about three-fourths of the time. But, he recalled, in the previous year he had attended ninety-three funerals and these depressed him. He admitted, "I get impatient. Life is so short and the art of making a comfortable earth is so long."[3]

But Reed refused to give up on the possibility that the American people would finally design a society that most nearly approximated the kingdom of God on earth. History was directed by an "unseen Power." The Jews and the Pilgrims modeled, sometimes imperfectly, the principle of cooperation working itself out in human transactions. This world would not end; it was being transformed into "a living, loving, comfortable earth." Evidences of such cooperation flourished: women's clubs, the Socialist Colony in Ruskin, Tennessee, the Parliament of Religions scheduled for 1900 in India — all indicated that God's leaven slowly prepared humanity for a new earth.[4] Comforted by these thoughts, Reed could affirm:

> It is a new day. . . . All good deeds are but splinters of the True Cross. . . . Shall we who have evil in us notwithstanding our good despise others? Shall we who have good in us notwithstanding our evil despair of others? Human nature as we see it on the street and in the newspapers is not a hopeless thing and it is not a finished thing. It is a blooming, growing thing. . . . It is our day."[5]

As unsettling as it was for Reed to experience what he considered humanity's obduracy and outright stupidity, he could never let go of his essential belief that in the historical process God shaped human nature in preparation for the coming kingdom on earth.

How should we measure Reed's importance in the Rocky Mountain region? To evaluate his influence, one must look to those who stood beside him when he was successful, when he failed, and when he was intractable. One might ask, when he died, who mourned him? Without dispute, one can say that the masses regarded Reed as their champion. He willingly spoke for them in the court of public opinion and in the shadow of the steeple. Reed tried to bridge the gap between the church and the workers, between the rich and the poor, and between politics and those whom politics forgot.

The idea of cooperation, with its emphasis on the people's participation, appealed to many nineteenth-century American reformers. With industrialization came employers who dictated work hours, products produced, and wages paid. Government helped industrial expansion along with liberal policies, economic subsidies, and the use of force against rebellious workers when necessary. The transformation from a largely agrarian nation to an urban, industrialized one culminated in the generation after 1899. The 1920 census reported that a majority of Americans, 51 percent, now lived in towns of 2,500 or more; with all its advantages and disadvantages, the city had become home for more than half the nation's citizens. For those Americans who felt excluded from the main economic and political stream, Reed stood out as a leader who boldly swam against the current, a man who believed that with applied intelligence and effort, one could improve society's organization. Reed understood humanity's limitations, but even so, he maintained that the world moved toward the kingdom of God on a zigzag course. He once said that a seeker after mercy could always find some, but it had no constant strength — it flowed unevenly. Any change that improved society occurred because God's spirit pulled humanity closer to his kingdom on earth, whether it manifested itself in laws to protect the weak or in individual acts of kindness.

Appropriately, the common folk who mourned Reed's death formed the most significant part of Reed's legacy. They represented his hope for a more comfortable world. Inasmuch as they recognized God's spirit within them, practiced brotherhood in their everyday lives, assumed the responsibilities of citizenship, and looked for ways to improve the lives of their neighbors, then they reflected the servant model that Reed had preached.

After a lengthy illness, the sixty-two-year-old Reed died on 30 January 1899 from a combination of inflammation of the intestines and colon and influenza. Reed's health had been declining for several years, and except for preaching on Sunday mornings, his activity had been limited during the last few months of 1898.[6] He had made his final public appearance on 11 December when he preached at the funeral of a friend, J. Q. Charles. In his

closing comments, Reed kept alive the idea that each person should strive
to contribute something to the growth of a new community:

> That which we call death is but a pause in the progress of life. . . . But
> when death comes after life had done its good, having enjoyed the
> summer, that is not violence. I don't think old age is to be sought after.
> I don't want to linger on the threshold of the stage. While I can be of
> any use then I am willing to remain.[7]

Life's justification rested on one's contribution to the larger human community, and the value of that contribution depended on the quality of one's
deeds. Philanthropy and public acclaim did not necessarily equal quality of
contribution. Reed looked for acts that best expressed servanthood in the
ordinary relationships among people: the kindness demonstrated in forgiveness; the support for victims of misfortune: the public-spirited person
who worked for the city or state without pay or recognition. These deeds
served as proof of God's presence in the world and nourished Reed's faith.

Any public figure's funeral contains a depth of emotion that can prejudice
an understanding of its significance, but even so, by considering the people
who came, the ceremony itself, and the later attempts to honor his memory,
we can learn something about Reed's impact on the Rocky Mountain West.
The *Rocky Mountain News* described Reed's funeral as "fit for the Father of
his country." The poor, the rich, the middle class, legislators, union leaders,
and businessmen came to the Broadway Temple. Each cause for which
Reed had fought — charity, political reform, labor, and socialism — was represented by mourners who attended the funeral or published their condolences. Sympathetic telegrams and letters arrived from across the country. Actors and theater associations, unions and individual laborers, the
common people, all expressed their sorrow because they had lost a friend.
The Denver newspapers printed these messages as they received them, including resolutions from the state House of Representatives and the Charity Organization Society .[8]

Two examples from the many condolences that came from outside Colorado illustrate the diverse sources. Jacob Huff of Pennsylvania, an author
and co-worker of Edward Bellamy, maintained that he contributed to a
journal with the names of Reed and Bellamy on its masthead. Huff placed
Reed in the same company with Bellamy and wrote, "Yet their deaths has
[sic] given the gospel of humanity an impetus which plutocracy and the
gates of monopolistic hell cannot prevent from sweeping to the outer con-
fines of civilization." Then a stage performer described how much actors

had appreciated Reed as a friend of the stage; they were inspired to find a preacher who would say "a kind word for them and defend their profession from a public pulpit or platform." People beyond Denver knew Reed as a voice for forgotten souls because of the wide distribution of his sermons.[9]

Labor leaders voiced their sorrow upon losing a soldier in the battle for workers' justice. Eugene Debs described Reed as "the tribune of the people, the friend of the toil — a soldier, a Socialist and a man." Colorado labor leader Otto F. Thum presented a portrait of Reed to the Denver Trades and Labor Assembly in 1904 and lauded Reed for his great humanity and support of Colorado's workers. The *Miners' Magazine* printed copies of Reed's sermons for years thereafter, and members of the Western Federation of Miners visited his grave when they met in Denver. When laborers gathered at the Fairmount Cemetery Reed memorial, Samuel Gompers said that while some ministers asserted the poor had strayed from the church, Reed "was never estranged from the poor. His pews were filled by men who marked every class from the beggar to the millionaire."[10]

In a bitter cold with temperatures below zero, the newspapers reported, people from all social classes and professions lined up to pass slowly by Reed's coffin. Among these mourners, the group most represented was the common folk. An African American, a poor elderly man, and an Italian immigrant indicated the masses' feelings about Reed's Denver ministry: "An old colored man, bright pearls on his black face, bent over and kissed the glass above the dead." Many could not get inside because of the crowd, but an old man in a faded overcoat with a red scarf said, "I never saw Myron Reed but I have read every one of his sermons for the last six years. . . . He was such a noble man. . . . Do you know a man did not have to see or hear Myron Reed to love him?" An Italian woman with a baby in her arms and only a shawl around her shoulders tried to get through the mob, but urged not to because of the baby she turned and in tears walked away. The *News* reported that never before in Denver's history had there been such an outpouring of sorrow. Noticeably absent were many Denver ministers.[11] Even in death, Reed's views on life and society inhibited some preachers from showing any public support for Reed the man or Reed the activist.

Ten thousand people tried to enter the Broadway Temple, which held only two thousand. The three thousand who managed to crowd inside sat in reverent silence. Participants included some of Colorado's most important political and religious leaders: Governor Charles S. Thomas served as a pall bearer; Father William O'Ryan of St. Leo's Catholic Church, Rabbi William S. Friedman of Temple Emanuel, and Tom Patterson were the principal speakers; Denver University's Chancellor W. F. McDowell gave the invocation; Reverend B. O. Aylesworth of the Central Christian Church read the 90th Psalm; and Reverend D. N. Beach of the First Congregational Church prayed the benediction. The funeral's participants symbolized Reed's eclecticism in theology and his concern for education. Father O'Ryan preached the sermon and described Reed as a man who pleaded for human rights and a liberty that would culminate in "an unreached ideal America."[12] He appealed to the mourners to remember Reed's lesson:

> There are no creeds to be outlawed, no colors of skin debarred. Mankind is one in its rights and wrongs — one right, one hope, one guard. By his life he taught, by his death we learn the great reformer's creed. The right to be free, and the hope to be just, and the guard against selfish greed.[13]

Rabbi Friedman and Tom Patterson eulogized Reed with anecdotes from their friendship with him and emphasized his character and work. Friedman conceded that Reed had his faults, but he also had a large sympathy for anyone in need and possessed a character that "was almost childlike in its confidence." Reed represented the true liberal, who saw the good in every human and the truth in every faith. Religion for Reed was not dogma but "voiced in the ringing eloquence of deed." Patterson recalled for the mourners the qualities that had attracted them to Reed: "What drew and bound him to us was his heart and soul. To his sympathies there was no limitation. Only his lack of means circumscribed his benevolence." A private burial ceremony followed at Fairmount Cemetery.[14]

The *News* published Reed's epigrams for several weeks in 1899, and Reverend Victor Southworth, a Denver minister, proposed to publish a collection of these sayings in booklet form, but none appeared. Herbert George, prominent Populist, reformer, and trustee of the Broadway Temple, said that no one could take Reed's place at the Temple. Neither Denver nor the West had a minister acceptable to the trustees who could command the resources necessary to succeed at the Broadway Temple. It closed after the funeral.[15]

Reed's energetic defense of equal opportunity, his voice that criticized injustice and the moneyed elite, and his ability to stir within the masses the possibilities of a better community attracted people from near and far. Perhaps funereal rhetoric embellished these qualities, but the primary theme reverberated with praise for an individual who treated everybody with respect and compassion, who addressed with word and deed the inequities in ordinary life, and who shared the flaws inherent in human existence. His popularity stimulated a drive to erect a suitable memorial, but his friends protested that he would not have approved of such a large expenditure for public display. Suggestions included a downtown statue, a park, or an art museum, but as time passed these projects faded. Finally, the Trades Assembly erected a monument at Reed's grave in Fairmount Cemetery and unveiled it on Memorial Day, 30 May 1900. James E. Faulkner, Trades Assembly representative in charge of the ceremony, said in his dedication, "We dedicate this monument to a man of the people. . . . He believed that the laborer was entitled to the fruits of his labor; to a decent home, reasonable hours of labor, and a few of the comforts of life." Workers, union men, businessmen, old soldiers, and ex-Populist Governor Davis Waite made up the crowd. Again, Father O'Ryan and Rabbi Friedman were the principal speakers.[16] The common folk most remembered Reed and his work.

When he left Indiana, Reed told his congregation that the evidences of Christianity walked the city streets. The streets formed Reed's laboratory, the place to observe life in all its mystery and promise. He associated more with mechanics and gamblers than with ministers, for in these people he saw the Christ feeling emerging — the hidden power of God. Reed wanted to treat life as God's gift, which meant that he had to share it with others. When he went fishing or camping, he tried to share without broadcasting his ministerial identity. A fishing companion who met Reed in Canada stopped to visit him when he traveled through Indianapolis. He asked for Reed and only then learned that he was a minister. Such behavior did not reveal an apprehension about his ministry; Reed simply believed that a man should be judged by his actions, not by his profession. Reed's friend of twenty years, James Whitcomb Riley, poet and Indianapolis author, said that Reed "enjoyed the harvest of the eye." Reed always tried to read the book of life by looking at the individuals who lived it before him: "He seemed infinitely touched by anything that showed such a man as Burns to be a true brother and fellow."[17]

Counted among the princes of the pulpit, Reed seems to have been lost to history, along with David Swing. The historian Ferenc Szasz has observed that in the popularization of the myth of the American West, one group that figured prominently in the myth had been totally ignored — the American clergy. Szasz lists six reasons for this oversight, but the most significant one contended that the Gilded Age West revealed a religious/ethnic pluralism that the East only later recognized.[18] When settlement began in the West, no denomination achieved the same prominence as did the Congregationalists, the Presbyterians, and the Episcopalians along the eastern seaboard. Several religious groups arrived in the West at about the same time — Protestants, Jews, and Catholics — but none gained dominance in any one area. Somehow, this religious pluralism obscured individuals like Reed, who had a significant impact on the western religious environment. Denver's population included a diverse mix of foreign nationalities and the West had an abundance of urban churches. The Congregational Church came to the Rocky Mountain region in the 1860s but did not gain the high visibility that it had on the East Coast. Reed never achieved any lasting recognition from the national Congregational Church, but he did earn local and national visibility and received recognition for his influential role in Gilded Age Denver.

A list of his public offices in 1893 reveals an impressive level of activity. He served the cause of charity as president of local and national charitable organizations. His interest in prison reform found expression on local and national boards of parole and prison reform. Reed always stood for humane treatment of animals and became the vice-president of the Humane Society. As president of the Colorado branch of the Indian Rights Association, Reed lobbied for their rights as American citizens who deserved more justice than they had received at the hands of the governmental bureaucracy. One incident that provoked Reed's intolerance for acts of brazen injustice involved some Indians who were killed by the game warden for hunting illegally. Reed grew impatient with the investigation's slow progress and threatened to hang the offenders himself if no just decision came forth.[19] These activities showed his devotion to causes for the masses and society's forgotten.

Reed left no significant writings about his theological musings; he placed more emphasis on action than on theory. His only published book, *Temple Talks*, contains but fifteen sermons, which he selected, including the sermons on socialism and the tramp. He published at least two other sermons: "Night and Sleep and Rest" in *The Cosmopolitan* (February 1897), and "Our Day" in *The Arena* (February 1899). The *Denver Post* reprinted the popular series, "The Evolution of the Tramp" in 1905, and the *News* published a series of Reed's sermons in 1911. Reed's followers bought his book and read his articles, but these writings do not accurately measure his legacy. He was the people's man. Rev. Camden M. Cobern, pastor of Trinity Methodist Church, remarked that he had had great differences with Reed on many subjects, but that "he loved the common people and was their spokesman. . . . He was the people's voice."[20]

A Denver astrologer attempted to shed some light on Reed by preparing an astrological chart of his life, showing that while he possessed the ability to make money, he would never keep it. His friends observed these tendencies and tried to protect him from giving away too much. Reed had limited financial success. His estate consisted of three hundred books, two book-cases, a writing desk, a gun and hunting outfit, a gold watch, and an interest in the copyright on his book, *Temple Talks*. His wife received an insurance policy, largely paid for by friends, that guaranteed some income. She died at her daughter's Denver home in 1907.[21]

While many admired Reed and respected his achievements, they also recognized his shortcomings, which probably prevented greater successes. His inclination to speak his opinions plainly, often without much tact, alienated those who could have been allies in a common cause. When the pressures became too great, when he felt strong disappointment over the new community's lack of progress, he grew despondent and escaped with alcohol. His impatience with detail often turned long-term projects into short-term ones because he would either withdraw or resign. His relentless independence together with his impetuosity prevented him from establish-ing any enduring organization to carry forward his work for a cooper-ative community.[22] Thus, the Denver Charity Organization Society re-mained Reed's single enduring institutional legacy. But few Coloradans recall Reed's role in establishing what later became the United Fund.

Rabbi Friedman in his eulogy said that Reed desired to see a city "orna-mented with parks, replete with play grounds, adorned with an audito-rium." Reed's wish came true during the Progressive Era mayoralty of Rob-ert W. Speer, who held that office in 1904–12, and then again in 1916–1918. Speer, a friend and supporter of Reed, made no attempt to resurrect Reed's cooperative principle. He did, however, fulfill Reed's description of the good citizen who left something to benefit future generations. Speer put together a coalition of businessmen and politicians who supported a "city beautiful" movement. He built city parks with play areas and twelve play-grounds for the children. Anyone could take advantage of the cultural events staged in the new municipal auditorium; the city limited the admis-sion cost from twenty-five cents to one dollar. The new auditorium hosted everything from circuses and revivals to grand opera and trade shows. Reed would have approved of this universal offering of culture.[23]

Reed's lasting importance did not depend on institutions, movements, or material monuments; rather it resided in the lives of the people he touched. In the generations immediately after him, he left laborers with the hope that not all churches or religious leaders would desert their cause. He left the poor with the belief that someone would challenge the powerful cap-italists to approve shorter working hours and higher wages to permit a more comfortable life. He left the rich and powerful with the haunting notion that not all churchmen or citizens would remain passive about the exploitative tendencies of wealth — rebellion could happen if there were no measure of justice. Reed might have possessed that hope, described by Christopher Lasch, that supports "a trusting attitude toward life" in contrast to ongoing despair. Earnest individuals could make society more just, but how would they do so? Reed left no immediate answer for his admirers.[24]

In *Reflections on the End of an Era*, Reinhold Niebuhr expressed a biting criticism of the "erroneous estimate of human nature." Niebuhr pointed out that even wise men do not know to what extent life's impulses can defy reason and "the dictates of conscience." Reed, too, misjudged the degree of goodness in humankind. He thought that teaching the truth of servanthood and preparing the mind to receive this truth would eventually draw all like-minded people together into one cooperative commonwealth. Reed believed that individuals required time to accept the principles revealed in Christ's life, and he expected that differences would be resolved as the community reasoned together guided by their common objective. But his high expectations that this idealistic method would solve complex problems, such as conflict between capitalism and labor, collapsed into pessimism when no solution appeared. Yet, even in times of deep despair, Reed publicly proclaimed a message of hope for the future, although he did not expect to live to see it happen. He wrote: "The human society that compels a tramp to be, is considered by the best heads and hearts to be out of order. Such a state of society needs prompt reconstruction. Such a society the twentieth century will set in order." It did not come to pass, but Reed would have exhorted his listeners nevertheless: "Hold onto the American idea."[25]

Myron Reed, a Congregationalist minister from Indiana and a descendant of Vermont abolitionists, became a Rocky Mountain radical who challenged the premises of the dominant power groups in Denver — the capitalists and their political supporters. His death silenced not only a voice of Christian Socialism in the West, but a force for humanitarian religion that embraced all people regardless of social status, race, or creed. He showed that not all people who came West were driven by the urge to rape the land and dispossess the Native Americans. For Reed, the West offered a new beginning, an opportunity to practice cooperative living that could offer a comfortable life for all people. Even though Reed did not accomplish all of his goals in Colorado, his work certainly placed him among the leading figures in state politics, religion, labor activity, and social issues. He often said that one should read history through the lives of its great figures. The people he admired — Edward Bellamy, Eugene Debs, Henry Demarest

Lloyd, John Brown, Henry George, Henry Ward Beecher — live on because of their deeds and their writings. Others he admired — Emma Abbot,
David Swing, and O. C. McCulloch — are not in the historical canon. To
study Reed, maverick and the people's voice, opens another page in American society and the history of dissent in the West. Myron Reed must be
more than a footnote in the history of the Rocky Mountain West.[26]

Notes

CHAPTER I

1. "Reed On Socialism," *Rocky Mountain News*, 19 December 1892, p. 2.

2. "One Doctrine For All," *Rocky Mountain News*, 16 December 1895, p. 4; Myron W. Reed, *Temple Talks* (Indianapolis and Kansas City: The Bowen–Merrill Company, 1898), 59.

3. Stephen J. Leonard and Thomas J. Noel, *Denver: Mining Camp to Metropolis* (Niwot, CO: University Press of Colorado, 1990), xii; Glenn Chesney Quiett, *They Built the West: An Epic of Rails and Cities* (New York: D. Appleton–Century Company, 1934), 143–44, 162; Lawrence H. Larsen, *The Urban West at the End of the Frontier* (Lawrence: The Regents Press of Kansas, 1978), 17; Gunther Barth, *Instant Cities: Urbanization and the Rise of San Francisco and Denver* (1975; reprint, Albuquerque: University of New Mexico Press, 1988), 155, 158–60; Robert L. Perkin, *The First Hundred Years: An Informal History of Denver and the Rocky Mountain News* (Garden City, NY: Doubleday and Company, 1959), 17, 30–31, 43, 51, 54.

4. Barth, *Instant Cities*, 160; Lyle W. Dorsett and Michael McCarthy, *The Queen City: A History of Denver*, 2nd ed. (Boulder, CO: Pruett Publishing Company, 1986), 95.

5. "A Better World," *Rocky Mountain News*, 1 November 1886, p. 1; Reed, *Temple Talks*, 54–59.

6. For Reed's biography see William P. Fishback, Collection of Clippings Relating to Reverend Myron W. Reed, n.d., Indiana State Library, Indianapolis, Indiana; "Biography of Myron W. Reed," and W. P. Fishback, "Memorial of Myron W. Reed, 1883–1899," both in Myron W. Reed, Miscellaneous Items Concerning Myron W. Reed, 1883–1899, Collected and Compiled by Edgar A. Burton (1871–1951), Western History Department, Denver Public Library, Denver, Colorado; Myron W. Reed, Dictation of Rev. Myron Reed, H. H. Bancroft Collection, University of California, Berkeley, California; Richard E. Leach, "Myron Winslow Reed," *The Trail* 19 (November 1926): 3–7; for reference to abolition, see "Win We

Will," *Rocky Mountain News*, 15 July 1894, p. 1; see Reed eulogies in the *Denver Post*, *Rocky Mountain News*, and *Denver Republican*, 31 January and 1, 2 February 1899.

7. For examples of Memorial Day sermons, see Fishback, Collection of Clippings; "The Boys In Blue," *Rocky Mountain News*, 26 May 1884, p. 6; for Sherman's visit, see "Sherman In The City," 3 July 1889, p. 1; "The Camp Fire," 3 July 1889, p. 6; "Sherman Received," 4 July 1889, p. 1, all in the *Rocky Mountain News*.

8. Myron W. Reed, Myron W. Reed Papers (five letters), Chicago Historical Society, Chicago, Illinois.

9. "Myron Reed Is Dead," *Indianapolis News*, 30 January 1899, p. 1; Paul Reed and thesis prize, "Honors For The Sire," *Rocky Mountain News*, 18 October 1894, p. 5; "Mrs. L. P. Carter, Philanthropist's Daughter, Is Dead," *Denver Post*, 29 September 1933, p. 39.

10. Reed, Myron W. Reed Papers (five letters); Mrs. Myron Reed, *One Life: One Law* (New York: John W. Lovell Company, 1890); Ferenc M. Szasz, "'New Thought' and The American West," *Journal of the West* 23 (January 1984): 83–90.

11. See "Oldfish On Myron Reed," in Fishback, Collection of Clippings.

12. "A Better World," *Rocky Mountain News*, 1 November 1886, p. 1.

13. Thomas J. Noel, "Denver Boosters and Their 'Great Braggart City'," *Colorado Heritage* (Autumn 1995): 2, 6; William N. Byers, *Encyclopedia of Biography of Colorado* (Chicago: The Century Publishing and Engraving Company, 1901), 1: 187–90; Perkin, *The First Hundred Years*, 15, 44, 84, 134–40; Dorsett and McCarthy, *The Queen City*, 1–5; Leonard and Noel, *Denver*, 29–30.

14. Byers, *Encyclopedia*, 1:45; Perkin, *The First Hundred Years*, 120–24; Quiett, *They Built the West*, 149–50.

15. Dorsett and McCarthy, *The Queen City*, 6–9; Leonard and Noel, *Denver*, 7–8; Quiett, *They Built the West*, 143–44; "Co-Founder's Street Plan Left Legacy of Confusion," *Rocky Mountain News*, souvenir edition, 22 April 1984, p. 96A.

16. Dorsett and McCarthy, *The Queen City*, 6–9; Clyde Lyndon King, *The History of the Government of Denver with Special Reference to its Relations with Public Service Corporations* (Denver: Fisher Book Company, 1911), 14–15; Carl Abbott et al., *Colorado: A History of the Centennial State*, rev. ed. (Boulder: Colorado Associated University Press, 1982), 62–69; Carl Ubbelohde et al., *A Colorado History*, 5th ed. (Boulder, CO: Pruett Publishing Company, 1982), 99–102.

17. Leonard and Noel, *Denver*, 24–25; Perkin, *The First Hundred Years*, 253–55; for more on Gilpin see Larsen, *The Urban West*, 2–3, 111–14, 121.

18. Dorsett and McCarthy, *The Queen City*, 10–14; Leonard and Noel, *Denver*, 25; Byers, *Encyclopedia*, 1:99, 440–42;, Ubbelohde, *A Colorado History*, 144–45; Perkin, *The First Hundred Years*, 255–57.

19. Dorsett and McCarthy, *The Queen City*, 14, 18–19; for additional references, see Leonard and Noel, *Denver*, 29.

20. Leonard and Noel, *Denver*, 164, 167–81; Dorsett and McCarthy, *The Queen City*, 14–20; Byers, *Encyclopedia*, 1:192–95; Quiett, *They Built the West*, 162–65, 167–68, 190–92.

21. Dorsett and McCarthy, *The Queen City*, 34–43; Leonard and Noel, *Denver*, 17–20, 27–28, 66; Barth, *Instant Cities*, 165–66; Richard Hogan, *Class and Community in Frontier Colorado* (Lawrence: University of Press Kansas, 1990), 2–3; David Brundage, *The Making of Western Labor Radicalism: Denver's Organized Workers, 1878–1905* (Urbana and Chicago: University of Illinois Press, 1994), 10–11. Chivington defended his action twenty years later in "Sand Creek," 7 October 1885, p. 4; for another version, see "The Sand Creek Massacre," 11 March 1888, p. 15, both in the *Rocky Mountain News*.

22. Byers, *Encyclopedia*, 1:51; Dorsett and McCarthy, *The Queen City*, 21–24; Leonard and Noel, *Denver*, 34–37; Quiett, *They Built the West*, 155–56.

23. Quiett, *They Built the West*, 157–60; Abbott, *Colorado*, 82–86; Dorsett and McCarthy, *The Queen City*, 21.

24. Dorsett and McCarthy, *The Queen City*, 22–23.

25. Ibid., 23; Quiett, *They Built the West*, 115, 122, 160–61, 164; Abbott, *Colorado*, 84–86; Perkin, *The First Hundred Years*, 307–9.

26. Dorsett and McCarthy, *The Queen City*, 23–25; Abbott, *Colorado*, 86; Barth, *Instant Cities*, 213–16.

27. Leonard and Noel, *Denver*, 39–41; Dorsett and McCarthy, *The Queen City*, 57–60; Larsen, *The Urban West*, 102–3; Perkin, *The First Hundred Years*, 305–10; Byers, *Encyclopedia*, 1:84–90.

28. Leonard and Noel, *Denver*, 42.

29. Ibid., 21, 44; "Democratic Doctrine," 17 February 1880, p. 4; "This Beats All," 1 January 1880, p. 1; for articles about the Utes, see "The Utes Must Go," 3 February 1880, p. 2, and 19 February 1880, p. 8; editorial, 22 February 1880, p. 4; "The Ute," 29 February 1880, p. 3, all in the *Rocky Mountain News*; Abbott, *Colorado*, 100.

30. LeRoy R. Hafen, *Colorado and Its People: A Narrative and Topical History of the Centennial State* (New York: Lewis Historical Publishing Co., Inc., 1948), 2:343; Byers, *Encyclopedia*, 1:98–101.

31. Ellen Arguimbau, comp., and Joseph A. Brennan, ed., "Guide to the Thomas M. Patterson Family Papers" (Western Historical Collections, University of Colorado Libraries, Boulder, Colorado, 1977), 3; Byers, *Encyclopedia*, 1:213–16; Robert Earl Smith, "Thomas M. Patterson: Colorado's Crusader," (Ph.D. diss., University of Missouri, 1973), chapter 1; Sybil Downing and Robert E. Smith, *Tom Patterson: Colorado Crusader for Change* (Niwot: University Press of Colorado, 1995), chapters 1–3; Perkin, *The First Hundred Years*, 380–83; James Edward Wright, *The Politics of Populism: Dissent in Colorado* (New Haven: Yale University Press, 1974), 53.

32. Mary Fonda Adams, "Thomas M. Patterson: Some Aspects of His Political Career," (M.A. thesis, University of Colorado, 1933), 4.

33. "A Wasted Opportunity," *Rocky Mountain News*, 26 July 1874, p. 2; Smith, "Thomas M. Patterson," 31.

34. Byers, *Encyclopedia*, 1:214; Perkin, *The First Hundred Years*, 382; Downing and Smith, *Tom Patterson*, 16–22; King, *The History of the Government of Denver*, 87.

35. Hafen, *Colorado and Its People*, 2:345–49; Colin B. Goodykoontz, "Some Con-

troversial Questions Before the Colorado Constitutional Convention of 1876," *Colorado Magazine* 17 (January 1940): 1–17; Ubbelohde, *A Colorado History*, 151–55; Abbott, *Colorado*, 127.

36. "The Fourth; A Day Long to be Remembered in Denver," 6 July 1876, p. 1; "The President's Proclamation Declaring Colorado A State," 2 August 1876, p. 1, both in the *Rocky Mountain News*; Perkin, *The First Hundred Years*, 382; Robert Earl Smith, "Thomas M. Patterson, Colorado Statehood and the Presidential Election of 1876," *Colorado Magazine* 53 (Spring 1976): 153–61; Wilbur Fisk Stone, *History of Colorado* (Chicago: Clarke Publishing Company, 1918), 1:423–27; Ubbelohde, *A Colorado History*, 151–52, 155–56.

37. Downing and Smith, *Tom Patterson*, 193–203; Fitz-Mac (James Mac Carthy), *Political Portraits* (Colorado Springs: The Gazette Printing Company, 1888), 20–29; Perkin, *The First Hundred Years*, 380, 382–83, 435–36.

38. Dorsett and McCarthy, *The Queen City*, 44–46, 111–17; Leonard and Noel, *Denver*, 69–70; for more on Elizabeth Byers, see Perkin, *The First Hundred Years*, 171–72.

39. See chapter 4, this volume, for a discussion of charity in Denver.

40. Larsen, *The Urban West*, 17.

41. "The Building Boom," 1 January 1880, pp. 1, 4; "This Beats All," 1 January 1880, p. 1; "The Land of Promise," 1 January 1880, p. 10; "Agriculture," 1 January 1880, p. 19; "The People's Pride," 1 January 1880, p. 22; "The Public Library," 14 November 1885, p. 1; "An Assured Success," 18 November 1885, p. 3, all in the *Rocky Mountain News*; Dorsett and McCarthy, *The Queen City*, 88–90; Brundage, *The Making of Western Labor Radicalism*, 18–19; Gunther Barth, "Metropolism and Urban Elites in the Far West," in *The Age of Industrialism in America: Essays in Social Structure and Cultural Values*, ed. Frederic Cople Jaher (New York: Free Press, 1968), 172–73, 177.

42. Dorsett and McCarthy, *The Queen City*, 87–90; Leonard and Noel, *Denver*, 29, 44; Byers, *Encyclopedia*, 1:41–42; Brundage, *The Making of Western Labor Radicalism*, 18–24; "Denver's Twelve Railroads," *Rocky Mountain News*, 7 February 1880, p. 4.

43. For statistics see Abbott, *Colorado*, 335–36; Leonard and Noel, *Denver*, 41–42, 44; Dorsett and McCarthy, *The Queen City*, 59–61; "This Beats All," 1 January 1880, p. 1; "The Land Of Promise," 1 January 1880, p. 10, both in the *Rocky Mountain News*; Byers, *Encyclopedia*, 1:84–90.

44. Byers, *Encyclopedia*, 41–42; Dorsett and McCarthy, *The Queen City*, 87–90; Leonard and Noel, *Denver*, 49; Brundage, *The Making of Western Labor Radicalism*, 18–24.

45. For quotations see Paul Porchea, *The Musical History of Colorado* (Denver: Charles Westley, Publisher, 1889), 69, 85; Dorsett and McCarthy, *The Queen City*, 49; Perkin, *The First Hundred Years*, 356–57; Robert H. Latta, "Denver in the 1880s," *Colorado Magazine* 18 (July 1941): 134; William B. Thom, "Stage Celebrities in Denver Theatres," *The Trail* 19 (April 1927): 8–13 and (May 1927): 8–14; "The Mikado," 21 December 1885, p. 2; "Twin Graces of Zeus: Music and the

Drama as they Reign in Denver," 11 January 1880, p. 5; "Music and Drama," 25 January 1880, p. 8, all in the *Rocky Mountain News*.

46. Porchea, *The Musical History of Colorado*, 82, 85, 116; "The Glenarm Club," in Fishback, Collection of Clippings; for program examples, see the *Rocky Mountain News*: 5 October 1884, p. 7; 16 October 1884, p. 2; 17 November 1886, p. 2; 2 November 1887, p. 8; 6 September 1888, p. 9; 17 October 1888, p. 8; 13 October 1889, p. 12; 28 October 1889, p. 5; 8 February 1891, p. 12.

47. "Among the Artists," 18 January 1880, p. 8; "Art and Artists," 1 February 1880, p. 5; "Fine Art in Denver," 10 June 1888, p. 3; "Denver Art League," 29 August 1892, p. 8; "Culture in Colorado," 22 June 1890, p. 12; "Public Libraries," 18 May 1890, p. 12; "Art Gallery for Denver," 24 January 1897, p. 4; and "Western Art Museum Swells Gallery Growth," souvenir edition, 22 April 1984, p. 94A, all in the *Rocky Mountain News*.

48. "Culture in Colorado," *Rocky Mountain News*, 22 June 1890, p. 12.

49. Dorsett and McCarthy, *The Queen City*, 61, 65, 68–74, 80; Larsen, *The Urban Frontier*, 41; Brundage, *The Making of Western Labor Radicalism*, 19.

50. Abbott, *Colorado*, 126–27; for Reed's nomination see, "Naming Winners," *Rocky Mountain News*, 7 October 1886, p. 2; for negative views, see the *Denver Republican*: "The Democratic Ticket," 7 October 1886, p. 4; editorial, 13 October 1886, p. 4; "Myron Reed In Indiana," 20 October 1886, p. 4.

51. Larsen, *The Urban West*, 19, 48, 51, 97–98; Barth, *Instant Cities*, 153, 155.

52. Dorsett and McCarthy, *The Queen City*, 80–82; Larsen, *The Urban West*, 17, and chapter 6, "The Application of Technology"; see the following articles in the *Rocky Mountain News*: "Colorado's Main Product [silver]," 4 September 1880, p. 4; "The Gospel of the West [irrigation]", 5 January 1885, p. 4; "Eastern Colorado," 1 July 1888, p. 12; "Colorado Railroads," 31 October 1886, p. 12; "Over 200,000 People," 18 May 1890, p. 4; "Solid Men Speaking: Capitalists and Merchants Do Not Deign to Consider the Future as Problematical," 2 January 1890, p. 5.

53. Henry Steele Commager, *The American Mind: An Interpretation of American Thought Since the 1880s* (New Haven: Yale University Press, 1950), 41.

54. For comments about the use of government force, see David L. Montgomery, *Worker's Control in America: Studies in the History of Work, Technology, and Labor Struggles* (Cambridge: Cambridge University Press, 1979), 158; Mark Twain quoted in Larzer Ziff, *The American 1890s: Life and Times of a Lost Generation* (New York: The Viking Press, 1966), 71.

55. Dorsett and McCarthy, *The Queen City*, 94–99; Leonard and Noel, *Denver*, 45–46, 103–4, 204; Wright, *The Politics of Populism*, 44, 54–62, 167, 250–55.

56. Wright, *The Politics of Populism*, 64, 72, 142, 194–98, 206, 225.

57. Ibid., 226–29, 265–66; Foster Rhea Dulles and Melvyn Dubofsky, *Labor in America: A History*, 4th ed. (Arlington Heights, IL: Harlan Davidson, Inc., 1984), 166–70; David Montgomery, *The Fall of the House of Labor: The Workplace, the State, and American Labor Activism, 1865–1925* (Cambridge: Cambridge University Press, 1987), 5. For information on these reformers, see Ray Ginger, *The Bending Cross: A*

Biography of Eugene Victor Debs (New Brunswick, NJ: Rutgers University Press, 1949); Arthur Lipow, *Authoritarian Socialism in America: Edward Bellamy and the Nationalist Movement* (Berkeley: University of California Press, 1982); Nick Salvatore, *Eugene V. Debs: Citizen and Socialist* (Urbana: University of Illinois Press, 1982); John L. Thomas, *Alternative America: Henry George, Edward Bellamy, Henry Demarest Lloyd and the Adversary Tradition* (Cambridge: Harvard University Press, 1983); "Edward Bellamy And Equality," 25 December 1897, p. 5; "Bellamy's Dream Of An Empire," 19 June 1898, p. 23, both in the *Rocky Mountain News.*

CHAPTER 2

1. See "Myron Reed's New Friend," in William P. Fishback, Collection of Clippings Relating to Reverend Myron W. Reed, n.d., Indiana State Library, Indianapolis, Indiana.

2. Fitz-Mac (James Mac Carthy), *Political Portraits* (Colorado Springs: The Gazette Printing Company, 1888), 94.

3. "Churches and Church Goers," 5 October 1885, p. 1; "May Leave Denver," 16 December 1891, p. 5, both in the *Rocky Mountain News*; Wilbur Fisk Stone, ed., *History of Colorado* (Chicago: S. J. Clarke Publishing Company, 1918), 1:656; on Reed's appearance and pulpit mannerisms, see George S. Cottman, comp., Scrapbook Collection, 9 vols., n.d., Indiana State Library, Indianapolis, Indiana, 6:61–65; Fitz-Mac, *Political Portraits*, 86–95.

4. Myron W. Reed, Myron W. Reed Papers (five letters), Chicago Historical Society, Chicago, Illinois.

5. "Memorial to M. W. Reed," *Indianapolis Journal*, 21 February 1899, p. 8.

6. Ibid.; Reed told this story on several occasions; for one example, see "And There Are Others," *Rocky Mountain News*, 12 April 1897, p. 5.

7. "Memorial to M. W. Reed," *Indianapolis Journal*, 21 February 1899, p. 8; "And There Are Others," 12 April 1897, p. 5, and "Love Rules The World," 20 April 1896, p. 8, both in the *Rocky Mountain News*; also see Myron W. Reed, Dictation of Rev. Myron Reed, Denver Arapahoe County, 1885, 1887, H. H. Bancroft Collection, University of California, Berkeley, California; Edgar A. Burton, "Biography of Myron W. Reed," chapter 2, and W. P. Fishback, "Memorial of Myron W. Reed," 1–2, in Myron W. Reed, Miscellaneous Items Concerning Myron W. Reed, 1883–1899, collected and compiled by Edgar A. Burton, Western History Department, Denver Public Library, Denver, Colorado (hereafter cited as Burton Files); Richard E. Leach, "Myron Winslow Reed," *The Trail* 19 (November 1926): 3.

8. Burton, "Biography of Myron W. Reed," chapter 2, and Fishback, "Memorial of Myron W. Reed," 1–2, Burton Files; "Slaves Of Government," *Rocky Mountain News*, 6 July 1896, p. 8.

9. Arthur Cushman McGiffert, Jr., *No Ivory Tower: The Story of The Chicago Theological Seminary* (Chicago: The Chicago Theological Seminary, 1965), 27–31, 40–

42; see "Ought To Be Done," *Rocky Mountain News*, 24 March 1890, p. 8, for Reed's reference to Haven; D. H. Meyer has a brief biographical sketch of Haven in *The Instructed Conscience: The Shaping of the American National Ethic* (Philadelphia: University of Pennsylvania Press, 1972), 150–51, and see also 116–17, 159–60.

10. McGiffert, *No Ivory Tower*, 27–31, 40–42.

11. Ibid., 30–31.

12. Myron W. Reed, Recollections of Myron W. Reed, Minister of Broadway Temple, 1895–1899, Manuscript, Gift of Mrs. W. J. Mummery, 1944, Western History Department, Denver Public Library, Denver, Colorado; "Myron Reed's New Friend," in Fishback, Collections of Clippings; Leach, "Myron W. Reed," 4–5; "Reminiscences of Reed," *Indianapolis News*, 9 March 1899, p. 2; *History of the Indianapolis Presbytery*, By a Committee of Presbytery and published by the Presbytery (Indianapolis: The Church at Work Publishing Company, circa 1887), Indiana State Library, Indianapolis, Indiana.

13. "Reminiscences of Reed," *Indianapolis News*, 9 March 1899, p. 2; Genevieve Weeks, *Oscar Carleton McCulloch, 1843–1891: Preacher and Practitioner of Applied Christianity* (Indianapolis: Indiana Historical Society, 1976), 83; Stephen C. Noland, comp., *Indianapolis Literary Club: Summarized Record, 1877–1934* (Indianapolis, 1934), 22–24, 26.

14. Weeks, *Oscar Carleton McCulloch*, 104–6, 112–14, 170–79, 189; George Willis Cooke, "The Institutional Church," *The New England Magazine* 14 (August 1896): 645–50; Frederick Doyle Kershner, Jr., "A Social and Cultural History of Indianapolis, 1860–1914" (Ph.D. diss., University of Wisconsin, 1950), 218–19, 281–82; Aaron Ignatius Abell, *The Urban Impact on American Protestantism, 1886–1900* (1943; reprint, Hamden and London: Archon, 1962), 152–53; Oscar McCulloch, *The Tribe of Ishmael: A Study in Social Degradation* (Indianapolis: Carlon & Hollenbeck, 1888); Guy T. Justis, *Twenty-Five Years of Social Welfare, 1917–1942* (Denver: The Denver Community Chest, 1943), 15–16.

15. Weeks, *Oscar Carleton McCulloch*, 49; see memorial sermon, "Tribute of a Friend," *Indianapolis News*, 16 December 1891, p. 5.

16. Myron W. Reed, *A Review of Matthew Arnold's "Literature and Dogma"* (Milwaukee: Des Forges, Lawrence & Company, Printers, 1874), 4–5; "Matthew Arnold's Work," *Rocky Mountain News*, 23 April 1888, p. 1.

17. Reed, *Matthew Arnold's "Literature and Dogma,"* 7, 10, 20; cf. "Cant and Platitudes," *Rocky Mountain News*, 7 May 1888, p. 1.

18. Reed, *Matthew Arnold's "Literature and Dogma,"* 9.

19. Ibid., 10, 13, 14 (quotation); for Reed's references to Bushnell's idea of reconciliation, see "God In Christ," 13 June 1887, p. 1, and "Figures Of The Truth," 14 May 1888, p. 1, both in the *Rocky Mountain News*; Winthrop S. Hudson, *Religion in America: An Historical Account of the Development of American Religious Life* (New York: Charles Scribner's Sons, 1965), 176–77, 270–72; William R. Hutchison, *The Modernist Impulse in American Protestantism* (1976; reprint, New York: Oxford Uni-

versity Press, 1982), 43–48; H. Shelton Smith, Robert T. Handy, and Lefferts A. Loetscher, *American Christianity: An Historical Interpretation with Representative Documents* (New York: Charles Scribner's Sons, 1963), 2:70–71, 260–61.

20. Reed, *Matthew Arnold's "Literature and Dogma,"*, 17–18.

21. Ibid., 20–23, 21 (for Arnold quotation).

22. See Martin E. Marty, *Righteous Empire: The Protestant Experience in America* (New York: The Dial Press, 1970), 88.

23. Reed, Miscellaneous Items, see "Biography of Myron W. Reed," Burton Files.

24. "Mr. Reed's Resignation," *Indianapolis News*, 3 March 1884, p. 4.; Clifton J. Phillips, *Indiana in Transition: The Emergence of an Industrial Commonwealth, 1880–1920* (Indianapolis: Indiana Historical Bureau and Indiana Historical Society, 1968), 440–41.

25. "Rev. M. W. Reed's Last Day," *Indianapolis Journal*, 31 March 1884, p. 7.

26. Ibid.

27. Ibid.; "Farewell Exercises," *Indianapolis News*, 31 March 1884, p. 3; also see Reed's expression of Jesus' ministry in "More Humanity In Man," *Rocky Mountain News*, 23 December 1895, p. 8.

28. "Religious Remarks," *Rocky Mountain News*, 6 April 1884, p. 3.

29. Ibid.

30. Denver as the Capital," *Denver Republican*, 4 October 1888, p. 4; Gunther Barth, "Metropolism and Urban Elites in the Far West," in *The Age of Industrialism in America: Essays in Social Structure and Cultural Values*, ed. Frederic Cople Jaher (New York: Free Press, 1968), 172–73; Lyle W. Dorsett and Michael McCarthy, *The Queen City: A History of Denver*, 2nd ed. (Boulder, CO: Pruett Publishing Company, 1986), 57, 60–72, 87–90; Lawrence H. Larsen, *The Urban West at the End of the Frontier* (Lawrence: The Regents Press of Kansas, 1978), 8, 17.

31. "Reed's Religion," *Rocky Mountain News*, 7 April 1884, p. 6.

32. Ibid.

33. Ibid.

34. See editorial, *Rocky Mountain News*, 7 April 1884, p. 4.

35. Hudson, *Religion in America*, 274.

36. Hutchison, *The Modernist Impulse*, 43–48, 79, 84–85; Hudson, *Religion in America*, 175–78; Smith et al., *American Christianity*, 270–75; for Bushnell on institutions, see George M. Fredrickson, *The Inner Civil War: Northern Intellectuals and the Crisis of the Union* (1965; reprint, New York: Harper & Row, Publishers, Harper Torchbooks, 1968), 25–26.

37. Hutchison, *The Modernist Impulse*, 82, 95–99; Hudson, *Religion in America*, 270; for a New Theology heresy trial, see "The New Theology," *Indianapolis News*, 2 October 1886, p. 1; "Shades of Andover," *Rocky Mountain News*, 29 December 1886, p. 1.

38. Hutchison, *The Modernist Impulse*, 82, 95–99; Marty, *Righteous Empire*, 194–95.

39. Winthrop S. Hudson, *The Great Tradition of the American Churches* (1953; re-

print, New York: Harper & Row, Publishers, Harper Torchbooks, 1963), 160, 161–62, 165, 171, 193–94; see Hutchison, *The Modernist Impulse*, 48, and Hudson, *Religion in America*, 294, for inclusion of David Swing among the "Princes of the Pulpit."

40. Sydney E. Ahlstrom, *A Religious History of the American People* (New Haven: Yale University Press, 1972, 738–40; see quotations in Hudson, *The Great Tradition of the American Churches*, 162–66.

41. Hudson, *The Great Tradition of the American Churches*, 186–93; Jean B. Quandt, "Religion and Social Thought: The Secularization of Postmillennialism," *American Quarterly* 25 (October 1973): 397–98; Jacob H. Dorn, "The Social Gospel and Socialism: A Comparison of the Thought of Francis Greenwood Peabody, Washington Gladden, and Walter Rauschenbusch," *Church History* 62 (March 1993): 87–90.

42. Hutchison, *The Modernist Impulse*, 48–68.

43. Ibid., 60–64, 74; Hudson, *Religion in America*, 279.

44. "Going Around Logs," *Rocky Mountain News*, 20 October 1890, p. 7. Swing said that Reed had produced more original thought and expression than any other American preacher; see "He Was Loved Here," *Indianapolis Journal*, 31 January 1899, p. 8, and Hutchison, *The Modernist Impulse*, 49, 68. Swing's move to an independent church could have inspired Reed to establish the Broadway Temple.

45. "Religious Remarks," *Rocky Mountain News*, 6 April 1884, p. 3.

46. Rose Lee Smith, Scrapbook, 1890–1892 Manuscript, Western History Department, Denver Public Library, Denver, Colorado; "Religious Remarks," 6 April 1884, p. 3, and "Minds of Breadth," 13 October 1890, p. 2, both in the *Rocky Mountain News*.

47. "A Modern Pilgrim," 1 February 1892, p. 8; "A Remarkable Book," 8 October 1888, p. 1; "Congregational Creed," 26 November 1888, p. 1, all in the *Rocky Mountain News*.

48. "A Modern Pilgrim," *Rocky Mountain News*, 1 February 1892, p. 8.

49. Ibid.

50. Ibid.

51. Ibid.; "Myron Reed Is Dead," *Indianapolis News*, 30 January 1899, p. 1.

52. Harris Elwood Starr, "Beecher, Henry Ward (June 24, 1813 – Mar. 8, 1887)," in *Dictionary of American Biography*, rev. ed., ed. Allen Johnson (New York: Charles Scribner's Sons, 1964): 129–35; note criticisms of Chicago ministers who refused expressions of sympathy for Beecher, 9 March 1884, p. 4; 13 March 1887, p. 4; 20 March 1887, p. 4, all in the *Rocky Mountain News*.

53. For Beecher, see "A Noble Life," *Rocky Mountain News*, 14 March 1887, p. 5, and "Eulogizing Rev. Mr. Beecher," *Denver Republican*, 14 March 1887, p. 5; for the plain explanation see "Thou Art the Man," *Rocky Mountain News*, 13 April 1885, p. 3; Hudson, *Great Tradition*, 173; Marty, *Righteous Empire*, 181.

54. Rev. Myron Reed, Clippings File, Colorado Historical Society, Denver, Colorado; Burton Files; Fishback, Collection of Clippings; Leach, "Myron Winslow Reed," *The Trail*, 3–7; "Death Of Myron W. Reed," *Indianapolis Journal*, 31 January

1899, p. 8; "Myron Reed Is Dead," 30 January 1899, p. 1, and "Reminiscences of Reed," 9 March 1899, p. 2, both in the *Indianapolis News*; editorial, *Times*, 14 March 1887, p. 2; "Will Not Succeed Beecher," *Republican*, 3 September 1887, p. 6; the *News*'s introductions to Reed's sermons briefly describe the audiences; for a New York press endorsement of Reed, see "Myron W. Reed," 18 January 1888, p. 4; editorial, 19 December 1887, p. 4, both in the *Rocky Mountain News*.

55. "Pungent Preachers," 3 July 1887, p. 2; "As Others See Us," 5 May 1889, p. 18; see 15 May 1887 editorial, p. 12, all in the *Rocky Mountain News*; for the 1881 quotation, see "As A Pulpit Orator," *Indianapolis Journal*, 31 January 1899, p. 8; "Myron W. Reed, Great Preacher," *Indianapolis Star*, 26 February 1905, p. 15.

56. "A Portrait of Myron Reed," *(Aspen) Rocky Mountain Sun*, 23 April 1887, p. 2.

57. "As Others See Us," *Rocky Mountain News*, 5 May 1889, p. 18.

58. Reed's friend, the Reverand Victor Southworth, compiled Reed's epigrams for publication, but there is no evidence they were ever actually published; the *Rocky Mountain News* printed Southworth's collection in February and March of 1899; also see Ferenc M. Szasz, "Myron Reed: Colorado Epigrammatist," *Southwestern American Literature* 13 (Fall 1987): 26–40, and Ferenc Morton Szasz, *The Protestant Clergy in the Great Plains and Mountain West, 1865–1915* (Albuquerque: University of New Mexico Press, 1988), 197; Myron W. Reed, Clippings File, Western History Department, Denver Public Library, Denver, Colorado; Reed, Recollections; Fishback, Collection of Clippings; "Sermon By Myron Reed," *Indianapolis News*, 4 June 1898, p. 9.

59. "Myron Reed Is Dead," *Indianapolis News*, 30 January 1899, p. 1; for a favorable comparison with Twain, see Reed, Clippings File, Colorado Historical Society.

60. Myron W. Reed, *Evolution of the Tramp*, series of sermons preached in January and February 1886, published by the *Rocky Mountain News*, 1886; "Evolution of the Tramp," 15 January 1905, sec. 2, p. 8, 22 January 1905, sec. 2, p. 8, 29 January 1905, sec. 2, p. 9, 5 February 1905, sec. 5, p. 3, all in the *Denver Post*; "Barnum The Showman," 19 April 1891, p. 12, "Sara Bernhardt," 26 April 1891, p. 12, "The World's Fair," 29 March 1891, p. 12, "The War Cloud, "5 April 1891, p. 12, all in the *Denver Republican*; Myron Reed, "Night and Sleep and Rest," *Cosmopolitan*, 22 (February 1897): 437–44.

61. "Gould And His Gold," 5 December 1892; "The Law Of Mutual Aid (Death of Pullman)," 25 October 1897, p. 5; "John Brown," 6 December 1886, p. 1; "All Honor Bobby Burns," 20 July 1896, p. 8; for Burns and God, see "Conception Of God," 14 April 1890, p. 8, and "A Mistake about It," 7 July 1890, p. 8; "Kingsley Was King," 12 December 1891, p. 8; "Minnie Freeman," 23 January 1888, p. 1; other examples are "Victor Hugo," 25 May 1885, p. 8; "Lessons Of Hugo's Life," 27 April 1896, p. 8; "Henry George And Labor," 1 November 1897, p. 2; "Ingersoll Has A God," 28 September 1896, p. 5, all in the *Rocky Mountain News*.

62. Hudson, *Great Tradition*, 161; Hutchison, *The Modernist Impulse*, 83.

63. "God Guideth," *Rocky Mountain News*, 18 October 1886, p. 1.

64. "God In Christ," *Rocky Mountain News*, 13 June 1887, p. 1.

65. "Conception Of God," *Rocky Mountain News*, 14 April 1890, p. 8.

66. "Modern Times," *Rocky Mountain News*, 26 September 1887, p. 1.

67. "Rev. Myron W. Reed," *Rocky Mountain News*, 18 February 1889, p. 2; for servanthood, see "Rev. M. W. Reed's Last Day," *Indianapolis Journal*, 31 March 1884, p. 7; for Biblical references see Matthew 26:27; Mark 10:43–44; Luke 22:26–27; John 13:16.

68. Thomas Bender, *Community and Social Change in America* (1978; reprint, Baltimore: The Johns Hopkins University Press, 1982), 8, 10–11, 17–18, 28, 33–34.

69. "One Doctrine For All," *Rocky Mountain News*, 16 December 1895, p. 4.

70. "Covenant Of The People," 17 September 1888, p. 1; "Force Of Reason," 1 April 1889, p. 9; "Helping Humanity," 21 December 1885, p. 7; for "What ought to be will be, " see, "God Guideth," 18 October 1886, p. 1, and "No Backward Steps," 24 October 1887, p. 6, all in the *Rocky Mountain News*.

71. "History of the First Congregational Church of Denver, Colorado," comp. Mrs. Alice W. Gardner, unpublished manuscript, 1931, First Plymouth Congregational Church, Denver, Colorado, 16–17.

72. "Modern Times," 26 September 1887, p. 1; "No Backward Steps," 24 October 1887, p. 6; "Conception Of God," 14 April 1890, p. 8; "Loyalty To Leaders," 8 March 1886, p. 3; "Human Side Of Jesus," 9 December 1895, p. 8; "One Doctrine For All," 16 December 1895, p. 4; "More Humanity In Man," 23 December 1895, p. 8; "America's Mission," 2 May 1892, p. 8, all in the *Rocky Mountain News*.

73. For a brief biographical sketch of R. W. Woodbury, see Dorsett and McCarthy, *The Queen City*, 62; "Good Will," *Rocky Mountain News*, 25 October 1887, p. 8

74. "Good Will," *Rocky Mountain News*, 25 October 1887, p. 8.

CHAPTER 3

1. Lyle W. Dorsett and Michael McCarthy, *The Queen City: A History of Denver*, 2nd ed. (Boulder, CO: Pruett Publishing Company, 1986), 65–67, 80.

2. Carl Abbott et al., *Colorado: A History of the Centennial State*, rev. ed. (Boulder: Colorado Associated University Press, 1982), 126–27; Fitz-Mac (James Mac Carthy), *Political Portraits* (Colorado Springs: The Gazette Printing Company, 1888), 29; on Reed's disputed result, see note 40, this chapter; for Patterson's campaign rhetoric and the *News's* endorsement, see "Dedicating the Wigwam: Powerful Presentation of the Issues of the Campaign," 21 August 1888, p. 2, and "The Ticket of the People," 13 September 1888, p. 10, all in the *Rocky Mountain News*.

3. Thomas M. Patterson, "Address of Hon. Thos. M. Patterson at the Opening of the Manufacturers' Exposition at Denver, Colorado, October 7, 1886" (Denver: Executive Committee, The Times Printing Works, 1886), 14–16, located at Western History Department, Denver Public Library, Denver, Colorado; "Inaugurated," *Rocky Mountain News*, 8 October 1886, p. 1; "The Exposition," *Denver Republican*, 7 October 1886, p. 4; "The Exposition," *Denver Times*, 7 October 1886, p. 2.

4. Patterson, "Address," 15.

5. Ibid., 14–16.

6. Myron W. Reed, Miscellaneous Items Concerning Myron W. Reed, 1883–1899, collected and compiled by Edgar A. Burton, Western History Department, Denver Public Library, Denver, Colorado; for allegations against Blaine, see John A. Garraty, *The New Commonwealth, 1877–1890* (New York: Harper & Row, Publishers, Harper Torchbooks, 1968), 241, 285–86.

7. "Suspend Sentence," *Rocky Mountain News,* 22 June 1885, p. 8; for scriptural reference, see Genesis 18:25.

8. "Suspend Sentence," *Rocky Mountain News,* 22 June 1885, p. 8; for scriptural reference, see Matthew 20:26.

9. "The Church In Politics," *Rocky Mountain News,* 17 November 1885, p. 4.

10. Ibid.

11. "The People's Peril," *Rocky Mountain News,* 2 November 1885, p. 3.

12. Ibid.

13. Ibid.

14. Thomas M. Patterson, Family Papers, 1865–1925, Western Historical Collections, University of Colorado Libraries, Boulder, Colorado.

15. Mary Fonda Adams, "Thomas M. Patterson: Some Aspects of His Political Career," (M.A. thesis, University of Colorado, 1933), 6; Ellis Meredith, "Three Distinguished Figures of the Early *Rocky Mountain News,*" *Colorado Magazine* 27 (January 1950): 43; Fitz-Mac, *Political Portraits,* 20–29; Robert L. Perkin, *The First Hundred Years: An Informal History of Denver and the Rocky Mountain News* (Garden City, NY: Doubleday and Company, 1959), 385–90; Sybil Downing and Robert E. Smith, *Tom Patterson: Crusader for Change* (Niwot: University Press of Colorado, 1995), x, 65, 78–79, 82–83, 94, 99–100, 187–90.

16. "Fully Organized," 6 October 1886, p. 2, and "Greystone Receives," 5 October 1886, p. 3, both in the *Rocky Mountain News.*

17. "Fully Organized," *Rocky Mountain News,* 6 October 1886, p. 2.

18. Ibid.; "The Democratic Convention," 6 October 1886, p. 4; "What It Means," 4 October 1886, p. 4; "Choose Good Men," 6 September 1886, p. 4, all in the *Rocky Mountain News*; editorial, *Denver Times,* 14 October 1886, p. 2; "The Democratic Ticket," 7 October 1886, p. 4; editorial, 22 October 1886, p. 4; "Plain Words To Democrats," 29 October 1886, p. 4; editorial, 30 October 1886, p. 4, all in the *Denver Republican.*

19. "Naming Winners," *Rocky Mountain News,* 7 October 1886, p. 2.

20. Ibid., p. 6; Robert Gordon Dill, *The Political Campaigns of Colorado* (Denver: John Dove, Book and Job Printer, 1895), 108–13; "The Democratic Ticket," *Rocky Mountain News,* 7 October 1886, p. 4; "Reminiscences of Reed," *Indianapolis News,* 9 March 1899, p. 2; George S. Cottman, comp., *Indiana Scrapbook Collection,* Indiana State Library, Indianapolis, Indiana, 6:61–65; on Symes, see Fitz-Mac, *Political Portraits,* 11–19.

21. "Naming Winners," *Rocky Mountain News*, 7 October 1886, p. 6; James Edward Wright, *The Politics of Populism: Dissent in Colorado* (New Haven: Yale University Press, 1974), 64; on the tariff issue, see 8 October 1886, p. 4; 13 October 1886, p. 4, 18 October 1886, p. 4, in the *Denver Republican*.

22. "Naming Winners," 7 October 1886, p. 6; for Charleston, see "City By The Sea," 3 September 1886, p. 1, and "Cheered By Charity," 7 September 1886, p. 1; all in the *Rocky Mountain News*; for comments from Indiana, see "A Good Democrat," 11 October 1886, p. 1, and editorials, 9 October 1886, p. 4, and 11 October 1886, p. 2, all in the *Indianapolis News*; for anecdote, see editorials: 7 October 1886, p. 4; 8 October 1886, p. 4; 13 October 1886, p. 4; and "Myron Reed In Indiana," 20 October 1886, p. 4, all in the *Denver Republican*.

23. "The Church In Politics," *Rocky Mountain News*, 17 November 1885, p. 8; for the quotation, see the *Denver Times* editorial of 16 October 1886, p. 2.

24. "Preacher On Politics," 4 October 1886, p. 6; "What It Means," 4 October 1886, p. 4; "A Sound Sermon," 5 October 1886, p. 4; "Earnest Independents," 3 September 1886, p. 2, all in the *Rocky Mountain News*; editorial, *Denver Republican*, 6 October 1886, p. 4; for Indianapolis criticism of political ministers, see Frederick Doyle Kershner, Jr., "A Social and Cultural History of Indianapolis, 1860–1914," (Ph.D. diss., University of Wisconsin, 1950), 208.

25. "The Preacher In Politics," *Denver Times*, 9 October 1886, p. 2.

26. "The Democratic Ticket," 7 October 1886, p. 4; editorials, 8 October 1886, p. 4; 13 October 1886, p. 4, all in the *Denver Republican*.

27. See editorials, 8 October 1886, p. 4; "In Politics," 9 October 1886, p. 4; 13 October 1886, p. 4, all in the *Denver Republican*.

28. "The Democratic Ticket," 7 October 1886; "In Politics," 9 October 1886, p. 4; "Myron Reed In Indiana," 20 October 1886, p. 4; "Reed's Record," 27 October 1886, p. 4, all in the *Denver Republican*; for Indianapolis, see 11 October 1886, p. 2, and 22 October 1886, p. 2, both in the *Indianapolis News*.

29. "Politics And Pulpit," *Rocky Mountain News*, 11 October 1886, p. 1; editorial, *Denver Times*, 11 October 1886, p. 2; "In Politics," 11 October 1886, p. 4; editorial, 16 October 1886, p. 4; "Mr. Reed's Boom For Reed," 17 October 1886, p. 13, all in the *Denver Republican*; note that a *Republican* editorial, "Christian Hypochondriacs," appeared beside the report of Reed's sermon and emphasized that the church always had been strongest when it never compromised with the state.

30. "Politics and Pulpit," *Rocky Mountain News*, 11 October 1886, p. 1; note that quotations are from the *News* version.

31. Ibid.; "The Preacher In Politics," *Rocky Mountain News*, 11 October 1886, p. 4; "Myron Reed In Indiana, *Denver Republican*, 20 October 1886, p. 4.

32. George Brown Tindall and David E. Shi, *America: A Narrative History*, brief 3rd ed. (New York: W. W. Norton & Company, 1993), 2:A30.

33. "Political," *Denver Times*, 15 October 1886, p. 1; "The Democratic Ticket," *Denver Republican*, 7 October 1886, p. 4.

34. "Political," *Denver Times*, 15 October 1886, p. 1; "The Democratic Ticket," *Denver Republican*, 7 October 1886, p. 4.

35. "History of the First Congregational Church of Denver, Colorado," comp. Mrs. Alice W. Gardner, unpublished manuscript, First Plymouth Congregational Church, Denver, Colorado, 1931, 14, 14b; Irene M. Titus, *A Short History of First Plymouth Congregational Church* (Englewood, CO: First Plymouth Congregational Church, n.d.), 6.

36. Downing and Smith, *Tom Patterson*, 191; "Knights of Labor Endorse," 11 October 1886, pp. 1, 8; "Roused For Reed: Workingmen of Indiana Indorse the People's Candidate for Congress," 26 October 1886, p. 3, both in the *Rocky Mountain News*; "To Colorado Wage-Workers," 23 October 1886, p. 4; "To Workingmen," 27 October 1886, p. 4; "Reed And Grant," 23 October 1886, p. 4; "An Insult To The Clergy," 21 October 1886, p. 4; editorials and "To Colored Voters, 30 October 1886, p. 4, all in the *Denver Republican*; Wright, *The Politics of Populism*, 54–55, 57; for a brief sketch of Hill, see Fitz-Mac, *Political Portraits*, 61–78; for another Patterson sarcasm directed at Hill, see "A Liar And Traitor To His Party," *Rocky Mountain News*, 26 October 1888, p. 4.

37. "Reed And Grant," 23 October 1886, p. 4; see editorial, 24 October 1886, p. 12, both in the *Denver Republican*; see "The Boys In Blue," 26 May 1884, p. 6, and "Reed On Grant," 26 October 1886, p. 9, both in the *Rocky Mountain News*. In response to the *Denver Republican*, Reed included favorable remarks about Grant in a campaign speech at Golden; see "Reed And Right," 26 October 1886, p. 1, in the *Rocky Mountain News*. See also Wright, *The Politics of Populism*, 60; William S. McFeely, *Grant: A Biography* (New York: W. W. Norton & Company, 1981), 489–93.

38. "Parson Reed In Politics: Scathing Review of His Position by a Member of His Congregation," *Denver Republican*, 24 October 1886, p. 1; "With A Ring In His Nose," 25 October 1886, p. 4; for railroads, see "Telling Truths," 30 October 1886, p. 3; "Pooled Issues," 26 June 1887, p. 3, all in the *Rocky Mountain News*.

39. "Frank Goudy At Boulder," *Denver Republican*, 27 October 1886, p. 1; for a brief article on Goudy, see Fitz-Mac, *Political Portraits*, 79–85.

40. Dill, *Political Campaigns*, 102, 113. "The Day In Colorado," 3 November 1886, p. 4; the roosters adorned this page, "Right For Reed" 4 November 1886, p. 1; "Reed And Symes," 4 November 1886, p. 4; "Victory," 4 November 1886, p. 8; "Still For Reed," 5 November 1886, p. 1; "Rough On Symes," 7 November 1886, p. 1; "Still In Front," 8 November 1886, p. 1; "Still In Sight," 9 November 1886, p. 1; "Hold For The Right," 10 November 1886, p. 1; "That Voice Wins [Symes]," 11 November 1886, p. 1; "Preacher In Politics," 16 November 1886, p. 1, all in the *Rocky Mountain News*; "Symes Is Safe," *Denver Republican*, 5 November 1886, p. 1; "Very Close," *Denver Times*, 3 November 1886, p. 4; see editorial that declared Reed "would be . . . much out of his element," *Indianapolis News*, 3 November 1886, p. 2; "The Soul Before the Body," *Denver Republican*, 8 November 1886, p. 2; "Songs And Singing," *Rocky Mountain News*, 8 November 1886, p. 1.

41. "Preacher In Politics," *Rocky Mountain News*, 16 November 1886, p. 1.

42. Henry George, *Progress and Poverty: An Increase into the Cause of Industrial Depressions and of Increase of Want with Increase of Wealth . . . the Remedy* (1879; reprint, New York: Robert Schalkenbach Foundation, 1958), 552; John L. Thomas, *Alternative America: Henry George, Edward Bellamy, Henry Demarest Lloyd and the Adversary Tradition* (Cambridge: Harvard University Press, 1983), 220–23; for references to George, see "The Boys In Blue," 26 May 1884, p. 6; "Words," 13 February 1888, p. 1, in which Reed said that George's questions had never been answered; "Henry George And The Land," 1 November 1897, p. 2, all in the *Rocky Mountain News*; George visited Denver in 1890, see "The Glenarm Club," 25 January 1890, p. 9; "Mr. George's Lecture," 28 January 1890, p. 3, both in the *Denver Times*.

43. "Dedicating The Wigwam," 21 August 1888, p. 2; "Democrats In Session," 12 September 1888, pp. 1–2; "The Ticket Of The People," 13 September 1888, p. 10; see Reed's speech, "The Graystone Club," 8 June 1888, p. 6, all in the *Rocky Mountain News*. Wright, *The Politics of Populism*, 68–72; for Cleveland and the tariff, see Garraty, *The New Commonwealth*, 245–46.

44. "Myron Reed At Glenwood," 20 October 1888, p. 1; "Brass Tags In Colorado," 31 October 1888, p. 4; also see ""Myron Reed At Gilman," 17 October 1888, p. 1; "Brass Tag Labor," 26 October 1888, p. 4; "Brass Tag Labor," 31 October 1888, p. 3; for examples of campaign speeches, see 3 October 1888, p. 5; 9 October 1888, p. 5; 5 November 1888, p. 5, all in the *Rocky Mountain News*; Wright, *The Politics of Populism*, 71, 83–84.

45. Wright, *The Politics of Populism*, 51, 55, 62, 65, 72–74; Dill, *Political Campaigns of Colorado*, 132.

46. Reed spoke at the state Democratic convention, 26 September 1890, p. 2, platform on p. 4; "Be Confident," 27 September 1890, p. 4, both in the *Rocky Mountain News*. Dill, *Political Campaigns of Colorado*, 149. "Parson Reed In Politics," *Denver Republican*, 24 October 1886, p. 1. In a letter to W. P. Fishback, 20 September 1886, Reed commented that he had a "slim chance . . . of being governor of Colorado"; see "Myron Reed's Dog 'John': His Life And Death," in Myron W. Reed, Recollections of Myron W. Reed, Minister of Broadway Temple, 1895–1899 Manuscript, Western History Department, Denver Public Library.

47. Wright, *The Politics of Populism*, 103, 109, 110, 114, 117–19; Dill, *Political Campaigns of Colorado*, 135–60; for De La Matyr and the Greenback–Labor party, see "The People's Party," 18 September 1884, p. 6; "The Union Labor Club," 30 July 1888, p. 8; "The Union Labor Club," 8 August 1888, p. 8; "The 'Independents'," 22 August 1890, p. 4; "A Ticket Named," 22 August 1890, p. 5; all in the *Rocky Mountain News*; for a brief history of Colorado third parties, see Leah M. Bird, "Minor Political Parties in Colorado" *Colorado Magazine* 19 (November 1942): 208–13.

48. Wright, *The Politics of Populism*, 44, 54–62, 85, 102, 125, 251–53.

49. Ibid., 136–37, 250–55; Lynn Marie Olson, "The Essence of Colorado Populism: An Analysis of the Populists and the Issues in 1892," (M.A. thesis, University of Northern Colorado, 1971), vi–vii, 45–51, 69; for information on Herbert

George, see Fitz-Mac, "Herbert George: Western Era Maker," *The Great Divide*, January 1893, 224.

50. Wright, *The Politics of Populism*, 138–53; Leon W. Fuller, "Governor Waite and His Silver Panacea," *Colorado Magazine* 10 (March 1933): 41–47; Leon W. Fuller, "Colorado's Revolt Against Capitalism," *Mississippi Valley Historical Review* 21 (December 1934): 345–47, 349, 359; Jane Werner, "The Press and the Populists," *Colorado Magazine* 47 (Winter 1970): 46–47; G. Michael McCarthy, "Colorado's Populist Leadership," *Colorado Magazine* 48 (Winter 1971): 31, 38–39; for Patterson's role, see Downing and Smith, *Tom Patterson*, 65–80; Adams, "Thomas Patterson, Some Aspects of His Political Career," 32–34, 69–80. Olson also emphasized anti-monopolism; see "The Essence of Colorado Populism," vii.

51. Wright, *The Politics of Populism*, 151–52; Gene Clanton, *Populism: The Humane Preference in America, 1890–1900* (Boston: Twayne Publishers, 1991), xiii, 80–85; Lawrence Goodwyn, *The Populist Moment: A Short History of the Agrarian Revolt in America* (New York: Oxford University Press, 1978), xxi; Robert C. McMath, Jr., *American Populism: A Social History, 1877–1898* (New York: Hill and Wang, 1993), 19–49; Norman Pollack, *The Populist Response to Industrial America: Midwestern Populist Thought* (Cambridge: Harvard University Press, 1962), 13–24; see "Plea For Fair Play," *Rocky Mountain News*, 16 October 1893, p. 5; for reference to the church as the site of the first suffrage meeting, see Ellis Meredith's letter in the *Denver Post*, 5 February 1899, p. 11.

52. Dill, *Political Campaigns of Colorado*, 161–206; "Labor Legislation," 16 August 1892, p. 8; "Denver In Congress," 27 August 1892, p. 8; "Reed For Congress," 30 August 1892, p. 2; "Will Wire Myron," 1 September 1892, p. 3; "Myron W. Reed," 2 September 1892, p. 4; "Myron Reed Named," 2 September 1892, p. 5; "Mr. Reed For Congress," 15 September 1892, p. 4; "Man Of The People," 15 September 1892, p. 5; "Myron W. Reed," 18 September 1892, p. 12; "Press Opinion: The Rev. Myron W. Reed," 24 September 1892, p. 4; "Mr. Reed's Candidacy," 2 October 1892, p. 12, all in the *Rocky Mountain News*. For the fusion effort, see Downing and Smith, *Tom Patterson*, 65–80.

53. "He Can't Run," 5 October 1892, p. 1; "Mr. Reed Declines," 5 October 1892, p. 4, both in the *Rocky Mountain News*; on the new church, see "History of the First Congregational Church of Denver," 15–17; Titus, "A Short History of First Plymouth Congregational Church," 5.

54. John Robert Morris, "Davis Hanson Waite: The Ideology of a Western Populist" (Ph.D. diss., University of Colorado, 1965), 58, 105–8; Wright, *The Politics of Populism*, 170; Downing and Smith, *Tom Patterson*, 81–82; "No Time To Smile," *Rocky Mountain News*, 24 July 1893, p. 8.

55. "Myron W. Reed Resigns," 31 August 1893, p. 5; for views that punishment should fit the crime, see Reed's "Known By Numbers: Fate of the Prisoner in the State Penitentiary," 30 October 1893, p. 8; see the report of J. S. Appel, president of the State Board of Pardons, "Reform Needed: The Indeterminate Sentence Advocated," 16 December 1894, p. 16, all in the *Rocky Mountain News*; Myron W. Reed,

Clippings File, Western History Department, Denver Public Library, Denver, Colorado; Morris, "Davis Hanson Waite," 58, 216.

56. Wright, *The Politics of Populism*, 161, 170–80, 194; on Waite, see Dill, *Political Campaigns of Colorado*, 207–57.

57. "Silver The Theme," *Rocky Mountain News*, 11 July 1893, p. 1; Peter J. Frederick, *Knights of the Golden Rule: The Intellectual as Christian Social Reformer in the 1890s* (Lexington: The University of Kentucky Press, 1976), 84, 101.

58. "In Darkness," 30 June 1893, p. 1; "Tuesday's Meeting," 9 July 1893, p. 1; "Secret Of Strength," 17 July 1893, p. 8; "Object Of Tuesday's Meeting," 9 July 1893, p. 12; "To-Day's Convention," 11 July 1893, p. 1; "Silver The Theme," 11 July 1893, p. 3, all in the *Rocky Mountain News*. The *News* promised "full and exhaustive reports" of the contest between the silverites and the goldbugs ("Congress: The Most Absorbing and Important Session of the National Congress Since the War," 17 August 1893, p. 3). See also Dill, *Political Campaigns of Colorado*, 215; for political parties, see "On This Date," *Denver Post*, 2 November 1993, p. 8B.

59. "Myron Will Accept," 16 June 1894, p. 2; "The Nominations," 6 September 1894, p. 2; "Myron Reed Talks: He Did Not Get Nicholson's Telegram Until Too Late," 8 September 1894, p. 2; note Reed's efforts for the Populists, see "Wyoming And Montana," 19 September 1894, p. 8; "Populist Meetings," 20 October 1894, p. 12; for Patterson's opposition to Waite, see "Good Bye, Waite," 1 September 1894, p. 1; "The Future," 1 September 1984, p. 12; "Waiteism," 6 September 1894, p. 4, all in the *Rocky Mountain News*; Wright, *The Politics of Populism*, 64, 72, 142, 194–98, 206, 225.

60. "Carnegie's Purpose," *Rocky Mountain News*, 26 February 1894, p. 2; for scripture reference, see 4 Matthew.

61. "Politics Of Today," 24 September 1894, p. 1; "Myron W. Reed Resigns," 7 June 1894, p. 1, both in the *Rocky Mountain News*.

62. Henry O. Morris, *Waiting for the Signal: A Novel* (Chicago: The Schulte Publishing Company, 1897); see Reed's review in the *Rocky Mountain News*, 18 September 1898, p. 22.

63. "One More Conference," 12 March 1897, p. 1; "Led Captive Into An Enemy's Camp," 20 March 1897, p. 1; "Why He Is A Candidate," 22 March 1897, p. 5; "Populists Betrayed By Their Allies," 6 April 1897, p. 1, all in the *Rocky Mountain News*; King, *The History of the Government of Denver*, 124–27, 187–90.

64. Bird, "Minor Political Parties in Colorado," 208–13.

CHAPTER 4

1. "In A Practical Way," *Rocky Mountain News*, 25 November 1889, p. 6.

2. George M. Fredrickson, *The Inner Civil War: Northern Intellectuals and the Crisis of the Union* (1965; reprint, New York: Harper & Row, Publishers, Harper Torchbooks, 1968), 213; see also "The Pauper Question," *Rocky Mountain News*, 11 November 1889, p. 4.

3. For Smiley quotation, see Lyle W. Dorsett and Michael McCarthy, *The Queen City: A History of Denver*, 2nd ed. (Boulder, CO: Pruett Publishing Company, 1986), 44.

4. Ibid., 44–46, 111–17; Harold M. Parker, Jr., comp., "Religion in Colorado: A Bibliography," in *Faith on the Frontier: Religion in Colorado Before 1876*, ed. Louisa Ward Arps (Boulder, CO: Weekley Enterprises, Inc., 1976), 1–2, 61–62; Stephen J. Leonard and Thomas J. Noel, *Denver: Mining Camp to Metropolis* (Niwot: University Press of Colorado, 1990), 68–70; Robert L. Perkin, *The First Hundred Years: An Informal History of Denver and the Rocky Mountain News* (Garden City, NY: Doubleday and Company, 1959), 171–72.

5. Dorsett and McCarthy, *The Queen City*, 50, 114–17; for her work among the poor, see Rachel Wild Peterson, *The Long-Lost Rachel Wild, or Seeking Diamonds in the Rough* (Denver: Reed Publishing Company, 1906); for Reed at Uzzell's People Tabernacle, see "Church And Charity," 9 February 1886, p. 9; for Christmas dinner, see "Youthful Banqueters," 28 December 1888, p. 2, both in the *Rocky Mountain News*.

6. Genevieve C. Weeks, *Oscar Carleton McCulloch, 1843–1891: Preacher and Practitioner of Applied Christianity* (Indianapolis: Indiana Historical Society, 1976), 88, 184–85.

7. Ibid., 187.

8. Ibid., 188–89; for giving the money away, see "Death Of Myron W. Reed," *Indianapolis Journal*, 31 January 1899, p. 8. Reed served on the COS central committee; see "The Charity Organization," *Indianapolis News*, 15 November 1883, p. 1.

9. "Denver's Demands," *Rocky Mountain News*, 24 November 1884, p. 8.

10. "Charity's Cause," 26 November 1884, p. 5; "Problems of Poverty," 25 November 1884, p. 8, both in the *Rocky Mountain News*.

11. "Problems of Poverty," *Rocky Mountain News*, 25 November 1884, p. 8.

12. "Combined Charities," 1 December 1884, p. 8; for results of this first combined canvas, see "Gratifying Generosity," 25 December 1884, p. 2; note the second annual meeting, "Charity's Cause," 7 December 1885, p. 8, all in the *Rocky Mountain News*.

13. For a description of boom-and-bust cycles in Denver, see David Thomas Brundage, "The Making of Working-Class Radicalism in the Mountain West: Denver, Colorado, 1880–1903" (Ph.D. diss., University of California, Los Angeles, 1982), 18–21.

14. "World's Work," 29 June 1885, p. 3; "Poverty And Prosperity," 3 August 1885, p. 6, both in the *Rocky Mountain News*; for the story of Joseph, see Genesis 37, 38–47.

15. "Home Helpfulness," 28 September 1885, p. 3; note similar comment about enough foreigners in "Charity's Beginning," 16 January 1888, p. 1, both in the *Rocky Mountain News*.

16. "Seeking To Save," 19 October 1885, p. 3; "Sacrificing Self," 23 November 1885, p. 3; for another comment on the need of a friend, see "Exercise By Proxy," 3 October 1887, p. 1, all in the *Rocky Mountain News*.

17. For references to attendance at National Conferences on Charity, see "A Wise World," 23 August 1886, p. 1; "Reed Has Returned," 2 June 1890, p. 5; for Reed as president of the National Conference, see "May Leave Denver," 16 December 1891, p. 5; "Public Benefaction," 23 June 1892, p. 4; "Aids In Almsgiving," 24 June 1892, pp. 5–6, all in the *Rocky Mountain News*.

18. "The Poor," 20 February 1888, p. 1; "The Associated Charities," 10 January 1886, p. 10; "Churning For Charity," 27 April 1886, p. 8, all in the *Rocky Mountain News*.

19. "The Poor," 20 February 1888, p. 1; "The Associated Charities," 10 January 1886, p. 10, both in the *Rocky Mountain News*.

20. Fredrickson, *The Inner Civil War*, 213–15; Roy Lubove, *The Professional Altruist: The Emergence of Social Work as a Career, 1880–1930* (1965; reprint, Cambridge: Harvard University Press, 1971), 1–21; Bernard Rosen, "Social Welfare in the History of Denver" (Ph.D. diss., University of Colorado, 1976), 213–14, 218; for criticism of the "friendly visitor," see Walter I. Trattner, *From Poor Law to Welfare State: A History of Social Welfare in America*, 3rd ed. (New York: Free Press, 1984), 97–98; "The Ante-Room Of Hell," *Rocky Mountain News*, 19 November 1888, p. 1.

21. "The Ante-Room Of Hell," *Rocky Mountain News*, 19 November 1888, p. 1; for the story, see "Citizen Myron W. Reed," in Myron W. Reed, Clippings File, Colorado Historical Society, Denver, Colorado.

22. "The Organized Charities," *Rocky Mountain News*, 30 April 1888, p. 1. The Denver Charity Organization Society had its roots in the joint effort to raise funds in 1887, but it began as a federated society in 1889; see the "First Annual Report, November 24, 1889," in "Annual Reports of the Charity Organization Society of Denver, Colorado: 1889–1908," University of Colorado Libraries, Boulder, Colorado; Guy T. Justis, *Twenty-five Years of Social Welfare: 1917–1942* (Denver: Denver Community Chest, 1943), 15; Rosen, "Social Welfare in the History of Denver," 219. Note also the following references: "Denver Had First 'UF' in 1887," *Denver Post*, 5 October 1963, Religion Section, p. 3; "Denver's United Fund Got Its Start in 1889," *Rocky Mountain News*, 6 October 1963, p. 8.

23. "The Organized Charities," *Rocky Mountain News*, 30 April 1888, p. 1.

24. Ibid.; "Pauperism Is Dear," *Rocky Mountain News*, 15 December 1890, p. 5.

25. Editorials, 30 April 1888, p. 4, and 1 May 1888, p. 4; for "genteel poverty," see "Pride and Poverty," 13 August 1885, p. 1; for Reed's participation in sundry charitable efforts, see "The Kindergarten," 19 September 1886, p. 1; "Educate Children," 25 March 1889, p. 8; "Woman's Hospital," 10 May 1887, p. 10; editorial, 10 November 1888, p. 10; "Saving The Girls," 31 December 1887, p. 5; "For The Hospital Fund (Union soldier's home)," 25 June 1888, p. 2, all in the *Rocky Mountain News*; "The Cause of Charity," *Denver Republican*, 30 September 1889, p. 3.

26. "Associated Charities," 25 November 1888, p. 12; "[Associated] City Charities," 25 November 1888, p. 15; "The Charities," 26 November 1888, p. 4; "United Denver Charities," 26 November 1888, p. 2, all in the *Rocky Mountain News*; Lubove, *The Professional Altruist*, 7; Fredrickson, *The Inner Civil War*, 213; see the

reference to Mrs. Josephine Shaw Lowell in "Scientific Charity," *Rocky Mountain News*, 18 August 1889, p. 12.

27. "Victims Of Civilization," 21 January 1889, p. 8; "Pulpits Improving," 27 January 1890, p. 4; "Pauperism Is Dear," 15 December 1890, p. 5, all in the *Rocky Mountain News*; Lubove, *The Professional Altruist*, 6–10.

28. "The Investigation Office," 16 January 1889, p. 1; "Only A Misunderstanding," 17 January 1889, p. 2; "Charitable Work," 18 January 1889, p. 4; "The Investigation Office," 18 January 1889, p. 4, all in the *Rocky Mountain News*; "The Investigation Office," *Denver Republican*, 16 January 1889, p. 8; "Rev. Myron Reed's Answer," 16 January 1889, p. 5; "The Dean And The Charities," 18 January 1889, p. 4, both in the *Denver Times*; see George N. Rainsford, "Dean Henry Martin [sic] Hart and Public Issues," *Colorado Magazine*, Summer 1971, 204–20.

29. "Associated Charities," 22 January 1889, p. 6; "No More Imposition," *Rocky Mountain News*, 29 January 1889, p. 2. Rosen concluded that the society came about because businessmen insisted that charitable societies should solicit funds through one central agency, but while this might have been a factor, my reading led me to conclude that Denver's society resulted from the mixture of a desire for controlled solicitation and the altruism embodied in people like Uzzell, Jacobs, and Reed; see Rosen, "Social Welfare in the History of Denver," 219–20.

30. "No More Imposition," *Rocky Mountain News*, 29 January 1889, p. 2; "First Annual Report, November 24, 1889," p. 3, in "Annual Reports of the Charity Organization Society of Denver, Colorado: 1889–1908."

31. "First Annual Report, November 24, 1889," pp. 2, 5, in "Annual Reports of the Charity Organization Society of Denver, Colorado: 1889–1908"; "Catholic Charities," *Rocky Mountain News*, 5 February 1889, p. 5.

32. "Organized Charity," *Rocky Mountain News*, 26 February 1889, p. 2.

33. Ibid.

34. "He Puts It Plainly," *Rocky Mountain News*, 10 November 1890, p. 5.

35. "Reed Will Resign," 12 November 1890, p. 7; "Works of Charity," 18 November 1890, p. 9; "Annual Charity Meeting," 24 November 1890, p. 7; for return as president, see "Charities," 20 November 1892, p. 13; "Citizens," 21 November 1892, p. 3; for a later report of the neglect of charities, see "Charity Work Neglected," 14 March 1898, p. 8; all in the *Rocky Mountain News*.

36. "H. A. W. Tabor For Postmaster," *Rocky Mountain News*, 14 January 1898, p. 1; Leonard and Noel, *Denver*, 103–4, 204; Duane A. Smith, *Horace Tabor: His Life and the Legend* (1973; reprint, Boulder, CO: Pruett Publishing Company, 1981), 259–78, 308–9, 318.

37. Dorsett and McCarthy, *The Queen City*, 94–99; 115; Leonard and Noel, *Denver*, 103; James Edward Wright, *The Politics of Populism: Dissent in Colorado* (New Haven: Yale University Press, 1974), 167; for the "Bottoms," see "Immersed In Filth," 15 September 1890, p. 6; "Experts On Smells," 15 August 1890, p. 8; "No Silver Lining," 30 November 1891, p. 5; for Uzzell's run for the Board of Super-

visors on the Taxpayers' Ticket in 1897 and his reference to the "Bottoms," see "Reverend Tom's Opinion, " 31 March 1897, p. 4, all in the *Rocky Mountain News*.

38. "A Call For Charity," *Rocky Mountain News*, 6 July 1893, p. 8.

39. "Help Is Asked For," 19 July 1893, p. 8; "Organizing Relief," 21 July 1893, p. 2; "Bread Money Given: Food Distributed to the Hungry of the City Yesterday," 24 July 1893, p. 3; "Working Men Meet: Address to 3,000 People at Lincoln Park Last Evening," 24 July 1893, p. 3; "Aid Is Organized," 25 July 1893, p. 1, all in the *Rocky Mountain News*; see Forest Lowell White, "The Panic of 1893 in Colorado" (M.A. thesis, University of Colorado, 1932), 66, 68–76.

40. "Camp Opens To-day," 27 July 1893, p. 2; "Will Shut The Camp," 30 July 1893, p. 1; "Arata Lynched," 27 July 1893, pp. 1, 3, all in the *Rocky Mountain News*; White, "The Panic of 1893 in Colorado," 66, 68–76; Dorsett and McCarthy, *The Queen City*, 100–1; Leonard and Noel, *Denver*, 104–5; William Alexander Platt, "The Destitute In Denver," *Harper's Weekly*, 19 August 1893), pp. 787–88.

41. "Will Shut The Camp," 30 July 1893, p. 1; for Populists' claim that opponents closed the camp for political reasons, see "Will Break Camp," 8 August 1893, p. 3, both in the *Rocky Mountain News*.

42. The relief committee circulated a general statement to discourage people from coming to Denver for assistance. See "Preparing For Work," 12 July 1893, p. 8; "Work For The Charitable," 22 July 1893, p. 4; "The Relief Meeting," 25 July 1893, p. 4; "The Unemployed," 23 July 1893, p. 12; for aid to New York, see "On To The Battle: New York Invaded From Colorado," 23 August 1893, p. 1; for Coxeyites in Denver, see the issues 25 May and 9 June 1894, all in the *Rocky Mountain News*; for more on the Coxeyites, see Leonard and Noel, *Denver* , 104–5; Carlos A. Schwantes, *Coxey's Army: An American Odyssey* (Lincoln: University of Nebraska Press, 1985), 209–21, esp. 214–17.

43. "Organized Charity," 18 February 1894, p. 12; "No Time To Smile," 24 July 1893, p. 8, both in the *Rocky Mountain News*.

44. "Why Are Ye Idle," 26 February 1894, p. 3; "To Roost At Home," 14 May 1894, p. 8; for Coxey's followers in Denver, see "Wish To Join Coxey," 26 March 1894, p. 3; for sympathetic editorials, see "Coxey's Army," 10 April 1894, p. 4; "Liberty And Labor," 14 May 1894, p. 4; "Coxey In Irons," 23 May 1894, p. 4, all in the *Rocky Mountain News*; Schwantes, *Coxey's Army*, chapter 13.

45. See the criticism in "Scientific Charity," 17 September 1893, p. 12; "Must Get Work," 18 June 1894, p. 8; for accusation that Board Of Public Works too slow to begin projects, see "Men Must Starve," 10 July 1894, p. 8; for the Maverick Restaurant, see "Five-Cent Meals," 17 August 1893, p. 8; for annual rabbit hunts, see "Great Rabbit Slaughter," 1 January 1895, p. 8, all in the *Rocky Mountain News*.

46. "Why Are Ye Idle," *Rocky Mountain News*, 26 February 1894, p. 3.

47. "Rev. Myron Reed Ill," 5 March 1894; for Reed's departure for Hot Springs, Arkansas, see "Too Many Buttons," 15 March 1894, p. 3; for Reed's return after illness, see "To Roost At Home," 14 May 1894, p. 8; "Reed's Resignation," 21 Au-

gust 1894," p. 3; "Was Its Father," 24 August 1894, p. 4, all in the *Rocky Mountain News.*

48. Dorsett and McCarthy, *The Queen City,* 64, 82–86; Leonard and Noel, *Denver,* 110–11; "Business Proclamation," *Rocky Mountain News,* 1 October 1898, p. 16; "Festival of Mountain and Plain Expressed Joy," *Boulder Daily Camera,* 23 July 1980, p. 20A.

49. "Sentiment," 24 January 1898; "Voice Of The People," 25 January 1898, p. 4, both in the *Rocky Mountain News.*

50. "Welcomed Him Back," *Rocky Mountain News,* 8 September 1890, p. 3.

51. "Charity Is Not Cheap," *Rocky Mountain News,* 21 December 1896, p. 8.

52. Ibid.

53. "The Poor," *Rocky Mountain News,* 20 February 1888, p. 1.

CHAPTER 5

1. Henry F. May, *Protestant Churches and Industrial America* (1949; reprint, New York: Harper & Row, Publishers, Harper Torchbooks, 1967), 93–94.

2. Ibid, 55–56, 165.

3. "Work and Wages," *Rocky Mountain News,* 14 February 1887, p. 1.

4. "The Law of Wages," 20 February 1893, p. 2; "No Child Labor," 7 December 1891, p. 2; for editorial support, see "Child Labor," 12 April 1892, p. 4; "Improvident Injustice," 1 February 1886, p. 3, all in the *Rocky Mountain News.*

5. "The Law of Wages," 20 February 1893, p. 2, and "Work and Wages," 14 February 1887, p. 1, both in the *Rocky Mountain News.*

6. Joseph R. Buchanan, *The Story of a Labor Agitator* (New York: The Outlook Company, 1903), 48; David Brundage, *The Making of Western Labor Radicalism: Denver's Organized Workers, 1878–1905* (Urbana and Chicago: University of Illinois Press, 1994), 32–34, 57, 63–64. Reed supported the women's eight-hour movement in a mass meeting of the Knights of Labor; see "Substantial Relief," *Rocky Mountain News,* 21 April 1890, p. 8. See also Leon Fink, *Workingmen's Democracy: The Knights of Labor and American Politics* (1983; reprint, Urbana: University of Illinois Press, Illini Books, 1985), 3–17; Gerald N. Grob, *Workers and Utopia: A Study of Ideological Conflict in the American Labor Movement 1865–1900* (Chicago: Northwestern University Press, 1961), 34–38; Foster Rhea Dulles and Melvyn Dubofsky, *Labor in America: A History,* 4th ed. (Arlington Heights, IL: Harlan Davidson, Inc., 1984), 120–32.

7. See "Barbers' Business," 26 May 1886, p. 8, and "For Some People," 3 July 1893, p. 8, both in the *Rocky Mountain News.*

8. Patricia Nelson Limerick, "The Adventures of the Frontier in the Twentieth Century," in *The Frontier in American Culture,* ed. James Grossman (Berkeley: University of California Press, 1994), 89–95.

9. "Denver's Demands," 24 November 1884, p. 8, and "Labor and Leisure," 21 February 1887, p. 1, both in the *Rocky Mountain News;* for Cooper Union, see

Thomas Bender, *New York Intellect: A History of Intellectual Life in New York City, from 1750 to the Beginnings of Our Own Time* (Baltimore: The Johns Hopkins University Press, 1987), 114–16.

10. "Rational Recreation," 5 October 1885, p. 3, and "Labor In Leisure," 21 February 1887, p. 1, both in the *Rocky Mountain News*; David Thomas Brundage, "The Making of Working-Class Radicalism in the Mountain West: Denver, Colorado, 1880–1903" (Ph.D. diss., University of California, Los Angeles, 1982), 38.

11. Irvin G. Wyllie, *The Self-Made Man in America: The Myth of Rags to Riches* (1954; reprint, New York: The Free Press, 1966), 21–33, 40–46, 57–60, 143–46; May, *Protestant Church and Industrial America*, 199–200; Winthrop S. Hudson, *Religion in America: An Historical Account of the Development of American Religious Life* (New York: Charles Scribner's Sons, 1965), 294–95, 305.

12. "Why Workingmen Don't Go To Church," *Rocky Mountain News*, 27 December 1885, p. 16; May, *Protestant Churches and Industrial America*, 119–21.

13. "Pulpit and People," 5 January 1885, p. 8; "Reed Talks: He Does Not Think the Church Understands Man," 16 October 1890, p. 2; "Going To Church," 25 April 1892, p. 3, all in the *Rocky Mountain News*.

14. "Going To Church," 25 April 1892, p. 3; "Churches and Church Goers," 5 October 1885, p. 1, both in the *Rocky Mountain News*.

15. Joseph R. Buchanan, *The Story of a Labor Agitator*, 49, 68–69 (for dynamite reference); "De La Matyr," in *A Biographical History of Eminent and Self-Made Men of the State of Indiana* (Cincinnati: Western Biographical Publishing Company, 1880), 1:28–31; "Evans Chapel (Grace Church)," in *The Methodist, Evangelical, and United Brethren Churches in the Rockies, 1850–1976*, ed. J. Alton Templin, Allen D. Breck, and Martin Rist (Denver: The Rocky Mountain Conference of the United Methodist Church, 1977), 104–5; Gene Ronald Marlatt, "Joseph R. Buchanan: Spokesman for Labor During the Populist and Progressive Eras" (Ph.D. diss., University of Colorado, 1975), 193–94; James Edward Wright, *The Politics of Populism: Dissent in Colorado* (New Haven: Yale University Press, 1974), 25, 114, 227; for examples of the *News*'s attitude toward Buchanan, see "Printers On The Strike" and "Boycotting 'Buck'," 20 May 1885, p. 4; "Less Labor," 3 May 1886, p. 8; "Wise Workingmen," 5 May 1886, p. 4; "The Strikers' Meeting," 11 May 1886, p. 4; "Blatant Bluster," 18 May 1886, p. 8.

16. Buchanan, *The Story of a Labor Agitator*, 135–41; see De La Matyr's sermon, "Source of the Peril of Dynamite," *Rocky Mountain News*, 23 February 1885, p. 8; see Reed's sermon, "Courageous Comment," *Rocky Mountain News*, 23 February 1885, p. 3; for more on De La Matyr, Reed, and the Knights of Labor, see Brundage, *The Making of Western Labor Radicalism*, 63–64; for an interpretation of the evolution of the Labor Day holiday, see Michael Kazin and Steven J. Ross, "America's Labor Day: The Dilemma of a Worker's Celebration," *Journal of American History* 78 (March 1992): 1294–1301, 1322.

17. Buchanan, *The Story of a Labor Agitator*, 140. Buchanan claimed five hundred state socialists marched in this parade; see Marlatt, "Joseph R. Buchanan," 175;

"The Labor Parade," *Rocky Mountain News*, 23 February 1885, p. 4. Demonstrations of workers' importance to the productive process had their roots in the early nationalist period, see Sean Wilentz, *Chants Democratic: New York City & the Rise of the American Working Class, 1788–1850* (New York: Oxford University Press, 1984), 90–91.

18. "Courageous Comment," *Rocky Mountain News*, 23 February 1885, p. 3.

19. Ibid.; "The Labor Parade," *Rocky Mountain News*, 23 February 1885, p. 4.

20. "Rev. George [sic] De La Matyr's Sermon," *Rocky Mountain News*, 23 February 1885, p. 8.

21. "Courageous Comment," *Rocky Mountain News*, 23 February 1885, p. 4; David Montgomery, *Workers' Control in America: Studies in the History of Work, Technology, and Labor Struggles* (Cambridge: Cambridge University Press, 1979), 158–59; Samuel Yellen, *American Labor Struggles* (New York: Harcourt, Brace and Company, 1936), xi–xiv.

22. "Stock Speculators," *Rocky Mountain News*, 29 September 1884, p. 8.

23. Ibid. By "natural and beneficent laws," Reed evidently was referring to what he believed was an inherent tendency within man — a God-given law — toward cooperation.

24. Ibid.

25. Buchanan, *The Story of a Labor Agitator*, 79–126; see p. 99 for reference to Union Pacific settlement. See also "A Strike Settled," *Rocky Mountain News*, 16 August 1884, p. 8; Dulles and Dubofsky, *Labor in America*, 132; "Source of Strikes," *Rocky Mountain News*, 3 November, 1884, p. 8.

26. "Source Of Strikes," *Rocky Mountain News*, 3 November 1884, p. 8; for the role of absentee ownership in Denver's industrialization, see Brundage, *The Making of Western Labor Radicalism*, 17–18.

27. "Source Of Strikes," 3 November 1884, p. 8; cf. a later sermon by Reed on the topic of the combinations of capitalists, "For Some People" 3 July 1893, p. 8, both in the *Rocky Mountain News*.

28. Alan Dawley, *Struggles for Justice: Social Responsibility and the Liberal State* (Cambridge: The Belknap Press of Harvard University Press, 1991), 17; John A. Garraty, *The New Commonwealth, 1877–1890* (New York: Harper & Row, Publishers, 1968), 79, 128–30; Brundage, "The Making of Working-Class Radicalism in the Mountain West," 35.

29. For the *News*'s comments, see editorial on a Cleveland, Ohio, Knights of Labor meeting, 11 May 1886, p. 4; see also Frederick Jackson Turner, *The Frontier in American History* (1947; reprint Tucson: The University of Arizona Press, 1986), 1–38.

30. For Strong, see Daniel T. Rodgers, *The Work Ethic in Industrial America, 1850–1920* (1974; reprint, Chicago: The University of Chicago Press, Phoenix Books, 1978), 67–70; May, *Protestant Churches and Industrial America*, 113–16; Sidney E. Ahlstrom, *A Religious History of the American People* (New Haven: Yale University Press, 1972), 798–99.

31. Brundage, "The Making of Working-Class Radicalism," 15, 18–21.

32. Rodgers, *The Work Ethic*, 223–26, quotation on page 223; Dawley, *Struggles for Justice*, 27.

33. Rodgers, *The Work Ethic*, 225–28; see also Mark Pittenger, "The Great Evasion: Religion and Science in the Socialism of Edmond Kelly," *Journal of American Culture* 14 (Spring 1991): 15.

34. Lyle W. Dorsett and Michael McCarthy, *The Queen City: A History of Denver*, 2nd ed. (Boulder, CO: Pruett Publishing, 1986), 94–99, 111–17; Brundage, "The Making of Working-Class Radicalism," 20, 33–39.

35. "The Evolution of the Tramp," *Rocky Mountain News*, 7 April 1886, p. 2, announced the publication of the "The Evolution of Tramp" sermons in booklet form; later, the *Denver Post* published these sermons in weekly installments. See "Evolution of the Tramp," 15 January 1905, p. 8, section 2; 22 January 1905, p. 8, section 2; 29 January 1905, p. 9, section 2; 5 February 1905, p. 3, section 5.

36. See the abridged version in Myron W. Reed, *Temple Talks* (Indianapolis: The Bowen–Merrill Company, 1898), 9–20; titles and dates of the four sermons published weekly in the *Rocky Mountain News* were "Trials of Tramps," 11 January 1886, p. 8; Talking of Tramps," 25 January 1886, p. 7; "Improvident Injustice," 1 February 1886, p. 3; "Samson's Slaughter," 8 February 1886, p. 3.

37. "Trials Of Tramps," *Rocky Mountain News*, 11 January 1886, p. 8. In the abridged version, Reed wrote, "He would last in a mine as long as he would last at foot-ball"; see Reed, *Temple Talks*, 15.

38. "Trials Of Tramps," *Rocky Mountain News*, 11 January 1886, p. 8; see Rodgers, *The Work Ethic*, 78–81 for British socialist William Morris's views on machines and workers' livelihood, but Reed wanted to manage machines for man's benefit.

39. "Talking Of Tramps," *Rocky Mountain News*, 25 January 1886, p. 7; for reference to Cardinal Manning, see "The Poor," 20 February 1888, p. 1, both in the *Rocky Mountain News*; for a brief biography of Cardinal Manning, see Malachi B. Martin, "Manning," in *McGraw–Hill Encyclopedia of World Biography*, (New York: McGraw Inc., 1973), 7:148–49.

40. "Talking Of Tramps," *Rocky Mountain News*, 25 January 1886, p. 7. Carlyle was the source of the remark "If they will not work, let them suffer"; see Rodgers, *The Work Ethic*, 224. For more information about the "Friendly Inn," see Genevieve Weeks, *Oscar Carleton McCulloch, 1843–1891: Preacher and Practitioner of Applied Christianity* (Indianapolis: Indiana Historical Society, 1976), 177.

41. "Talking Of Tramps," *Rocky Mountain News*, 25 January 1886, p. 7.

42. Ibid.

43. Ibid.

44. "Improvident Injustice," *Rocky Mountain News*, 1 February 1886, p. 3; for John Ruskin, see Rodgers, *The Work Ethic*, 76–77.

45. Ibid.

46. "Samson's Slaughter," *Rocky Mountain News*, 8 February 1886, p. 3.

47. Ibid.

48. Ibid.; also see "Freedom Of Speech," *Rocky Mountain News*, 14 November 1887, p. 1.

49. "Samson's Slaughter," *Rocky Mountain News*, 8 February 1886, p. 3.

50. Paul T. Ringenbach, *Tramps and Reformers, 1873–1916: The Discovery of Unemployment in New York* (Westport, CT: Greenwood Press, Inc., 1973), xiii–xv, 18–19, and chapter 2.

51. Guy T. Justis, *Twenty-Five Years of Social Welfare, 1917–1942* (Denver: The Denver Community Chest, 1943), 15; Dorsett and McCarthy, *The Queen City*, 111, 113; for wage labor, see Christopher Lasch, *The True and Only Heaven: Progress and its Critics* (New York: W. W. Norton & Company, 1991), 206–8.

52. "The Transition Period," 27 February 1886, p. 2; "Talk With A Tramp," 5 September 1886, p. 14; "The Apotheosis Of The Tramp," 6 October 1895, p. 12; "Again The Tramp," 19 April 1896, p. 12, all in the *Rocky Mountain News*.

53. "Barbers' Business," 26 May 1886, p. 8; "Abbott's Answers," 5 July 1886, p. 4, both in the *Rocky Mountain News*, 5 July 1886, p. 4; Howard H. Quint, *The Forging of American Socialism: Origins of the Modern Movement* (Columbia: University of South Carolina Press, 1953), 99–112; Peter J. Frederick, *Knights of the Golden Rule: The Intellectual as Christian Social Reformer in the 1890s* (Lexington: University of Kentucky Press, 1976), 36–37, 56–77, 84–98.

54. "Will Not Succeed Beecher," *Denver Republican*, 3 September 1887, p. 8. In May 1887 Reed said that profit-sharing had not yet become fashionable, but when it comes in it never goes out; see "Labor's Leader," *Rocky Mountain News*, 16 May 1887, p. 1.

55. For the views of the *Rocky Mountain News* about the eight-hour movement before the Haymarket Affair, see "Tackling Time," 29 April 1886, p. 1; "Labor Leavers," 2 May 1886, p. 1; for editorial comment, see 3 May 1886, p. 4; "Less Labor," 3 May 1886, p. 8.

56. For views after the Haymarket bombing, see "Bombs and Blood," 5 May 1886, p. 1; "A Mad Mob," 6 May 1886, p. 1; "Death's Doom," 7 May 1886, p. 1; "A Better World," 1 November 1886, p. 1, all in the *Rocky Mountain News*; Reed, *Temple Talks*, 39–59; for the Haymarket Affair, the church, and the Knights of Labor, see May, *Protestant Churches and Industrial America*, 100–3; Dulles and Dubofsky, *Labor in America*, 116–19, 139.

57. "Raising Red Flags," *Rocky Mountain News*, 10 May 1886, p. 1; for another comment on the quality of immigrants, see "Brakemen Brothers," *Rocky Mountain News*, 4 June 1886, p. 3; for nativism, see John Higham, *Strangers in the Land: Patterns of American Nativism, 1860–1925*, 2nd ed. (New York: Atheneum, 1981), 52–56, 64–65; for Bellamy, see Arthur Lipow, *Authoritarian Socialism in America: Edward Bellamy and the Nationalist Movement* (Berkeley: University of California Press, 1982), 21–22.

58. "Raising Red Flags," *Rocky Mountain News*, 10 May 1886, p. 1. For Ely, see Mark Pittenger, *American Socialists and Evolutionary Thought, 1870–1920* (Madison: The University of Wisconsin Press, 1993), 34.

59. "Curbstone Comment," *Rocky Mountain News*, 16 May 1886, p. 1.

60. "A Better World," *Rocky Mountain News*, 1 November 1886, p. 1.

61. "The Burlington Strike," *Rocky Mountain News*, 5 March 1888, p. 1; see editorials, 6 March 1888, p. 4, for a denunciation of Pinkertons and a plea for moderation so that the strike would end soon and not affect business.

62. "From Myron Reed," *Rocky Mountain News*, 23 January 1893, p. 5. The *News* had urged arbitration in a local labor dispute and applied the principle to national labor problems; see "Local Labor Troubles," 18 May 1890, p. 12; "Freedom of Speech," 14 November 1887, p. 1, both in the *Rocky Mountain News*. On strikes and Christian socialists, see James Dombrowski, *The Early Days of Christian Socialism in America* (1936; reprint, New York: Octagon Books, 1966), 28–29.

63. Vernon H. Jensen, *Heritage of Conflict: Labor Relations in the Nonferrous Metals Industry up to 1930* (Ithaca, NY: Cornell University Press, 1950), 38–53; Wright, *The Politics of Populism*, 179–80; George G. Suggs, Jr., "Catalyst for Industrial Change: The WFM, 1893–1903," *Colorado Magazine* 45 (Fall 1968): 322–27; Merrill Hough, "Leadville and the Western Federation of Miners," *Colorado Magazine* 49 (Winter 1972): 20–21; for an eyewitness account, see Emil W. Pfeiffer, "The Kingdom of Bull Hill," *Colorado Magazine* 12 (September 1935): 168–72.

64. Jensen, *Heritage of Conflict*, 38–53; Wright, *The Politics of Populism*, 179–80. In February the *Rocky Mountain News* asked for arbitration, "Arbitrate the Matter," 26 February 1894, p. 4; see also the *News* articles "Lockout The Word," 2 April 1894, p. 3; "Bloodshed At Cripple," 27 May 1894, p. 1; "Afraid of the Springs: Cripple Creek Miners Fear Violent Treatment," 17 June 1894; and Melvyn Dubofsky, "The Origins of Western Working-Class Radicalism, 1890–1905," in *The Labor History Reader*, ed. Daniel J. Leab (Urbana and Chicago: University of Illinois Press, 1985), 245.

65. "Laws Favor Wealth," *Rocky Mountain News*, 4 June 1894, p. 8.

66. Ibid.

67. "Rev. Myron W. Reed," *Rocky Mountain News*, 1 June 1894, p. 1. Reed had asked for a six-weeks leave of absence in March due to his health. The church granted his request and reduced his salary from $500 to $300 per month. This unilateral action by the congregation might have been a factor in his resignation. In Indianapolis he had expressed some displeasure and a threat when the church there reduced his salary: "[those] who were responsible might live to regret it." He later resigned to come to Denver. See "Too Many Buttons," *Rocky Mountain News*, 15 March 1894, p. 3; "Reminiscences of Reed," *Indianapolis News*, 1 March 1899, p. 2.

68. "Business And Anarchy," *Rocky Mountain News*, 7 June 1894, pp. 1–2.

69. See these reactions to Reed's statement about Jesus as an anarchist: "Christ And Anarchy," 23 July 1894, p. 5; "Missouri Heard From," 24 July 1894, p. 3; "Calls It Myronism," 29 July 1894, p. 6; "Ho Ho, My Sisters!," 15 September 1894, p. 5, all in the *Rocky Mountain News*.

70. "Business And Anarchy," *Rocky Mountain News*, 7 June 1894, pp. 1–2.

71. "Rev. Myron W. Reed," *Rocky Mountain News*, 7 June 1894, p. 4; note labor's

support, "The Bricklayers' Union," 14 June 1894, p. 2; see letters from United Mine Workers in Blossburg, New Mexico, from American Railway Union, La Junta, Colorado, and from Populist Party, Indianapolis, 16 June 1894, p. 2, all in the *Rocky Mountain News.*

72. Lipow, *Authoritarian Socialism*, 78–80.

73. "Myron Will Accept," 16 June 1894, p. 2, contains Reed's conditional acceptance if nominated; "The Wicked Man," 21 June 1894, p. 4; "Myron Reed Talks," 8 September 1894, p. 2; "Federated Labor," 16 September 1894, p. 5; for Reed's speech, see "How Gompers Did It," 13 December 1894, p. 8, all in the *Rocky Mountain News.*

74. "Win We Will," *Rocky Mountain News*, 15 July 1894, pp. 1–2; on Debs, see Nick Salvatore, *Eugene Debs: Citizen and Socialist* (Urbana and Chicago: University of Illinois Press, 1982), 132–39.

75. "Eight Hours Is Enough," *Rocky Mountain News*, 11 March 1895, p. 8; see an earlier address by Reed to the Retail Clerks' Association, "[Eight-]Hour Service," *Rocky Mountain News*, 30 June 1890, p. 3; note an editorial "The Eight-Hour Day," *Rocky Mountain News*, 26 March 1896, p. 4, that supported eight hours for municipal projects; see also David L. Lonsdale, "The Eight-Hour Day," *Colorado Magazine* 43 (Fall 1966): 339–53; David Lawrence Lonsdale, "Movement for an Eight Hour Day in Colorado, 1893–1913" (Ph.D. diss., University of Colorado, 1963); LeRoy R. Hafen, *Colorado and its People: A Narrative and Topical History of the Centennial State*, (New York: Lewis Historical Publishing Company, 1948), 2:327.

76. "Eight Hours is Enough," *Rocky Mountain News*, 11 March 1895, p. 8.

77. Ibid.; "Laborer Not A Machine," *Rocky Mountain News*, 18 March 1895, p. 8.

78. See "Independent Church," 8 June 1894, p. 5; for practical religion, see "An Industrial Age," 27 June 1887, p. 1, both in the *Rocky Mountain News*; for options in the 1890s, see Dubofsky, "The Origins of Western Working-Class Radicalism," 232.

CHAPTER 6

1. "Reform And Business," *Rocky Mountain News*, 27 January 1896, p. 8.

2. Paul A. Carter, *The Decline and Revival of the Social Gospel: Social and Political Liberalism in American Protestant Churches, 1920–1940* (Ithaca, NY: Cornell University Press), 4–5.

3. Jacob H. Dorn, "The Social Gospel and Socialism: A Comparison of the Thought of Francis Greenwood Peabody, Washington Gladden, and Walter Rauschenbusch," *Church History* 62 (March 1993): 88.

4. "The Nationalists," 1 December 1890, p. 12; "Views On Nationalism," 9 December 1889, p. 5; "His Prophetic Eye," 29 September 1890, p. 6, all in the *Rocky Mountain News*; for Emerson, see Myron W. Reed, Myron W. Reed Papers (five letters), Chicago Historical Society, Chicago, Illinois.

5. Myron W. Reed, *Temple Talks* (Indianapolis and Kansas City: The Bowen–Merrill Company, 1898), 55; Arthur Lipow, *Authoritarian Socialism in America: Ed-*

ward Bellamy and the Nationalist Movement (Berkeley: University of California Press, 1982), 44–46; "Samson's Slaughter," 8 February 1886, p. 8; "Sifting the Heart," 17 November 1890, p. 8; "Equality of The Race," 18 May 1896, p. 8, all in the *Rocky Mountain News*.

6. "Shooting Socialists," 4 May 1886, p. 1; "A Mad Mob," 6 May 1884, p. 1; "Imported Socialists," 6 May 1886, p. 4; "Socialist Scare [Cincinnati]," 9 May 1886, p. 1; "The Anarchists," 16 October 1887, p. 9; "Denver Anarchists," 8 November 1887, p. 6; "Causes For Social Disorder," 13 November 1887, p. 12; "What Is The Remedy," 15 November 1888, p. 4, all in the *Rocky Mountain News*.

7. Gene Ronald Marlatt, "Joseph R. Buchanan: Spokesman for Labor During the Populist and Progressive Eras" (Ph.D. diss., University of Colorado, 1975), 176–83; Joseph R. Buchanan, *The Story of a Labor Agitator* (New York: The Outlook Company, 1903), 254–59; for activities of the League, see "Will He Do It!" (Reed's arrival in Denver), 12 April 1884, p. 2; "Ministers In The Movement," 26 December 1885, p. 4; "The Social League," 26 December 1885, p. 5; "The Preachers," 13 February 1886, p. 2; "The League: An Intensely Interesting Address by Rev. Myron W. Reed," 20 February 1886, p. 3, all in the *Labor Enquirer*; for local reaction, see "To Help Anarchists: Resolutions Passed by the Rocky Mountain Social League," *Rocky Mountain News*, 19 September 1887, p. 8.

8. "Raising Red Flags," 10 Monday May 1886, p. 1; "A Better World," 1 November 1886, p. 1; "Locksley Hall," 25 February 1887, p. 3; "The Commonwealth," 7 March 1887, p. 1; for Arkins, see "He Sleeps," 22 August 1894, pp. 1, 8; all in the *Rocky Mountain News*; Robert L. Perkin, *The First Hundred Years; An Informal History of Denver and the Rocky Mountain News* (Garden City, NY: Doubleday and Company, 1959), 360–61, 378, 383–84.

9. For an example of Van Ness's preaching on socialism, see "Socialistic Studies," *Rocky Mountain News*, 2 September 1889, p. 5.

10. "Pulpit And People," 5 January 1885, p. 8; "Kingsley Was King," 12 December 1892, p. 8; "One Of God's Workers," 2 December 1895, p. 8, all in the *Rocky Mountain News*; for Kingsley, see Henry F. May, *Protestant Churches and Industrial America* (1949; reprint, New York: Harper & Row, Publishers, Harper Torchbooks, 1967), 148–49; John C. Cort, *Christian Socialism: An Informal History* (Maryknoll, NY: Orbis Books, 1988), 141–46.

11. "Kingsley Was King," *Rocky Mountain News*, 12 December 1892, p. 8.

12. Ibid.

13. "Pulpit And People," 5 January 1885, p. 8; "Human Side Of Jesus," 9 December 1895, p. 8; "I don't care," in "Sifting The Heart," 17 November 1890, p. 8, all in the *Rocky Mountain News*; for Robertson, see William R. Hutchison, *The Modernist Impulse in American Protestantism* (1976; reprint, New York: Oxford University Press, 1982), 80–85.

14. "Reed On Socialism," *Rocky Mountain News*, 19 December 1892, p. 2; for labor unrest, see Foster Rhea Dulles and Melvyn Dubofsky, *Labor in America: A History*, 4th ed. (Arlington Heights, IL: Harlan Davidson, Inc., 1984), 160–62.

15. "Reed On Socialism," *Rocky Mountain News*, 19 December 1892, p. 2.

16. Ibid.

17. Ibid.

18. Ibid.

19. Ibid.

20. Ibid.

21. Ibid.

22. James Edward Wright, *The Politics of Populism: Dissent in Colorado* (New Haven: Yale University Press, 1974), 54–55; Theodore Saloutos, "Radicalism and the Agrarian Tradition," and Michael Rogin, "Comment," in *Failure of a Dream? Essays in the History of American Socialism*, rev. ed., ed. J. H. M. Laslett and Seymour Martin Lipset (Berkeley: University of California Press, 1984), 52–81; Sybil Downing and Robert E. Smith, *Tom Patterson: Colorado Crusader for Change* (Niwot: University Press of Colorado, 1995), 75–80.

23. "All Racing To Win," *Rocky Mountain News*, 9 January 1893, p. 8; see Charles Sheldon, *In His Steps*, rev. ed. (Chicago: Advance Pubishing Co., 1899).

24. "Co-operation Talk," *Rocky Mountain News*, 16 January 1893, p. 5.

25. For Knights of Labor cooperatives, see David Brundage, *The Making of Western Labor Radicalism: Denver's Organized Workers, 1878–1905* (Urbana and Chicago: University of Illinois Press, 1994), 85–86; for Shakers, see "Close To The Ideal," 13 October 1890, p. 7; "Co-operative City," 18 July 1894, p. 8; "People's Union," 3 August 1894, p. 6, all in the *Rocky Mountain News*.

26. "Pool Of Politics," *Rocky Mountain News*, 6 November 1893, p. 2.

27. Ibid.; for the APA, see Wright, *The Politics of Populism*, 191–93. Wright noted that Patterson's *News* criticized the APA in nearly every issue in September and October 1894. *News* quotation is in Downing and Smith, *Tom Patterson*, 187–89. See also "Rev. Myron W. Reed," *Rocky Mountain News*, 25 January 1894, p. 3; John Higham, *Strangers in the Land: Patterns of American Nativism, 1860–1925*, 2nd ed. (New York: Atheneum, 1981), 80–87.

28. "Laws Favor Wealth," 4 June 1894, p. 8; "Rev. Myron W. Reed Resigns," 7 June 1894, p. 1, both in the *Rocky Mountain News*.

29. "Glad Of The Rest," *Rocky Mountain News*, 10 June 1894, p. 8.

30. Ibid.

31. "Independent Church," *Rocky Mountain News*, 8 June 1894, p. 5.

32. William P. Fishback, Collection of Clippings Relating to Reverend Myron W. Reed, n.d., Indiana State Library, Indianapolis, Indiana; for state Senate appointment as chaplain, see editorial, *Rocky Mountain News*, 4 January 1895, p. 4.

33. See inside flyleaf of Reed, *Temple Talks*.

34. "Greeting to Reed," 4 February 1895, p. 1; for poverty story, see "Business and Anarchy," 7 June 1894, p. 1; for description and picture of the Broadway Theater, see "The Broadway Theater," 8 December 1889, p. 14, all in the *Rocky Mountain News*; "In The Pulpit Again," *Denver Post*, 4 February 1895, p. 3.

35. "Greeting To Reed," *Rocky Mountain News*, 4 February 1896, pp. 1–2.

36. Ibid.

37. Ibid.

38. Ibid.

39. Ibid.

40. Henry Demarest Lloyd, *Wealth Against Commonwealth* (New York: Harper and Brothers, 1894).

41. "Evils Of Competition," *Rocky Mountain News*, 27 May 1895, p. 5, note agreement with Laurence Gronlund and Edward Bellamy; see Mark Pittenger, *American Socialists and Evolutionary Thought, 1870–1920* (Madison: The University of Wisconsin Press, 1993), 53, 66–67; for Standard Oil centralization, see Alan Trachtenberg, *The Incorporation of America: Culture and Society in the Gilded Age* (1982; reprint, New York: Hill and Wang, 1988), 86.

42. "Notes Of His Vacation," *Rocky Mountain News*, 23 September 1895, p. 5.

43. See James Gilbert's Introduction in *The American Fabian* (Westport, CT: Greenwood Reprint Corporation, 1970); for mention of Reed, see *The American Fabian* 3 (January 1897): 12.

44. "Slaves Of Government," 6 July 1896, p. 8; "On The American Idea," 25 March 1895, p. 5; "And There Are Others," 12 April 1897, p. 5; also "Right Vs. Money," 28 February 1887, p. 1; "America's Mission," 2 May 1892, p. 8, all in the *Rocky Mountain News*.

45. "And There Are Others," *Rocky Mountain News*, 12 April 1897, p. 5.

46. "Meeting Of Extremes," *Rocky Mountain News*, 24 January 1896, p. 1; for the Candlelight Club, see Edward Ring, "Denver Clubs of the Past," *Colorado Magazine* 19 (July 1942): 140–41.

47. "Meeting of Extremes," *Rocky Mountain News*, 24 January 1896, p. 1.

48. "Love Rules The World," 20 April 1896, p. 8; "An Equal Opportunity," 26 October 1896, p. 5, both in the *Rocky Mountain News*.

49. "Equality Of The Race," *Rocky Mountain News*, 18 May 1896, p. 8.

50. "Union Of Wage Earners," 3 May 1897, p. 1; "Colony For Routt County," 31 December 1897, p. 1; "People's Union," 3 August 1894, p. 6, all in the *Rocky Mountain News*; Howard H. Quint, *The Forging of American Socialism: Origins of the Modern Movement* (Columbia: University of South Carolina, 1953), chapter 9.

51. Quint, *The Forging of American Socialism*, 282–85; Nick Salvatore, *Eugene V. Debs: Citizen and Socialist* (Urbana: University of Illinois Press, 1982), 161–62, 183.

52. James Dombrowski, *The Early Days of Christian Socialism in America* (1936; reprint, New York: Octagon Books, 1966), 75; Ray Ginger, *The Bending Cross; A Biography of Eugene Victor Debs* (New Brunswick, NJ: Rutgers University Press, 1949), 193–96; May, *Protestant Churches and Industrial America*, 259–60; Quint, *The Forging of American Socialism*, 285, 318; Salvatore, *Eugene V. Debs*, 161–69.

53. "Both Sides Considered," *Rocky Mountain News*, 11 January 1897, p. 5.

54. "Justice, Not Charity," *Rocky Mountain News*, 12 January 1897, p. 1.

55. Ibid.

56. "Co-operation The True Religion," 17 May 1897, p. 8; "To Try Socialism," 8 June 1897, p. 10; note Debs's Social Democracy, "Colonize By The Thousands," 15 June 1897, p. 2; "Social Democracy Colony," 17 November 1897, p. 8, all in the *Rocky Mountain News*; Quint, *The Forging of American Socialism*, 288–92.

57. "Denver's New Religion," 24 October 1896, p. 4; note W. D. P. Bliss's sermon at St. Mark's Church, "Scandalously Corrupt," 18 January 1897, p. 2, both in the *Rocky Mountain News*.

58. "Woman Pastor Selected," *Rocky Mountain News*, 3 February 1897, p. 5; Laurence Gronlund, *The New Economy: A Peaceable Solution of the Social Problem* (Chicago and New York: Herbert S. Stone and Company, 1898), 348–51; see also Pittenger, *American Socialists*, 61; Eliott Shore, *Talkin' Socialism: J. A. Wayland and the Role of the Press in American Radicalism, 1890–1912* (Lawrence: University Press of Kansas, 1988), 43–44; Reed mentioned in the *Coming Crisis*, 29 September 1892, p. 2; Brundage, *The Making of Western Labor Radicalism*, 71; for Gronlund's speech, see "Talked To The Point," *Rocky Mountain News*, 9 April 1894, p. 3.

CHAPTER 7

1. "Othello's occupation," 7 March 1898, p. 5; "Human Nature," 25 April 1898, p. 5, both in the *Rocky Mountain News*; Howard H. Quint, "American Socialists and the Spanish–American War," *American Quarterly* 10 (Summer 1958): 132–33; H. Wayne Morgan, *America's Road to Empire: The War with Spain and Overseas Expansion* (New York: Alfred A. Knopf, Inc., 1965), 103.

2. "Othello's occupation," 7 March 1898, p. 5; "The Annexation Question, Quality and Not Quantity," 14 March 1898, p. 5; "Words," 2 May 1898, p. 5; "The Rising Generation," 16 May 1898, p. 5; "Experience," 6 June 1898, p. 5; "The Deadly Parallel," 26 September 1898, p. 4; "Annexation," 28 November 1898, p. 5; all in the *Rocky Mountain News*; Quint, "American Socialists and the Spanish–American War," 138.

3. "Broadway Temple's Third Anniversary," 7 February 1898, p. 5; "The Making of Bread," 20 June 1898, p. 5, both in the *Rocky Mountain News*.

4. "Peace and War," 18 April 1898, p. 5; "Experience," 6 June 1898, p. 5; "The Parliament of Man, the Federation of the World," 9 May 1898, p. 5; "The Rising Generation," 16 May 1898, p. 5, all in the *Rocky Mountain News*.

5. "Hero Worship," *Rocky Mountain News*, 10 October 1898, p. 5.

6. "Rev. Myron Reed's Condition," 2 January 1899, p. 5; "Soul Ready To Depart," 30 January 1899, p. 1; "Denver's Most Popular Pastor Passes Away," 31 January 1899, pp. 1, 10, all in the *Rocky Mountain News*; "The Rev. Myron W. Reed Has Passed Away," *Denver Times*, 30 January 1899, p. 6; "Temple Passes With Its Leader," *Denver Republican*, 31 January 1899, pp. 1, 6; "Death Of Myron W. Reed," *Indianapolis Journal*, 31 January 1899, p. 8.

7. Myron W. Reed, Recollections of Myron W. Reed, Minister of Broadway Temple, 1895–1899, manuscript, Western History Department, Denver Public

Library, Denver, Colorado; "Funeral Fit For The Father Of His Country," *Rocky Mountain News*, 2 February 1899, p. 10.

8. "Funeral For The Father Of His Country," 2 February 1899, pp. 1, 10; "Obsequies At The Broadway," 1 February 1899, pp. 1–2, both in the *Rocky Mountain News*; for examples of messages, see copies of the *Denver Post* and the *Rocky Mountain News* in February and selected issues in March and April 1899.

9. For Huff, see "Volcano of Truth," and for the stage performers, see "Myron Reed As A Friend Of The Stage," in Reed, Recollections of Myron W. Reed.

10. Eugene Debs, "Reminiscences of Myron W. Reed," *The Comrade* 3 (November 1903): 34–35, and "Man Of The People Was Myron W. Reed," *Denver Post*, 29 November 1903, p. 3, section 2; "Applauds Name Of Myron Reed," 12 December 1904, p. 8; "Myron Reed, Friend Of Poor, Honored By People," 31 May 1905, p. 11, both in the *Rocky Mountain News*; for the WFM, see Vernon H. Jensen, *Heritage of Conflict: Labor Relations in the Nonferrous Metals Industry up to 1930* (Ithaca, NY: Cornell University Press, 1950), 48.

11. "Funeral Fit For The Father Of His Country," and "Shivered Out In The Street," in the *Rocky Mountain News*, 2 February 1899, pp. 1, 10; "The Tender Eulogy Of Tears," *Denver Post*, 1 February 1899, p. 1; "Deep Sorrow," *Denver Times*, 1 February 1899, p. 8; "Myron Reed's Funeral Was His Own Ideal," *Denver Republican*, 2 February 1899, pp. 1, 2, 5. Some ministers did preach about Reed's influence the Sunday following the funeral (see "Rev. Myron Reed The Subject Taken By Several Pastors," *Rocky Mountain News*, 6 February 1899, p. 3), and a few later described his funeral as pagan (see "Churches Need Mysticism," *Rocky Mountain* News, 14 February 1899, p. 4).

12. "Funeral Fit For The Father Of His Country," *Rocky Mountain News*, 2 February 1899, pp. 1, 10.

13. Ibid.

14. Ibid.

15. Ibid.; more information about Reed's funeral, resolutions from laborers and unions, epigrams, and miscellaneous items are in Reed, Recollections, and Myron W. Reed, Clippings File, Western History Department, Denver Public Library, Denver, Colorado.

16. "How To Subscribe To The Myron Reed Memorial," *Rocky Mountain News*, 13 February 1899, p. 4; "Reed Memorial Art Gallery," 7 Denver 1899, p. 10; "The Myron W. Reed Monument," 1 February 1899, p. 5, both in the *Denver Post*; for the monument's unveiling, see "Unveiling Of The Monument To Myron Reed At Fairmount," *Denver Times*, 30 May 1900, p. 2; "Rev. Myron W. Reed Remembered By The Masses With A Monument," *Rocky Mountain News*, 31 May 1900, p. 6.

17. Reed, Recollections; Myron W. Reed, Clippings File, Colorado Historical Society, Denver, Colorado; "Rev. M. W. Reed's Last Day," *Indianapolis Journal*, 31 March 1884, p. 7; "Good Will," *Rocky Mountain News*, 25 October 1887, p. 8.

18. Ferenc M. Szasz, "The Clergy and the Myth of the American West," *Church History* 59 (December 1990): 498, 503.

19. Reed, Clippings File, Western History Department, Denver Public Library, Denver, Colorado; "The Race Question," 19 January 1891, p. 7; "Will Avenge Indians," 15 November 1897, pp. 1, 5; "The Annexation Question, Quality and Not Quantity," 14 March 1898, p. 5, all in the *Rocky Mountain News*.

20. Myron W. Reed, *Temple Talks* (Indianapolis and Kansas City: The Bowen–Merrill Company, 1898); Myron Reed, "Night and Sleep and Rest," *The Cosmopolitan* 22 (February 1897): 437–44; Myron W. Reed, "Our Day," *The Arena* 21 (February 1899): 243–47; "The Evolution of The Tramp" began in the 15 January 1905 edition and ended in the 3 February 1905 edition of the *Denver Post*; for the series in the *News*, see "Myron W. Reed's Sermons," in the January, February, March, and April 1911 issues; "Rev. Camden M. Cobern," *Denver Republican*, 31 January 1899, p. 6.

21. For the astrological chart, see "How The Stars Influenced The Life of Myron Reed," 5 February 1899, p. 12; "Rev. Myron Reed's Estate," 7 February 1899, p. 10; "Widow Of Myron Reed Is Dead," 7 August 1907, p. 2, all in the *Denver Post*.

22. Myron W. Reed, Miscellaneous Items Concerning Myron W. Reed, 1883–1899, collected and compiled by Edgar A. Burton, Western History Department, Denver Public Library, Denver, Colorado.

23. Charles A. Johnson, *Denver's Mayor Speer: the forgotten story of Robert W. Speer, the political boss with a rather unsavory machine who transformed Denver into one of the world's most beautiful cities* (Denver: Green Mountain Press, 1969), 31–60; Lyle Dorsett and Michael McCarthy, *The Queen City: A History of Denver*, 2nd ed. (Boulder, CO: Pruett Publishing Company, 1986), 159–60; Edgar C. MacMechan, ed. *Robert W. Speer: A City Builder* (Denver: The Smith–Brooks Printing Company, 1919), 16, 35–48; for Friedman, see "Funeral Fit For The Father Of His Country," 2 February 1899, p. 10; for Speer and Reed, see "Good Will," both in the *Rocky Mountain News*, 25 October 1887, p. 8.

24. Casey Blake and Christopher Phelps, "History as Social Criticism: Conversations with Christopher Lasch," *Journal of American History* 80 (March 1994): 1332.

25. Reinhold Niebuhr, *Reflections on the End of an Era* (New York: Charles Scribner's Sons, 1934), 48; Myron Reed, "Night and Sleep and Rest," *The Cosmopolitan* 22 (February 1897): 438.

26. Paul Avrich wrote that to study De Cleyre opened another page in American history, and so it seems true with Reed; see Paul Avrich, *An American Anarchist: The Life of Voltairine de Cleyre* (Princeton: Princeton University Press, 1978), 16.

Selected Bibliography

NEWSPAPERS

Denver Post
Denver Republican
Denver Times
Indianapolis Journal
Indianapolis News
Indianapolis Star
Indianapolis Times
Labor Enquirer
Rocky Mountain News (Denver)
Rocky Mountain Sun (Aspen)
The Road

PRIMARY SOURCES

The American Fabian, volumes 1–3, 1895–1897. Introduction to the Greenwood reprint by James Gilbert. Westport, CT: Greenwood Reprint Corporation, 1970.
Annual Reports of the Charity Organization Society of Denver, Colorado. 1889–1908. University of Colorado Libraries, Boulder, Colorado.
The Arena: A Monthly Review of Social Advance. Boston: The Arena Company, 1894–1899.
Arguimbau, Ellen, comp., and John A. Brennan, ed. "Guide to the Thomas M. Patterson Papers." Western Historical Collections, University of Colorado Libraries, Boulder, Colorado, March 1977.
Bellamy, Edward. *Looking Backward*. 1888. Reprint, New York: New American Library, 1960.
———. *Equality*. 1897. Reprint, New York: Greenwood Press, 1969.

A Biographical History of Eminent and Self-Made Men of the State of Indiana. 2 vols. Cincinnati, OH: Western Biographical Publishing Company, 1880. S.v. "De La Matyr, Gilbert."

Buchanan, Joseph R. *The Story of a Labor Agitator.* New York: The Outlook Company, 1903.

Byers, William N. *Encyclopedia of Biography of Colorado.* Vol. 1. Chicago: The Century Publishing and Engraving Company, 1901.

Cooke, George Willis. "The Institutional Church." *The New England Magazine* 14 (August 1896): 645–660.

Dill, Robert Gordon. *The Political Campaigns of Colorado.* Denver: John Dove, Book and Job Printer, 1895.

Dunn, Jacob Piatt. *Indiana and Indianans: A History of Aboriginal and Territorial Indiana and the Century of Statehood.* 5 vols. Chicago and New York: The American Historical Society, 1919.

Fishback, William P. Collection of Clippings Relating to Reverend Myron W. Reed. (In collection of Indiana State Library, Indianapolis, Indiana.)

Fitz-Mac (James Mac Carthy). "Herbert George: A Western Era Maker." *The Great Divide* (January 1893): 224.

———. *Political Portraits.* Colorado Springs, CO: The Gazette Printing Company, 1888.

George, Henry. *Progress and Poverty: An Inquiry into the Cause of Industrial Depressions and of Increase of Want with Increase of Wealth . . . The Remedy.* 1879. Reprint, New York: Robert Schalkenbach Foundation, 1958.

George, Herbert. Scrapbooks, 1891–1905. (In collection of Western History Department, Denver Public Library, Denver, Colorado.)

Gronlund, Laurence. *The Co-operative Commonwealth: An Exposition of Socialism.* 1884. Reprint, Boston: Lee and Shepard Publishers, 1893.

———. *The New Economy: A Peaceable Solution of the Social Problem.* Chicago and New York: Herbert S. Stone and Company, 1898.

History of the Indianapolis Presbytery. By a Committee of Presbytery and Published by the Presbytery. Indianapolis: The Church at Work Publishing Company, c. 1887. (In collection of Indiana State Library, Indianapolis, Indiana.)

Indiana Scrap-book Collection. Compiled for and presented to the Indiana State Library in Remembrance of Benefits received by George S. Cottman. 9 vols., n.d.

Indianapolis Literary Club: Summarized Record, 1877–1934. Compiled by the secretary, Stephen C. Noland. Indianapolis, December 1934.

Lloyd, Henry Demarest. "Lords of Industry." *North American Review* 138 (June 1884): 535–553.

Lloyd, Henry Demarest. "The New Conscience." *North American Review* 147 (September 1888): 325–39.

———. *Wealth Against Commonwealth.* New York: Harper and Brothers, 1894.

McCulloch, Oscar. *The Tribe of Ishmael: A Study in Social Degradation.* Indianapolis: Carlon & Hollenbeck, 1888.

Morris, Henry O. *Waiting for the Signal: A Novel*. Chicago: The Schulte Publishing Company, 1897.

"Oscar C. McCulloch." *Harper's Weekly* (7 May 1892): 434.

Patterson, Thomas M. "Address of Hon. Thos. M. Patterson at the Opening of the Manufacturers' Exposition at Denver, Colorado, October 7, 1886." Denver: The Executive Committee, The Times Printing Works, 1886. (In collection of Western History Department, Denver Public Library, Denver, Colorado.)

——. Family Papers, 1865–1925. Western Historical Collections, University of Colorado Libraries, Boulder, Colorado.

Platt, William Alexander. "The Destitute in Denver." *Harper's Weekly*, (19 August 1893): 787–88.

Porchea, Paul. *The Musical History of Colorado*. Denver: Charles Westley, Publisher, 1889.

Reed, Mrs. Myron (Louise Lyon Reed). *One Life: One Law*. New York: John W. Lovell Company, 1890.

Reed, Myron W. Clippings File. Colorado Historical Society, Denver, Colorado.

——. Clippings File. Western History Department, Denver Public Library, Denver, Colorado.

——. Dictation of Rev. Myron Reed. Denver Arapahoe County, 1885, 1887. H. H. Bancroft Collection, University of California, Berkeley, California.

——. *Evolution of the Tramp*. Series of sermons preached in January and February 1886. Published by the *Rocky Mountain News*, 1886.

——. Miscellaneous Items Concerning Myron W. Reed, 1883–1899. Collected and compiled by Edgar A. Burton. Western History Department, Denver Public Library, Denver, Colorado.

——. Myron W. Reed Papers (five letters). Chicago Historical Society, Chicago, Illinois.

——. "Night and Sleep and Rest." *Cosmopolitan* (February 1897): 437–44.

——. Recollections of Myron W. Reed, Minister of Broadway Temple, 1895–1899. Western History Department, Denver Public Library, Denver, Colorado.

——. *A Review of Matthew Arnold's "Literature and Dogma."* Read before the Congregational and Presbyterian State Convention Assembled at Madison, Wis., October 17th, 1874. Milwaukee: Des Forges, Lawrence & Company, Printers, 1874.

——. *Temple Talks*. Indianapolis and Kansas City: The Bowen–Merrill Company, 1898.

——. *The Unspeakable Gift*. A sermon delivered in the First Presbyterian Church on 9 December 1877. Indianapolis: H. L. Benham, 1877.

Smiley, Jerome C. *History of Denver: With Outlines of the Earlier History of the Rocky Mountain Country*. Denver: J. H. Williamson and Company, Publishers, 1903.

Smith, Rose Lee. Scrapbook, 1890–1892. Western Department, Denver Public Library, Denver, Colorado.

Stone, Wilbur Fisk. *History of Colorado*, 4 vols. Chicago: The S. J. Clarke Publishing Company, 1918.

SECONDARY SOURCES

Abbott, Carl, Stephen J. Leonard, and David McComb. *Colorado: A History of the Centennial State*. Revised edition. Boulder: Colorado Associated University Press, 1982.
Abell, Aaron Ignatius. *The Urban Impact on American Protestantism, 1865–1900*. 1943. Reprint, Hamden and London: Archon, 1962.
Adams, Mary Fonda. "Thomas M. Patterson, Some Aspects of His Political Career." M.A. thesis, University of Colorado, 1933.
Ahlstrom, Sydney E. *A Religious History of the American People*. New Haven: Yale University Press, 1972.
Barth, Gunther. *Instant Cities: Urbanization and the Rise of San Francisco and Denver*. 1975. Reprint, Albuquerque: University of New Mexico Press, 1988.
Barth, Gunther. "Metropolism and Urban Elites in the Far West." In *The Age of Industrialism in America: Essays in Social Structure and Cultural Values*, edited by Fredric Cople Jaher, 158–87. New York: The Free Press, 1968.
Bender, Thomas. *Community and Social Change in America*. 1978. Reprint, Baltimore and London: Johns Hopkins University Press, Johns Hopkins Paperbacks, 1982.
Bird, Leah M. "Minor Political Parties in Colorado." *Colorado Magazine* 19 (November 1942): 208–13.
Blake, Casey, and Christopher Phelps. "History as Social Criticism: Conversations with Christopher Lasch." *Journal of American History* 80 (March 1994): 1310–32.
Brundage, David. *The Making of Western Labor Radicalism: Denver's Organized Workers, 1878–1905*. Urbana and Chicago: University of Illinois Press, 1994.
Brundage, David Thomas. "The Making of Working-Class Radicalism in the Mountain West: Denver, Colorado, 1880–1903." Ph.D. diss., University of California, Los Angeles, 1982.
Carter, Paul A. *The Decline and Revival of the Social Gospel: Social and Political Liberalism in American Protestant Churches, 1920–1940*. Ithaca, NY: Cornell University Press, 1954.
Clanton, Gene. *Populism: The Human Preference in America, 1890–1900*. Boston: Twayne Publishers, 1991.
Cole, G. D. H. *William Morris as a Socialist: A Lecture Given on 16th January 1957 to the William Morris Society at the Art Workers' Guild*. London: William Morris Society, 1960.
Cort, John C. *Christian Socialism: An Informal History*. Maryknoll, NY: Orbis Books, 1988.

Dawley, Alan. *Struggles for Justice: Social Responsibility and the Liberal State.* Cambridge: Belknap Press of Harvard University Press, 1991.

Destler, Chester McArthur. *American Radicalism, 1865–1901: Essays and Documents.* New London: Connecticut College, 1946.

Dombrowski, James. *The Early Days of Christian Socialism in America.* 1936. Reprint, New York: Octagon Books, 1966.

Dorn, Jacob H. "The Social Gospel and Socialism: A Comparison of the Thought of Francis Greenwood Peabody, Washington Gladden, and Walter Rauschenbusch." *Church History* 62 (March 1993): 82–100.

Dorsett, Lyle W., and Michael McCarthy. *The Queen City: A History of Denver.* 2nd ed. Boulder, CO: Pruett Publishing Company, 1986.

Downing, Sybil, and Robert E. Smith. *Tom Patterson: Colorado Crusader for Change.* Niwot: University Press of Colorado, 1995.

Dubofsky, Melvyn. "The Origins of Western Working-Class Radicalism, 1890–1905." In *The Labor History Reader,* edited by Daniel J. Leab, 230–53. Urbana and Chicago: University of Illinois Press, 1985.

Dulles, Foster Rhea, and Melvyn Dubofsky. *Labor In America: A History.* 4th ed. Arlington Heights, IL: Harlan Davidson, Inc., 1984.

Fellman, Michael. *The Unbounded Frame: Freedom and Community in Nineteenth Century American Utopianism.* Westport, CT: Greenwood Press, Inc., 1973.

Fink, Leon. *Workingmen's Democracy: The Knights of Labor and American Politics.* Urbana: University of Illinois Press, Illini Books, 1983.

Foner, Eric. "Why Is There No Socialism in the United States?" *History Workshop Journal* 17 (Spring 1984): 57–80.

Frederick, Peter J. *Knights of the Golden Rule: The Intellectual as Christian Social Reformer in the 1890s.* Lexington: University of Kentucky Press, 1976.

Fredrickson, George M. *The Inner Civil War: Northern Intellectuals and the Crisis of the Union.* 1965. Reprint, New York: Harper & Row, Publishers, Harper Torchbooks, 1968.

Fuller, Leon W. "Colorado's Revolt against Capitalism." *Mississippi Valley Historical Review* 21 (December 1934): 343–60.

———. "Governor Waite and His Silver Panacea." *Colorado Magazine* 10 (March 1933): 41–47.

Garraty, John A. *The New Commonwealth: 1877–1890.* New York: Harper & Row, Publishers, Harper Torchbooks, 1968.

Ginger, Ray. *The Bending Cross: A Biography of Eugene Victor Debs.* New Brunswick, NJ: Rutgers University Press, 1949.

Goodykoontz, Colin B. "Some Controversial Questions Before the Colorado Constitutional Convention of 1876." *Colorado Magazine* 17 (January 1940): 1–17.

Green James R. *Grass-Roots Socialism: Radical Movements in the Southwest, 1895–1943.* Baton Rouge: Louisiana State University Press, 1978.

Grob, Gerald N. *Workers and Utopia: A Study of Ideological Conflict in the American Labor Movement, 1865–1900.* Chicago: Northwestern University Press, 1961.

Gutman, Herbert. "Protestantism and the American Labor Movement: The Christian Spirit in the Gilded Age." *American Historical Review* 72 (October 1966): 74–101.

Hafen, LeRoy R., ed. *Colorado and Its People: A Narrative and Topical History of the Centennial State.* 4 vols. New York: Lewis Historical Publishing Company, 1948.

Handy, Robert T. "Christianity and Socialism in America, 1900–1920." *Church History* 21 (March 1952): 39–53.

Hicks, John D. *The Populist Revolt: A History of the Farmers' Alliance and the People's Party.* 1931. Reprint, Lincoln: University of Nebraska Press, Bison Books, 1961.

Higham, John. *Strangers in the Land: Patterns of American Nativism, 1860–1925.* 2nd ed. New York: Atheneum, 1981.

"History of the First Congregational Church of Denver, Colorado." Compiled by Mrs. Alice W. Gardner. Unpublished manuscript, First Plymouth Congregational Church, Englewood, Colorado, 1931.

Hogan, Richard. *Class and Community in Frontier Colorado.* Lawrence: University Press of Kansas, 1990.

Hopkins, Charles Howard. *The Rise of the Social Gospel in American Protestantism, 1865–1915.* New Haven: Yale University Press, 1967.

Hopkins, Walter S., Virginia Greene Millikin, Charles C. Mierow, and Robert P. Colwell. *The Bible and the Gold Rush: A Century of Congregationalism in Colorado.* Denver: Big Mountain Press, 1962.

Hough, Merrill. "Leadville and the Western Federation of Miners." *Colorado Magazine* 49 (Winter 1972): 19–34.

Hudson, Winthrop S. *The Great Tradition of the American Churches.* 1953. Reprint, New York: Harper & Row, Publishers, Harper Torchbooks, 1963.

Hudson, Winthrop S. *Religion in America: An Historical Account of the Development of American Religious Life.* New York: Charles Scribner's Sons, 1965.

Hutchison, William R. *The Modernist Impulse in American Protestantism.* 1976. Reprint, New York: Oxford University Press, 1982.

Jensen, Vernon H. *Heritage of Conflict: Labor Relations in the Nonferrous Metals Industry up to 1930.* Ithaca, NY: Cornell University Press, 1950.

Johnson, Charles A. *Denver's Mayor Speer: The forgotten story of Robert W. Speer, the political boss with a rather unsavory machine who transformed Denver into one of the world's most beautiful cities.* Denver: Green Mountain Press, 1969.

Justis, Guy T. *Twenty-Five Years of Social Welfare: 1917–1942.* Denver: Issued by The Denver Community Chest, 1943.

Katz, Michael B. *In the Shadow of the Poorhouse: A Social History of Welfare in America.* New York: Basic Books, Inc., 1986.

Kazin, Michael, and Steven J. Ross. "America's Labor Day: The Dilemma of a Workers' Celebration." *Journal of American History* 78 (March 1992): 1294–1323.

Kershner, Frederick Doyle, Jr. "A Social and Cultural History of Indianapolis, 1860–1914." Ph.D. diss., University of Wisconsin, 1950.

King, Clyde Lyndon. *The History of the Government of Denver with Special Reference to its Relations with Public Service Corporations*. Denver: The Fisher Book Company, 1911.

Larsen, Lawrence H. *The Urban West at the End of the Frontier*. Lawrence: The Regents Press of Kansas, 1978.

Larson, Robert W. *Populism in the Mountain West*. Albuquerque: University of New Mexico Press, 1986.

Lasch, Christopher. "Religious Contributions to Social Movements: Walter Rauschenbusch, The Social Gospel, and Its Critics." *Journal of Religious Ethics* 18 (Spring 1990): 7–25.

———. *The True and Only Heaven: Progress and Its Critics*. New York: W. W. Norton & Company, 1991.

Laslett, J. H. M., and Seymour Martin Lipset, eds. *Failure of a Dream? Essays in the History of American Socialism*. Rev. ed. Berkeley: University of California Press, 1984.

Latta, Maurice. "The Background for the Social Gospel in American Protestantism." *Church History* 5 (1936): 256–70.

Latta, Robert M. "Denver in the 1880s." *Colorado Magazine* 18 (July 1941): 131–37.

Lauck, W. Jett. *The Causes of the Panic of 1893*. Boston and New York: Houghton, Mifflin and Company, 1907.

Leach, Richard E. "Myron Winslow Reed." *The Trail* 19 (November 1926): 3–7.

Leonard, Stephen J., and Thomas J. Noel. *Denver: Mining Camp to Metropolis*. Niwot: University Press of Colorado, 1990.

Limerick, Patricia Nelson. "The Adventures of the Frontier in the Twentieth Century." In *The Frontier in American Culture*, edited by James Grossman, 89–95. Berkeley: University of California Press, 1994.

———. *The Legacy of Conquest: The Unbroken Past of the American West*. New York: W. W. Norton and Company, 1987.

Lipow, Arthur. *Authoritarian Socialism in America: Edward Bellamy and the Nationalist Movement*. Berkeley: University of California Press, 1982.

Lonsdale, David L. "The Fight for an Eight-Hour Day." *Colorado Magazine* 53 (Fall 1966): 339–53.

Lubove, Roy. *The Professional Altruist: The Emergence of Social Work as a Career, 1880–1930*. Cambridge: Harvard University Press, 1965.

MacMechan, Edgar C., editor. *Robert W. Speer: A City Builder*. Published by the Authority of the Council of the City and County of Denver. Denver: The Smith–Brooks Printing Company, 1919.

McCarthy, G. Michael. "Colorado's Populist Leadership." *Colorado Magazine* 48 (Winter 1971): 30–42.

McGiffert, Arthur Cushman, Jr. *No Ivory Tower: The Story of the Chicago Theological Seminary*. Chicago: Chicago Theological Seminary, 1965.

McMath, Robert C., Jr. *American Populism: A Social History, 1877–1898.* New York: Hill and Wang, 1993.

Marlatt, Gene Ronald. "Joseph R. Buchanan: Spokesman for Labor During the Populist and Progressive Eras." Ph.D. diss., University of Colorado, 1975.

Marty, Martin E. *Righteous Empire: The Protestant Experience in America.* New York: The Dial Press, 1970.

May, Henry F. *Protestant Churches and Industrial America.* 1949. Reprint, New York: Harper & Row, Publishers, Harper Torchbooks, 1967.

Meredith, Ellis. "Three Distinguished Figures of the Early Rocky Mountain News." *Colorado Magazine* 27 (January 1950): 34–49.

Meyer, D. H. *The Instructed Conscience: The Shaping of the American Ethic.* Philadelphia: University of Pennsylvania Press, 1972.

Montgomery, David. *The Fall of the House of Labor: The Workplace, the State, and American Labor Activism, 1865–1925.* Cambridge: Cambridge University Press, 1987.

——. *Worker's Control in America: Studies in the History of Work, Technology, and Labor Struggles.* Cambridge: Cambridge University Press, 1979.

Morgan, Arthur E. *Edward Bellamy.* New York: Columbia University Press, 1944.

Morris, John Robert. "Davis Hanson Waite: The Ideology of a Western Populist." Ph.D. diss., University of Colorado, 1965.

Niebuhr, H. Richard. *The Kingdom of God in America.* 1937. Reprint, New York: Harper and Brothers, Publishers, Harper Torchbooks, 1959.

Niebuhr, Reinhold. *Reflections on the End of an Era.* New York: Charles Scribner's Sons, 1934.

Noel, Thomas J. "Denver Boosters and Their 'Great Braggart City'." *Colorado Heritage* (Autumn 1996): 2–29.

Olson, Lynn Marie. "The Essence of Colorado Populism: An Analysis of the Populists and the Issues in 1892." M.A. thesis, University of Northern Colorado, 1971.

Parsons, Stanley B. *The Populist Context: Rural Versus Urban Power on a Great Plains Frontier.* Westport, CT: Greenwood Press, Inc., 1973.

Patai, Daphne, ed. *Looking Backward, 1988–1888.* Amherst: The University of Massachusetts Press, 1988.

Perkin, Robert L. *The First Hundred Years: An Informal History of Denver and the Rocky Mountain News.* Garden City, NY: Doubleday and Company, 1959.

Pfieffer, Emil W. "The Kingdom of Bull Hill." *Colorado Magazine* 12 (September 1935): 168–72.

Phillips, Clifton J. *Indiana in Transition: The Emergence of an Industrial Commonwealth, 1880–1920.* Indianapolis: Indiana Historical Bureau and Indiana Historical Society, 1968.

Pittenger, Mark. *American Socialists and Evolutionary Thought, 1870–1920.* Madison: The University of Wisconsin Press, 1993.

———. "The Great Evasion: Religion and Science in the Socialism of Edmond Kelly." *Journal of American Culture* 14 (Spring 1991): 13–18.

Pollack, Norman. *The Populist Response to Industrial America: Midwestern Political Thought.* Cambridge: Harvard University Press, 1962.

Quandt, Jean B. "Religion and Social Thought: The Secularization of Postmillennialism." *American Quarterly* 25 (October 1973): 390–409.

Quiett, Glenn Chesney. *They Built the West: An Epic of Rails and Cities.* New York: D. Appleton–Century Company, Incorporated, 1934.

Quint, Howard H. "American Socialists and the Spanish–American War." *American Quarterly* 10 (Summer 1958): 131–41.

———. *The Forging of American Socialism: Origins of the Modern Movement.* Columbia: University of South Carolina Press, 1953.

Rainsford, George N. "Dean Henry Martin [sic] Hart and Public Issues." *Colorado Magazine* 48 (Summer 1971): 204–20.

Rastall, Benjamin McKie. *The Labor History of the Cripple Creek District: A Study in Industrial Evolution.* Madison: Bulletin of the University of Wisconsin, No. 198, 1908.

Ring, Edward. "Denver Clubs of the Past." *Colorado Magazine* 19 (July 1942): 140–41.

Ringenbach, Paul T. *Tramps and Reformers, 1873–1916: The Discovery of Unemployment in New York.* Westport, CT: Greenwood Press, Inc., 1973.

Rodgers, Daniel T. *The Work Ethic in Industrial America, 1850–1920.* 1974. Reprint, Chicago: The University of Chicago Press, Phoenix Books, 1978.

Rosen, Bernard. "Social Welfare in the History of Denver." Ph.D. diss., University of Colorado, 1976.

Salvatore, Nick. *Eugene V. Debs: Citizen and Socialist.* Urbana and Chicago: University of Illinois Press, 1982.

Smith, Duane A. *Horace Tabor: His Life and the Legend.* 1973. Reprint, Boulder, CO: Pruett Publishing Company, 1981.

Smith, H. Shelton, Robert T. Handy, and Lefferts A. Loetscher. *American Christianity: An Historical Interpretation With Representative Documents.* 2 vols. New York: Charles Scribner's Sons, 1963.

Smith, Robert E. "The Anti-Imperialist Crusade of Thomas M. Patterson." *Colorado Magazine* 51 (Winter 1974): 28–42.

———. "Thomas M. Patterson: Colorado's Crusader." Ph.D. diss., University of Missouri, 1973.

———. "Thomas M. Patterson, Colorado Statehood, and the Election of 1876." *Colorado Magazine* 53 (Spring 1976): 153–62.

Suggs, George G., Jr. "Catalyst for Industrial Change: The WFM, 1893–1903." *Colorado Magazine* 45 (Fall 1968): 322–39.

Szasz, Ferenc M. "The Clergy and the Myth of the American West." *Church History* 59 (December 1990): 497–506.

———. "Myron Reed: Colorado Epigrammatist." *Southwestern American Literature* 13 (Fall 1987): 26–40.

———. " 'New Thought' and The American West." *Journal of the West* 23 (January 1984): 83–90.

———. *The Protestant Clergy in the Great Plains and Mountain West, 1865–1915.* Albuquerque: University of New Mexico Press, 1988.

Thom, William B. "As it Was in the '80s." *The Trail* 20 (July 1927): 3–9.

———. "Stage Celebrities in Denver Theatres Forty Years Ago." *The Trail* 19 (April 1927): 8–13.

———. "Stage Celebrities in Denver Theatres Forty Years Ago." *The Trail* 19 (May 1927): 8–14.

Thomas, John L. *Alternative America: Henry George, Edward Bellamy, Henry Demarest Lloyd and the Adversary Tradition.* Cambridge: Harvard University Press, 1983.

Titus, Irene M. *A Short History of First Plymouth Congregational Church.* Englewood, CO: First Plymouth Congregational Church, privately printed, n.d.

Trachtenberg, Alan. *The Incorporation of America: Culture and Society in the Gilded Age.* 1982. Reprint, New York: Hill and Wang, 1988.

Trattner, Walter I. *From Poor Law to Welfare State: A History of Social Welfare in America.* 3rd ed. New York: The Free Press, 1984.

Ubbelohde, Carl, Maxine Benson, and Duane A. Smith, eds. *A Colorado History.* 5th ed. Boulder, CO: Pruett Publishing Company, 1982.

Weeks, Genevieve. *Oscar Carleton McCulloch, 1843–1891: Preacher and Practitioner of Applied Christianity.* Indianapolis: Indiana Historical Society, 1976.

———. "Oscar C. McCulloch: Leader in Organized Charity." *Social Service Review* 39 (June 1965): 209–21.

———. "Oscar C. McCulloch Transforms Plymouth Church, Indianapolis, into an 'Institutional' Church." *Indiana Magazine of History* 44 (June 1968): 87–108.

———. "Religion and Social Work as Exemplified in the Life of Oscar C. McCulloch." *Social Service Review* 39 (March 1965): 38–52.

White, Forest Lowell. "The Panic of 1893 in Colorado." M.A. thesis, University of Colorado, 1932.

White, Ronald C., Jr., and C. Howard Hopkins. *The Social Gospel: Religion and Reform in Changing America.* Philadelphia: Temple University Press, 1976.

Wiebe, Robert H. *The Search for Order, 1877–1920.* New York: Hill and Wang, 1967.

Wilentz, Sean. *Chants Democratic: New York City & the Rise of the American Working Class, 1788–1850.* New York: Oxford University Press, 1984.

Wright, James Edward. *The Politics of Populism: Dissent in Colorado.* New Haven: Yale University Press, 1974.

Wyllie, Irvin G. *The Self-Made Man in America: The Myth of Rags to Riches.* 1954. Reprint, New York: The Free Press, 1966.

Yellen, Samuel. *American Labor Struggles.* New York: Harcourt, Brace and Company, 1936.

Index